Sod Ha'ibur

Origin of the Hebrew Calendar

Conflict between Rabban Gamliel and Rabbi Yehoshua

Richard K. Fiedler

Acharai Publications

Acharai Publications
HaTamid 6
Jerusalem 97500

ISBN 978-0-9903577-0-4

© Richard K. Fiedler 2014

sodhaibur@gmail.com

ור"ש בן לקיש מקפד על הדא מילתא חשש להיא הדא דא"ר לעזר דא"ר לעזר והיתה ידי על הנביאים החוזים שוא והקוסמים כזב בסוד עמי לא יהיו זה סוד העיבור.

And Rabbi Shimon ben Lakish became angry concerning this matter. He was troubled because of what Rabbi Eleazar said, for Rabbi Eleazar said: And my hand shall be against the prophets that see falsehood, and divine lies; they shall not be in the secret council of my people (Ezekiel 13:9). [They shall not be in the secret council of my people] – this refers to the "Secret of the Intercalation." (Talmud Yerushalmi, Rosh HaShanah, 2:6[1].)

---

[1] Translation Edward A. Goldman, *The Talmud of the Land of Israel, Volume 16: Rosh HaShanah*, p. 71.

The book's cover is from a painting done by my mother Saerree Fiedler, ז"ל. There is no end to my debt and the love I have for her and for my father, Louis P. Fiedler, ז"ל.

I had considerable assistance in writing this book from Yael Unterman, who edited this book. She transformed a work that sounded pretty good to me but that no one could understand into the book you see before you, which hopefully will be well received by those who are interested in the Hebrew Calendar.

Table of Contents

Preface 1

Author's Note...3

The Question and the Study..............................5

Hillel the Patriarch..17

The Moon and Lunar Visibility 37

The Molad..49

What's the Old Moon Got to Do With It? 59

The Rabban Gamliel/R' Yehoshua 73

The Dehiyyah Molad Zaqen 91

The Dehiyyot and Calendar Setup.................97

The Exilarch's Letter of 835 CE...................107

Setting the Scene 121

The Origin of the Hebrew Calendar 129

Till the Fat Lady Sings 139

Final Word..149

Appendix A: Molad of Tishrei Study..........153

Appendix B: Global Visibility Maps...........195

Appendix C: Three-Day Discrepancies 197

Preface

This book deals with the origin of the Fixed Hebrew Calendar, the very same one we use today to order our religious lives.

This is not a science-versus-Torah book. It lays out the primary Torah sources and makes them consistent with the knowledge that astronomers have acquired about the skies.

Nor is this a book of science versus mefarshim (Torah commentators or interpreters). Both Hazal (the Talmudic Sages) and later rabbinic interpreters utilized the best science that was available to them in their respective eras.

The advances made from the 15th century onward – specifically, those made by Nicolaus Copernicus and subsequently by Galileo, Kepler and Newton, along with mathematical advances in the 18th and 19th centuries – were supplemented by such tools as NASA's database of 6000 years of lunar data and such software programs as Sky View Café. All of these taken together have enabled me to reconstruct the skies seen by Hillel II, R' Hiyya, and Rabban Gamliel and R' Yehoshua thousands of years ago.

One of the most important foundations of my faith is the historicity of my people's relationship with God. There is a quote that I remembered as appearing in Max Planck's *Scientific Autobiography and Other Papers*, though now I cannot locate it (it might, in fact, be from elsewhere). In any event, it expresses the point well, remarking: "I don't believe the world is like Alice in Wonderland, where an apple is today edible and tomorrow not." There is a consistent order to the universe. It is the same moon I am seeing today, governed by the same laws, as that seen by Rabban Gamliel in 120 CE and Ezra in 450 BC.

This work is not so much a testimony to my own great cleverness as to the merit of my ancestors, of whose insights I am the recipient.

Robert H. van Gent, a Dutch astronomer, provided the custom Global Visibility Maps which confirmed these insights. Since these maps are often difficult to see, I have included links to PDFs in full color which should help to make them much more understandable.

I still recall the occasion when, by chance, I glanced at the date attributed to Hillel II and realized its astronomical significance. I remember bringing it to my study partner, Rabbi Yehoshua (Shuki) Reich, and his acknowledgment that perhaps my obsession with the Hebrew Calendar would indeed bear fruit. After giving many lectures on the topic, discussing it with dozens of friends and acquaintances, and working hard to translate it into language that is accessible to the interested layperson – all of which took years – this book finally represents that fruit.

It is like a detective story, and like any good detective story, the mystery is revealed at the end. The reader daunted by complicated calculations is invited to press on regardless, in order to discover the solution to the mystery.

Author's Note

In this work I have used all dates according to our modern (Gregorian) calendar. This is true even for dates earlier than the establishment of the Gregorian calendar in 1582. For example, Hillel II is credited with inaugurating the Fixed Hebrew Calendar in 358 CE. In this book, the Molad of Tishrei of that year is Saturday, September 20, 358 at 17:12. However, in the Julian calendar – the one in place at the time – this date would have been Saturday, September 19, 358 at 17:12. The reason the Gregorian system was used was to be consistent with the Apple's Numbers program, to make for smooth transitions to historical dates.

A note about terminology: The term "New Moon" in its current scientific use refers to the point at which the moon is closest to the sun, as seen from the Earth. At this point, the earth, moon, and sun lie on an approximate straight line. Because I wish to utilize the Jewish traditional meaning for the term "New Moon" (see below), I will henceforth refer to this lunar event as a "*Lunar Conjunction*" or simply "*Conjunction*." Scientifically strictly speaking, the word "*Conjunction*" refers to when these three heavenly bodies line up exactly; but I will suffice with defining it as their closest alignment of the month.

(It is important to realize that in the strict usage of the word, a Conjunction is synonymous with a solar eclipse. The moon, passing between the sun and earth, fully or partially blocks the sun from being seen.)

The term "New Moon" will be reserved in this work for use exclusively in the traditional Jewish sense of the word – i.e. referring to the first visible lunar crescent after the moon has closely passed the sun: the Crescent New Moon. The term "Old Moon" means the last visible crescent of the moon as it approaches the sun. Eventually the rising sun will prevent the moon from being seen in the sky at all, due to being much brighter.

Historically, the Molad was originally specified in terms of day, hours, and halakim (parts). At some point this was modified to clock notation, like the one I used above (Saturday, September 20, 358 at 17:12). One must realize that clock notation used with respect to the Molad presumes that the day ends at 17:59:59, and that the new day always starts at 18:00:00. This is by definition sunset, regardless if the sun actually set before or after that time.

The spreadsheet program used was Apple's Numbers. It has the capability of representing date and time as one value, even for dates which precede the Common Era.

The Question and the Study

A Lunar Puzzle in Jerusalem

It all began on Rosh HaShanah, 2002. The festival commenced on Friday evening, September 6, at which point Jews around the world entered not only the lunar month of Tishrei but also a new year – the year 5763.

I live in the Old City on HaTamid Street, a main thoroughfare used by Muslims from Silwan to travel through the Jewish quarter to the Al-Aqsa Mosque. Two days after Rosh HaShanah, on Sunday evening, I was surprised when my ears picked up the sound of our Muslim cousins on their way to the Al-Aqsa Mosque to begin their new month of Rajab.

What I was noticing was that they had established their new lunar month two days later than the start of our lunar month of Tishrei. Since Muslims and Jews both use a lunar calendar, this two-day discrepancy was unexpected. The Islamic calendar is based on lunar months, which begin when the thin New Crescent Moon is sighted in the western sky after sunset within a day or so after the Lunar Conjunction[2].

Originally, the Hebrew Calendar was similarly based, relying on two witnesses to report the sighting of the New Moon to the calendrical court in Jerusalem. However, at some point this was changed to a calculated, and hence fixed, calendar – supposedly by Hillel the Patriarch (aka Hillel II) in 358/9 CE. Minor differences could be expected, but two days seemed excessive. After all, Hillel II has been billed by many contemporary rabbis as a great

---

[2] As I mentioned in the author note – and it bears repeating – strictly speaking, in scientific terms, a Conjunction is an absolute alignment of the sun, moon, and earth, while the New Moon refers to their *closest* alignment each lunar month. We will however be using the term "*Lunar Conjunction*" or simply "*Conjunction*" for the closest alignment, and *New Moon* for the New Crescent Moon, as per its traditional definition.

mathematician in establishing the Fixed Hebrew Calendar. Why would his calculations then not line up Rosh HaShanah and the actual New Moon more successfully? A more successful mathematical model could have kept Hillel's calendar within a day of a calendar based upon the actual New Moon. It will be the conclusion of this book that this two-day discrepancy was an essential part of the design of this system and not an error at all.

Growing up, I found calendars ubiquitous, making their way to us from synagogues, schools and even, as I recall, funeral homes. I knew that somehow they were tied to the Molad[3] that I always heard announced in synagogue on the Shabbat before the new month; the gabbai (synagogue warden) would refer to a book for the correct date and time. People who take little interest in these matters tend to imagine that the Molad is the time of the actual New Moon, but I was soon to discover that the functioning of the Molad was more complex.

Returning now to my observations in 2002: The Molad of Tishrei for 2002 fell on Shabbat/Saturday at 12 hours and 982 halakim (parts out of 1080) – i.e. 6:54 AM Israel Standard Time. A quick check of NASA's published astronomy tables revealed the fact that the Lunar Conjunction fell on Saturday at approximately 5:10 AM Israel Standard Time. Thus, the time of the Molad and the time of the Conjunction were within two hours of each other. For astronomical purposes, the New Moon is regarded as the start of the lunar month. So were the Molad and the Conjunction and the beginning of the Hebrew month all the same thing, I wondered?

Well, this is certainly not true for Islam. For Islam, the Conjunction is not the start of the Islamic lunar month. The Islamic Calendar remains dependent on a local sighting of the "New Moon." Islam struggles with this issue due to its

---

[3] Literally "birth" or "born," referring to the moment of birth of the New Moon.

economic consequences.[4] Imagine if we did not know whether Rosh HaShanah would be observed on Monday or Tuesday until we actually saw the moon! Whereas the Conjunction occurs at the same instant across the earth, the New Moon does not. Thus, the start of Ramadan, for instance will not necessarily be the same day in different Muslim communities, because the sighting of the moon is not dependent on its sighting in one spot (for example Mecca), but rather on where one is located at the time the New Moon appears. For Jews, however, as the Rambam explains, Eretz Yisrael is the only location of interest in the determination of the Hebrew Calendar.[5]

I had been taught the widely held position that prior to Hillel II, the Jews were dependent on the report of an actual sighting of the New Moon in Eretz Yisrael and its acceptance by the Beit Din, the court; and that this was replaced by a fixed system, the origin of which is ascribed to Hillel II.

Since I could safely assume that the Islamic date was based on actual sighting, I became curious as to our calendar's methodology, which apparently was causing a discrepancy as large as two days from what it was ostensibly supposed to establish – the appearance of the New Moon.

I therefore studied the details carefully. Now, according to the rules of the Hebrew Calendar, the Molad is rounded back to the previous sunset – in this case, Friday evening, September 6, 2002. At this point, it was obviously

---

[4] For example, the tourist industry needs to know when to plan for holidays, work schedules need to be adjusted, the beginning of Ramadan needs to be determined properly. The issue of moon sighting has indeed caused much conflict for Muslims over the years, and today there are even advocates for deciding by calculation or by global sighting instead. See for example http://twocircles.net/2013aug05/hilal_hangover_why_indian_muslims_turn_moon_sighting_moon_fighting.html

[5] Hilchot Kiddush HaHodesh 1:8.

impossible for witnesses to see the New Moon, as even the Conjunction had yet to occur. On Saturday at sunset, the moon was 13 hours and 23 minutes old. I would learn later that according to the US Naval Observatory, the New Moon has never been observed when it is less than 15.5 hours old (we will develop this issue further in a subsequent chapter); hence no moon sighting Saturday evening. It follows that the first time the New Moon could have been sighted in Israel was Sunday evening, which was exactly what happened, thus validating the Islamic calendar as I mentioned.

Restating the initial question, why did Rosh HaShanah in the Hebrew Calendar based on Hillel II's system fall two days before the date that actual witnesses would establish? Was this an anomaly?

Molad of Tishrei Study

To seek an answer to this question, I decided to see how frequently the Molad of Tishrei, and the date of Rosh HaShanah established by it, corresponds with the date that the New Moon can actually first be seen by witnesses.

This gave rise to the study entitled **Molad of Tishrei,** part of which appears in the appendix of this book. In subsequent chapters, I will explain the details of the chart and its method of derivation.

The data was assembled spanning from the Molad of Tohu, 3761 BCE through 2020 CE. Within this span, conjunction data was only presented during the Common Era.

The chart that follows is only part of this study, more of it appearing in the appendix.

The spreadsheet file runs on Macintosh Computers using their Numbers spreadsheet program. This spreadsheet only contains Moladot from Tishrei. Conjunction data for the first 19 years is not shown, due to a glitch in Apple's Number program in handling entry of BCE data.

Year	Day	Hrs	Pts	Molad of Tishrei	Conjunction	Diff	Skew
1	Mon	5	204	Sep 6, 3761 23:11			
2	Fri	14	0	Aug 27, 3760 7:59			
3	Tue	22	876	Aug 16, 3759 16:48			
4	Mon	20	385	Sep 4, 3758 14:21			
5	Sat	5	181	Aug 23, 3757 23:10			
6	Wed	13	1057	Aug 13, 3756 7:58			
7	Tue	11	566	Sep 1, 3755 5:31			
8	Sat	20	362	Aug 21, 3754 14:20			
9	Fri	17	951	Sep 8, 3753 11:52			
10	Wed	2	747	Aug 28, 3752 20:41			
11	Sun	11	543	Aug 18, 3751 5:30			
12	Sat	9	52	Sep 6, 3750 3:02			
13	Wed	17	928	Aug 25, 3749 11:51			
14	Mon	2	724	Aug 14, 3748 20:40			
15	Sun	0	233	Sep 2, 3747 18:12			
16	Thu	9	29	Aug 23, 3746 3:01			
17	Mon	17	905	Aug 11, 3745 11:50			
18	Sun	15	414	Aug 30, 3744 9:22			
19	Fri	0	210	Aug 19, 3743 18:11			
5751	Thu	0	258	Sep 19, 1990 18:14	Sep 19, 1990 2:46	15h 28m	1d
5752	Mon	9	54	Sep 9, 1991 3:03	Sep 8, 1991 13:01	14h 2m	1d
5753	Sun	6	643	Sep 27, 1992 0:35	Sep 26, 1992 12:40	11h 56m	1d
5754	Thu	15	439	Sep 16, 1993 9:24	Sep 16, 1993 5:10	4h 14m	2d
5755	Tue	0	235	Sep 5, 1994 18:13	Sep 5, 1994 20:33	-2h 20m	2d
5756	Sun	21	824	Sep 24, 1995 15:45	Sep 24, 1995 18:55	-3h 9m	3d
5757	Fri	6	620	Sep 13, 1996 0:34	Sep 13, 1996 1:07	-0h 33m	2d
5758	Thu	4	129	Oct 1, 1997 22:07	Oct 1, 1997 18:52	3h 15m	2d
5759	Mon	12	1005	Sep 21, 1998 6:55	Sep 20, 1998 19:01	11h 55m	2d
5760	Fri	21	801	Sep 10, 1999 15:44	Sep 10, 1999 0:02	15h 42m	2d
5761	Thu	19	310	Sep 28, 2000 13:17	Sep 27, 2000 21:53	15h 24m	2d
5762	Tue	4	106	Sep 17, 2001 22:05	Sep 17, 2001 12:27	9h 39m	1d
5763	Sat	12	982	Sep 7, 2002 6:54	Sep 7, 2002 5:10	1h 45m	2d
5764	Fri	10	491	Sep 26, 2003 4:27	Sep 26, 2003 5:09	-0h 42m	2d
5765	Tue	19	287	Sep 14, 2004 13:15	Sep 14, 2004 16:29	-3h 13m	2d
5766	Mon	16	876	Oct 3, 2005 10:48	Oct 3, 2005 12:28	-1h 39m	2d
5767	Sat	1	672	Sep 22, 2006 19:37	Sep 22, 2006 13:45	5h 52m	1d
5768	Wed	10	468	Sep 12, 2007 4:26	Sep 11, 2007 14:44	13h 42m	1d
5769	Tue	7	1057	Sep 30, 2008 1:58	Sep 29, 2008 10:12	15h 47m	1d
5770	Sat	16	853	Sep 19, 2009 10:47	Sep 18, 2009 20:44	14h 3m	2d
5771	Thu	1	649	Sep 8, 2010 19:36	Sep 8, 2010 12:30	7h 6m	1d
5772	Tue	23	158	Sep 27, 2011 17:08	Sep 27, 2011 13:09	4h 0m	2d
5773	Sun	7	1034	Sep 16, 2012 1:57	Sep 16, 2012 4:11	-2h 14m	2d
5774	Thu	16	830	Sep 5, 2013 10:46	Sep 5, 2013 13:36	-2h 50m	2d
5775	Wed	14	339	Sep 24, 2014 8:18	Sep 24, 2014 8:14	0h 5m	2d
5776	Sun	23	135	Sep 13, 2015 17:07	Sep 13, 2015 8:41	8h 26m	2d
5777	Sat	20	724	Oct 1, 2016 14:40	Oct 1, 2016 2:12	12h 28m	2d
5778	Thu	5	520	Sep 20, 2017 23:28	Sep 20, 2017 7:30	15h 59m	1d
5779	Mon	14	316	Sep 10, 2018 8:17	Sep 9, 2018 20:01	12h 17m	2d
5780	Sun	11	905	Sep 29, 2019 5:50	Sep 28, 2019 20:26	9h 24m	2d
5781	Thu	20	701	Sep 17, 2020 14:38	Sep 17, 2020 13:00	1h 39m	2d

The chart is arranged according to the following column titles:

- Hebrew year, Day, Hours, Parts of the Molad according to the Hebrew calendar system.
- Gregorian date and time of the Molad of Tishrei.
- Gregorian date and time of its Lunar Conjunction in Jerusalem.
- Time difference between the Molad and the Conjunction. This Difference column is especially noteworthy because many, if not most, traditional Jewish commentators erroneously equate the Molad and the Conjunction (as I too believed, before the start of this study). We see from the table that the Molad of Tishrei is differentiated from the Conjunction, preceding it by a span of up to a maximum of 5 hours and 10 minutes, or following it by a span of up to a maximum of 16 hours and 17 minutes. Thus the Molad clearly is not synonymous with the Conjunction!
- Skew. The Molad imputes a virtual Re'iyah or sighting of the moon, and the Molad of Tishrei is the Hebrew day (without consideration of Rabbinical Dehiyyot[6]) on which Rosh HaShanah begins after sunset. Skew is the number of days from this virtual Re'iyah until the New Moon can actually be seen, again after sunset.

One would think that the goal of a calculated calendar would be to simulate the witness-based calendar as closely as possible. In other words, rather than wait for witnesses to appear and testify, it would be helpful if we could know in advance (and the more in advance the better) when the

---

[6] Dehiyyot are four rabbinical rules of postponement of Rosh HaShanah that help round off the date without affecting the Molad. They serve to prevent oddities from occurring, such as in the length of the year or in holidays that must not fall on particular days of the week so as not to cause various problems. They will be discussed later at length.

moon's sighting will be, as then we can make our plans around fixed festivals – as indeed we do today.

Considering that lunar months can only be 29 or 30 days long, one would expect Skews of 1, 0, or -1 – in other words, that the calculated Molad will fall on the day after, the same day, or the day before the real sighting, creating an even distribution or bell curve of deviation. This is where the results of my study become so surprising and significant. They clearly show that the motivation of whosoever designed the calculation could not have been to simulate the real sighting as accurately as possible. On the contrary, instead of falling before, after, or on it, the day[7] of the calculated Molad *always precedes* the day of the actual New Moon!

It should be noted that this chart is based on an approximate model only, and the data is not exact. "Skew" was approximated by the assumption that the New Moon would actually be seen if the time from the Conjunction to sunset exceeds 24 hours. The 24 hours is consistent with the statement of the Rambam, who writes:

> הלבנה נסתרת בכל חדש וחדש ואינה נראית כמו שני ימים או פחות או יתר, כמו יום אחד קודם שתדבק בשמש בסוף החדש וכמו יום אחד אחר שתדבק בשמש ותראה במערב בערב, ובליל שתראה בערב אחר שנסתרה הוא תחלת החדש.

The moon is hidden every month for around two days more or less – for approximately one day before and one day after it approaches the sun and is seen in the evening, in the West. That evening, when it becomes visible after being hidden, marks the new month.[8]

---

[7] Day starting at sunset and ending just before sunset of the morrow.

[8] Hilchot Kiddush HaHodesh 1:3. Note that other Jewish sources say that the moon is not seen for 24 hours (from the last visibility of Old Moon to the first visibility of New Moon), but that nonetheless the time from the Conjunction until the sighting of the New Moon is six hours. My tables show the time from the Lunar Conjunction to the New Moon to span on average 40 hours.

Before we move on to discuss the science of the chart, let us take note of how the Jewish sources and science will interface. It is the thesis of this book that we can accurately relate dates in this table to particular Jewish sources. One of the most well known of these sources is the conflict between Rabban Gamliel[9] and R' Yehoshua that appears in the Talmud[10], tractate Rosh HaShanah; and the figure of Rabban Gamliel will be of great importance in the coming pages.

Rabban Gamliel was not averse to science. On the contrary, the Mishnah[11] tells us that he had diagrams or models of the phases of the moon, providing illustrations for use during the questioning of the witnesses. He was the first in Jewish tradition to quantify the essential constant month of the Hebrew Calendar as 29 days, 12 hours and 793 halakim. This is an extremely close approximation of the average value of a Synodic Month[12]. This will be discussed further in later chapters.

From tractate Rosh HaShanah, 25a:

> אמר להם רבן גמליאל: כך מקובלני מבית אבי אבא: אין חדושה של לבנה פחותה מעשרים ותשעה יום ומחצה ושני שלישי שעה ושבעים ושלשה חלקים.

> Rabban Gamliel says: thus I learned from the house of my fathers, new moons are separated by 29 and a half days, two-thirds of an hour [720 halakim] plus 73 halakim.

---

[9] Also spelled Gamaliel. This was Gamliel II, also known as Gamliel of Yavne, who lived through the fall of the Second Temple; not to be confused with Gamliel I ("Gamliel HaZaqen"), his grandfather.

[10] In this work, "Talmud" will refer to the Talmud Bavli (Babylonian Talmud). Where the Yerushalmi (Jerusalem Talmud) is referred to, this will be made explicit.

[11] Rosh HaShanah 2:8

[12] The value cited by Rabban Gamliel is only a half a second greater than the contemporary scientific determination of the average Synodic Month. The number came from data collected by the Chaldeans, in ancient Babylonia.

Thus the source of the first four columns in the Molad of Tishrei study is Rabban Gamliel. Each Molad of Tishrei is 12 or 13 equidistant Moladot from every other Molad of Tishrei, for reasons explained below.

Rabban Gamliel also knew something about the next column, the Conjunction. The Conjunctions are not equidistant at all; they appear to vary randomly. Rabban Gamliel actually knew this fact too:

פעמים שבא בארוכה ופעמים שבא בקצרה.

Sometimes [the moon] travels a long route and sometimes [the moon] travels a short route. (ibid.)

Rabban Gamliel lacked the tools to calculate the actual path of the moon. It is modern science, and specifically Celestial Mechanics, that provide us with the numbers in the Conjunction column. We will explain more later.

Surprising Results

In just the small sample of the study brought above, looking at the final column it becomes clear that seeing the New Moon two days after the Molad is the norm and not an anomaly.

From my complete study of the Molad of Tishrei from 70 through 2018 CE, several surprising facts emerge:

Firstly, throughout the entire 2020 years of the study, the moon could not be seen on Rosh HaShanah except by virtue of Rabbinical Dehiyyot. Since the Dehiyyot were later additions to the Fixed Hebrew Calendar, the initial calendar system was designed in such a way that no one would ever see the moon on Rosh HaShanah! In fact, 26% of the time Tishrei begins one day before, and 70% of the time two days before, any possibility of seeing the moon.

As I wrote above, this is odd. Could they not have adopted a mathematical model that more closely approximated the moon's actual appearance? I will argue that the answer is no. This was done deliberately, for reasons I will later explain. The fact that the initial Fixed Hebrew Calendar was set up such that the majority of the time Tishrei began two days before the New Moon was not an error. On the contrary, this was one of the primary purposes of the adoption of the system, a point that will be established at greater length in a later chapter.

A second surprising fact emerging from the study alongside these one- and two-day discrepancies is that in almost 4% of the 2020 years studied, the New Moon could be sighted only a full three days after the day of the Molad, as the chart below demonstrates:

Discrepancy Skew	Count	Percentage	Conjunction Difference
1 Day	522	25.84%	11h 42m
2 Day	1420	70.30%	3h 25m
3 Day	78	3.86%	-3h 42m
	2020	100.00%	5h 10m

There are 78 cases of a three-day discrepancy over the 2020 years of the study. You can view the specific years in which they fall in a chart entitled "Three-Day Discrepancies," located in the appendix.

In this book, I will be taking a special interest in four of these 78 cases: the years 120, 198, 358, and 835 CE; and in the figures respectively associated with these dates: Rabban Gamliel, R' Hiyya, Hillel II, and the Exilarch. For these four points in time, to gain more accurate data I enlisted the aid of a Dutch astronomer, Robert H. van Gent, who provided me with very useful Global Visibility Charts. He also kindly made accessible to me the data for the years 1999 through 2018 CE, which were already prepared.

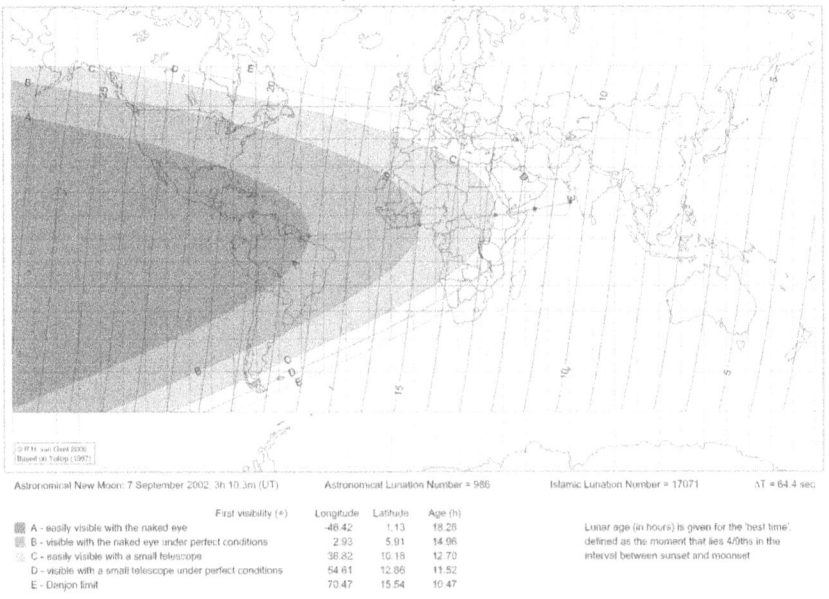

This is the van Gent chart for Saturday, September 7, 2002[13], the year I first began thinking about these issues. The darkest shaded area represents the locations where the moon could be seen by an average observer with the naked eye. Clearly, only with a telescope under perfect conditions could the moon be seen in Israel. Sightings by telescope are, of course, invalid for our purposes. We confirm, therefore, that on Saturday the moon could not be seen with the naked eye in Israel; hence, the Muslims' choice to start Rajab only on Sunday was, in fact, correct, as for them the local visibility of the moon is the sole determining factor.

Summary

This chapter documents my realization that the Fixed Hebrew Calendar was not merely a "high-tech" fixed

---

[13] http://www.sodhaibur.com/van-gent-maps/2002-09-07.pdf

version of the traditional Jewish system documented in the Talmud, which established the Hebrew months via the testimony of actual witnesses at the calendrical court. Far from it.

It was found that with this calendar in place, the New Moon could never actually be seen on the Molad of Tishrei. In fact, in a majority of the cases (70%), the Molad of Tishrei fell two days before witnesses would have any ability to see the New Moon. It was also noted that in special cases (less than 4% of the total), the New Moon was not visible until three days after the Molad.

Hillel the Patriarch

The Inauguration Myth

It is an almost universally held belief that the Hebrew Calendar as we know it today was initiated by a Patriarch named Hillel (known as Hillel II, to differentiate him from Hillel the Elder), in the year 358/9 CE. As Rabbi David Feinstein, Rosh Yeshivah of Mesivtha Tifereth Jerusalem notes in his book *The Jewish Calendar*, published 2003:

> This happened, Rambam writes, toward the end of the Talmudic period, in the times of Abaye and Rava. Ramban (*Sefer ha-Zechus*) gives more details about when this happened. It was in a time when the leader of the people was Hillel, a great-grandson of Rabbi Yehudah the Prince (Rabbeinu HaKodosh, the redactor of the Mishnah). Seeing the inevitable, Hillel and his court established the calendar for all future years, based on the known astronomical calculations and providing for all eventualities. This took place in the year 4119 from Creation, corresponding to the year 359 C.E. [sic.]

The author here cites the Rambam and the Ramban, two of our great medieval commentators. Whereas some rabbis might tell you that the source of this information is the Talmud, there is in fact no Talmudic mention of a Patriarch named Hillel, nor of the establishment of a Fixed Hebrew Calendar. This despite the fact that 358/9 CE is precisely the time when the Talmud Yerushalmi, and in its wake the Talmud Bavli, were soon to be redacted and disseminated – a perfect forum for promoting the calendar. After all, what is the purpose of a calendar if not to publicize the timing of shared events? Why then does it not merit some mention at least?

Likewise, neither a Patriarch named Hillel nor the establishment of a Fixed Hebrew Calendar is found in the

10th-century *Iggeret Rav Sherira Gaon*, a principal source of the history of the Talmudic period.

The only primary source, from which all later sources take their lead, is the mention of a certain "Hillel ben R' Yehuda" in the early 11th century, in a responsum of R' Hai Gaon cited by R' Avraham ben Hiyya:

> עד ימי הלל בר' יהודה בשנת תר'ע לשטרות, שמאותה שנה לא הקדימו ולא אחרו, אלא אחזו הסדר הזה אשר היה בידם.

> ...until the days of Hillel ben R' Yehuda, in the year 670 of the Seleucid era, from which year they did not bring forward or postpone, but kept to this cycle which was at hand ...

R' Hai Gaon's words have been widely assumed to be referring to the establishment of the Fixed Hebrew Calendar. The year cited corresponds to Hebrew Year 4119, or 358/9 CE.

It is a curious fact that the establishment of the Fixed Hebrew Calendar is here precisely dated as having happened in the year 358/9 CE. Few precisely dated historical halachic proclamations have been handed down to us by our Rabbis, so one might justifiably wonder what was special about this date and what Rabbi David Feinstein meant by the use of the word "inevitable" in his description of the transition from a witness-based calendar to one based on calculation.

There is no obvious reason why in 358 CE the dissemination of calendar information in Eretz Yisrael would have suddenly become more problematic than in previous times. Eretz Yisrael was not then in the focus of Roman hostile activity; on the contrary, soon afterwards, in 362 CE, the Roman Emperor Julian wanted to permit the Jews to rebuild the Temple. So the phrase "this happened" in the paragraph quoted above from *The Jewish Calendar* appears rather too simplistic, if not downright inaccurate.

Furthermore, the author's reliance on Rambam is unfounded. Rambam does not mention a Patriarch named

Hillel establishing a calendar; just the opposite. In Hilchot Kiddush HaHodesh (5:2), Rambam states:

ודבר זה הלכה למשה מסיני הוא, שבזמן שיש סנהדרין קובעין על הראייה ובזמן שאין שם סנהדרין קובעין על חשבון זה שאנו מחשבין בו היום ואין נזקקין לראייה.

> This is the law of Moses from Sinai, that when there is a Sanhedrin [in Eretz Yisrael] we establish the months on the basis of sightings, but when there is no Sanhedrin we use the calculation in our hands today and pay no attention to sightings.

In his discussion here of the calendrical system, the Rambam does not cite R' Hai Gaon, as the Ramban does, and there is no Hillel in the vicinity. Note, however, that he does believe that an essential element for the implementation of the calendar is the absence of a Sanhedrin. This belief has led many to the notion that the year 358 represented the disbanding of the Sanhedrin, and hence the implementation of the calculated calendar. In the Wikipedia entry on the Sanhedrin, for example, it is recorded that

> The final binding decision of the Sanhedrin was in 358, when the Hebrew Calendar was adopted.

Yet looking back at the conflict between Rabban Gamliel and R' Yehoshua, described in tractate Rosh HaShanah and occurring two centuries earlier, there does not appear to be any Sanhedrin council influencing Rabban Gamliel. This does not mean the Sanhedrin did not exist, but rather that perhaps it was not involved in routine calendrical decisions.

The aforementioned *Iggeret Rav Sherira Gaon* likewise makes no mention in this period of the disbanding of the Sanhedrin. I would claim, in fact, that rather than deducing that 358 marked the end of the Sanhedrin, we should understand that the reverse was true – the end of the Sanhedrin marked 358, so to speak. In other words, later commentators attempting to understand the Hillel story, and the supposed shift to the calculated calendar in 358 CE, artificially located the end of the Sanhedrin in this year to explain the reason for the shift.

Moving forward in our historical search for the inauguration of the calculated calendar, in the Exilarch's Letter of 835/6 CE, discovered in the Cairo Geniza, we find that Bavel – the Babylonian Diaspora – was still deferring to Eretz Yisrael for calendrical decisions, implying that the Hebrew Calendar had yet to be publicly implemented even at this late date.

Lastly, in 922 CE there was a major dispute between Saadia Gaon in Bavel and Rabbi Aaron ben Meir in Eretz Yisrael over the "Dehiyyah Molad Zaqen," a postponement rule that will be discussed in depth. Interestingly, neither Ben Meir nor Saadia indicate any knowledge of a Patriarch named Hillel, nor of the establishment of a Fixed Hebrew Calendar in 358 CE. In fact, Rabbi Menahem Kasher, in his magnum opus the *Torah Shelemah*, notes that Saadia argues that it dated from the time of Moshe Rabbeinu.

Of all the scholarly books written about the Jewish Calendar, few are as extensive and well documented as Sacha Stern's book *Calendar and Community, A History of the Jewish Calendar 2nd century BCE – 10th century CE*. Stern is a Professor of Rabbinic Judaism at the Department of Hebrew and Jewish Studies at University College London. On pages 175–179 of this work, Stern discusses the Hillel tradition and its advocacy by the Ramban and his disciples, the Ritva and the Rashba. Interestingly, he notes that in one of the Rashba's responsa (4:254) the latter states that he does not know the origin of the Hillel tradition. Indeed, Stern cites other traditions as to the origin of the calculated calendar – for instance, R' Isaac Israeli sets it at the end of the period of the Talmudic Sages, 499/500 CE. Stern notes:

> Another tradition appears in a baraita that, though cited only by Karaites, is ostensibly a genuine, albeit late, rabbinic work. This baraita is a sequel to M. RH 2:8-9,

and describes how the dispute between R' Gamliel of Yavneh (early 2nd century) and his opponents regarding the date of the Day of Atonement led to the institution, by R' Gamliel himself, of the fixed rabbinic calendar.

And Stern concludes his chapter on Hillel II:

> The very existence of a 'Hillel the Patriarch' in the mid-4th century may thus be treated as uncertain.

A New Perspective

Based on all of the above, as well as various proofs I plan to offer, my aim in this book is to completely overturn common thinking on this matter and refute the myth that, "In 358 CE, Hillel launched the calculated calendar." I will be arguing that it was created at an earlier time and publicly implemented at a later time, such that this myth is not useful in understanding either of these historical events.

The reader will notice that I have separated the two events that the Hillel myth conflated – the creation and the public revelation of the calendar. I now enlist my reader to share with me an important presumption. There does not appear to be any historical accuracy in the notion of a press release by the Public Relations Department of the Sanhedrin to the effect that, from a particular date, witnesses will no longer be accepted at the calendrical court and hereafter the Hebrew Calendar will be produced by a calculation. Instead, I am going to presume throughout this book that there was a period, most likely spanning centuries, where behind the curtain of the calendrical court the "Wizard of Oz," i.e. the Patriarch (Nasi), was accepting witnesses according to a pre-set criterion that they testify to the days *already specified* by the calculated Molad. In other words, the creation of the Fixed Hebrew Calendar harks back to a much earlier (for now unspecified) date, yet it remained hidden over a protracted span of time. Much that will be soon presented will validate this assumption.

As a clarifying note: in the search for, and description of, the creation and gradual implementation of the Fixed Hebrew Calendar, there are actually several different steps that needed to be considered:

1   The scientific basis, i.e., the length of an average lunar month (Synodic Month) and the fact that there are approximately 235 lunar months in 19 solar years.

2   The procedure used, for example rounding the result of the calculation back to the start of the day (from sunset onwards) when establishing Rosh HaShanah.

3   The implementation by the calendrical court, in secret.

4   The enactment of modifications, like the Dehiyyot or other rabbinical postponements.

5   The dissemination of the process into the public sphere, now no longer secret.

Hopefully the context will make each of the steps clear.

Events of the Year 358 CE

The question to be asked, in that case, is: "If neither the creation nor the public implementation of the Fixed Hebrew Calendar occurred in 358 CE, what, if anything, did happen in that year?"

As exhaustive as Stern's research was, he missed an important resource, one that helps us glimpse an answer to this question: lunar science. From a lunar astronomical point of view, the date of Rosh HaShanah 358 CE that prompted the statement about the days of Hillel ben R' Yehuda is, in fact, of great significance.

In our first chapter, we learned a surprising fact from the Molad of Tishrei study: that a few times each century, the Molad of Tishrei launches Rosh HaShanah three days before it would be possible for witnesses to actually see the moon. Here is a list of those years for the four-century period that interests us, spanning the years 120-358 CE.

We find nine years with a three-day discrepancy in this period, totaling about 4% of it – this is consistent with the 78 such years in the entire 2020 years of the study, also about 4%.

Year	Day	Hrs	Pts	Molad of Tishrei	Conjunction	Skew
3774	Sat	22	142	Sep 21, 0013 16:07	Sep 21, 0013 20:54	3d
3783	Mon	19	685	Sep 12, 0022 13:38	Sep 12, 0022 18:27	3d
3803	Mon	20	1076	Sep 1, 0042 14:59	Sep 1, 0042 18:40	3d
3819	Wed	22	410	Sep 4, 0058 16:22	Sep 4, 0058 19:36	3d
3835	Fri	23	824	Sep 7, 0074 17:45	Sep 7, 0074 20:35	3d
3844	Sun	21	287	Aug 29, 0083 15:15	Aug 29, 0083 19:23	3d
3881	Mon	21	601	Sep 9, 0120 15:33	Sep 9, 0120 19:04	3d
3897	Wed	22	1015	Sep 12, 0136 16:56	Sep 12, 0136 19:31	3d
3906	Fri	20	478	Sep 3, 0145 14:26	Sep 3, 0145 18:08	3d
3934	Thu	23	249	Sep 23, 0173 17:13	Sep 23, 0173 22:00	3d
3943	Sat	20	792	Sep 14, 0182 14:44	Sep 14, 0182 18:13	3d
3959	Mon	22	126	Sep 17, 0198 16:07	Sep 17, 0198 18:16	3d
4004	Fri	22	394	Sep 1, 0243 16:21	Sep 1, 0243 21:07	3d
4066	Wed	21	585	Sep 6, 0305 15:32	Sep 6, 0305 20:29	3d
4119	Sat	23	233	**Sep 20, 0358 17:12**	Sep 20, 0358 21:41	3d
4128	Mon	20	776	Sep 11, 0367 14:43	Sep 11, 0367 19:15	3d

I was amazed when I first noticed the year 358 CE (Hebrew year 4119) on this list, and this unanticipated fact provided one of my first major clues as to what was really going on.

The reader will see that the Molad of Tishrei for 358 CE (Hebrew year 4119) was Saturday, September 20, at 5:12 PM (i.e. Shabbat at 23 hours and 233 halakim). This is very late – it is almost at the end of the Hebrew day, just before sunset.

The operating principle of the Fixed Hebrew Calendar is that the Molad is always rolled back to the previous sunset and substituted for the actual sighting. This means that in Tishrei 4119, it was considered as if the moon had been sighted almost a full day earlier – 23 hours and 48 minutes, to be precise – than its calculated Molad.

The Ramban might have known the fact that the Molad of Tishrei 358 CE fell at almost the very end of a Hebrew day, though it is certainly an arduous calculation when you lack the computers that we have today. But in the absence of lunar science, the Ramban could not possibly have known the timing of the actual Lunar Conjunction in relation to the Molad, nor could he have known the exceptional orbit of the moon (a significant factor, as we will discuss below).

Today we are assisted by a developed lunar science which permits us to go back in time and to see the sky that Hillel ben R' Yehuda would have seen that year. Though I cannot insert a modern planetarium into this book, I can bring you some tables and maps.

Visible Old Moon, Molad Same Night

On the facing page is a table from data provided by the Sky View Café program. From this table it becomes apparent that on the day of the Molad it was impossible to actually see the New Moon.[14]

The table indicates that on September 19, 358 CE, a very bright (3.6%) Old Moon rose at 4:11 AM. The sun did not rise until 5:45 AM, meaning that this moon was visible for almost an hour and a half in the sky. Yet that evening, the Fixed Hebrew Calendar dictated the start of Rosh HaShanah. Although this means that we must consider it as if the New Moon was seen, in reality the New Moon was

---

[14] To verify the Molad you can use the link: http://www.realluach.com/mld.php?zone=mot&JS=3&y=4119&m=1. The difference in hours is due to my starting of the day after 6:00 PM at night.

The Moon of Hillel II – 358 CE

Molad of Tishrei	Sat, Sep 20, 17:12						
Conjunction	Sat, Sep 20, 21:56						

Moonrise	Illum %	Age	Sunrise	Sunset	Moonset	Illum %	Age	Note
Thu, Sep 18, 3:13	8.8%	2d 19h	Thu, Sep 18, 5:45					Old Moon still bright enough to be seen after sunrise.
Fri, Sep 19, 4:11	3.6%	1d 18h	Fri, Sep 19, 5:45	Fri, Sep 19, 18:02				Old Moon seen only before dawn for 1 hour and a half. Possible to walk 4 miles as per R' Hiyya in the Yerushalmi. Calculated day of Molad starts after sunset so moon is effectively sanctified that evening.
Sat, Sep 20, 5:11	0.6%	0d 17h	Sat, Sep 20, 5:46	Sat, Sep 20, 18:01	Sat, Sep 20, 17:45	–0d 4h		Moon very close to sun and hidden by its brightness.
				Sun, Sep 21, 17:59	Sun, Sep 21, 18:24	.9%	0d 20h	According to van Gent charts, no possibility of seeing moon on Sunday after sunset.
				Mon, Sep 22, 17:58	Mon, Sep 22, 19:04	4.5%	1d 21h	Moon seen by all viewers per van Gent chart.

Moon invisible for (total of)   3d 12h 13m
Sky View Café 5.8

Hillel the Patriarch 25

only seen after sunset September 22, 358 CE, three days later.

In fact, from the inception of the fixed calendar and to this very day, Old Moon and New Moon can *never* be seen on the same day. This point will be crucial in the coming pages. The 1st-2nd century Talmudic sage R' Yohanan ben Nuri knew this fact well. Clearly not privy to the secret use of the fixed calendar, R' Yohanan ben Nuri's surprise and dismay are palpable in the Mishnah's description of the following occurrence, which we will discuss in greater depth when we deal with the year 120 CE:

> משנה. מעשה שבאו שנים, ואמרו: ראינוהו שחרית במזרח וערבית במערב. אמר רבי יוחנן בן נורי: עדי שקר הם.
>
> Two witnesses came and said: "We saw the Old Moon in the morning and the New Moon in the evening." R' Yohanan ben Nuri said: "They are false witnesses!"[15]

People knew that whenever the Old Moon was seen in the morning, a new month could not yet start that evening. Jews and non-Jews alike knew this as most of the Semitic world was using a lunar calendar at the time. Amongst all the Semitic peoples, the New Moon was cause for a festival. It was common knowledge that lunar festivals, such as Rosh Hodesh, started a day or more after the Old Moon disappeared from being a fixture of the early morning sky, signaling the end of the lunar month. Thus, any farmer with an iota of common sense would not start his travels to the city to celebrate the lunar festival while there was still an Old Moon in the morning sky; but rather delay setting out until this was no longer the case. Otherwise, he would arrive early while they were still setting up!

Returning to 358 CE, this brings into question the Ramban's almost universally followed claim that that year marked the inauguration of the Fixed Hebrew Calendar. Ramban, of course, did not have any knowledge of the

---

[15] Rosh HaShanah 24b-25a.

lunar conditions in 358 CE; such was not contained in the note of Hai Gaon. We, however, do know these conditions, through our tools based on Celestial Mechanics.

For the Ramban and his myriad supporters, this calculated calendar system represented a good replacement for the witnessed system. But, as we have seen, it was not actually good at all. Rosh HaShanah 358 CE was established as falling a full three days before the New Moon could be seen – meaning that at dawn of that day, a bright Old Moon would be seen dominating the pre-sunrise skies.

For the Old Moon to be shining merrily Erev Rosh Hashanah would, I believe, have come as quite a shock to the people of that time. This is a bit of a historical conjecture, but one must remember that sun and moon were crucial cogs in the time system for those lacking our contemporary time tools. I am sure that folk wisdom of the time was aware that the New Moon could never be seen a mere twelve or so hours after the Old Moon was still visible in the pre-dawn skies. Rabbi Yohanan ben Nuri too, speaking earlier, in 120 CE, rejected such a scenario as ridiculous – and rightfully so.

The Missing New Moon

However, seeing the Old Moon and drawing conclusions was only a small part of the problem. After all, many had perhaps not noticed the Old Moon, well illuminated or not – arguably, people do not search the skies for the Old Moon they way they do for the New Moon. More impactful would have been what occurred over the coming days.

For anyone hearing that the moon was sanctified as Molad on Saturday morning, September 20, 358 CE, it would be a reasonable assumption that witnesses actually saw the New Moon the previous evening and testified at the court. People were familiar with the witness-based system. The absence of the Fixed Hebrew Calendar from the Talmud, and the fact that the only source we have for calculation is the obscure reference emerging over 600 years later in the quote from Avraham ben Hiyya, leads us to feel fairly confident that Jewish society at the time would not have been aware of a fixed calendar. It was a secret.

So let us leave then the few who might have seen the Old Moon on Friday morning and turn to the many who would undoubtedly notice that, despite the sanctification Saturday morning, no moon was seen either Saturday night or Sunday night, at a time when it should have been visible and growing brighter.

This would have created much confusion, as the continuation of the Mishnah we cited above, dealing with events two centuries previously, indicates:

> ועוד באו שנים ואמרו: ראינוהו בזמנו, ובליל עיבורו לא נראה. וקיבלן רבן גמליאל. אמר רבי דוסא בן הורכינס: עדי שקר הן.
>
> On another occasion, two witnesses came and said: "We saw [the Molad] at its proper time." The next night it was not seen. Rabban Gamliel accepted them, but R' Dosa ben Horkynos said: "They are false witnesses!"[16]

We understand this Mishnah better now. In a sighting-based case, we could not accept the notion that the moon was born on Friday night and yet seen neither on Saturday night nor on Sunday night. Nonetheless, in both Tishrei 120 CE and Tishrei 358 CE, based on the calculated calendar, it was presumed for all intents and purposes that the moon was "seen" Friday night, even though it still could not be seen on Saturday and Sunday night. This would cause anyone not in the know – such as R' Yehoshua, R' Yohanan ben Nuri, and R' Dosa ben Horkynos in the year 120 CE, or the ordinary masses in both 120 and 358 CE – to feel confusion, frustration, and even anger, as will be seen later.

---

[16] Rosh HaShanah 25a.

Significance of the Orbit

The fact that no moon at all was seen until after sunset on Monday, September 22, 358 CE, is borne out by modern astronomical science. Theoretically, according to the chart based on Sky View figures on page 25, the moon could have been seen Sunday evening after sunset, as the moon was 20 hours old and shone at a brightness of 0.9%. But there is another factor to be taken into account – the moon's orbit, which varies as it moves across the global map, affecting the possibility of sighting.

In the case of 358 CE, there was a very long path of 3½ days. Other years hold paths of 1½ days and 2½ days. This is consistent with another observer of the moon, Rabban Gamliel who indicates, in Rosh HaShanah 25a, a knowledge of the moon's varying orbit:

תניא, אמר להם רבן גמליאל לחכמים: כך מקובלני מבית אבי אבא: פעמים שבא בארוכה, ופעמים שבא בקצרה.

> Rabban Gamliel said to the Sages, "This I have received from the house of my father's fathers – [The moon] sometimes takes a long path and sometimes takes a short path."

Rabban Gamliel could not, however, know the exact path figures without modern lunar science.

Once again we turn to van Gent, who upon my request was kind enough to provide a graphic of the path of the moon for the year under discussion (below – and link to full map in this footnote[17]). Examining it, we learn that the moon of Tishrei 4119 (358 CE) was traveling in a very unusual extreme southern orbit, preventing any possibility of an actual sighting until a full three days after the calculated Molad had dictated the initiation of Rosh HaShanah. In fact, 358 CE was one of the most skewed years of all the 2020 years in the study.

---

[17] http://www.sodhaibur.com/van-gent-maps/lunvis_4119.pdf

Here is the excerpt from the Global Visibility Map for September 20, 358 CE. The Conjunction occurred at 21:56 Israel Standard Time. As shown on the map, the Conjunction was over Antarctica, as extreme south as one can get. Such an event happens in Tishrei only a few times each century.

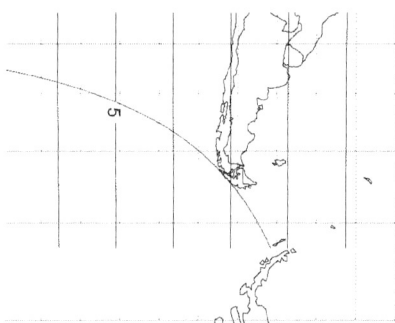

The next day was the 21st. On this, the day after the Lunar Conjunction, one might normally expect this map to show that the moon can be sighted; but not in this case. Neither of the dark grey parabolas A nor B covers the northern hemisphere, thus precluding any sighting in Eretz Yisrael.

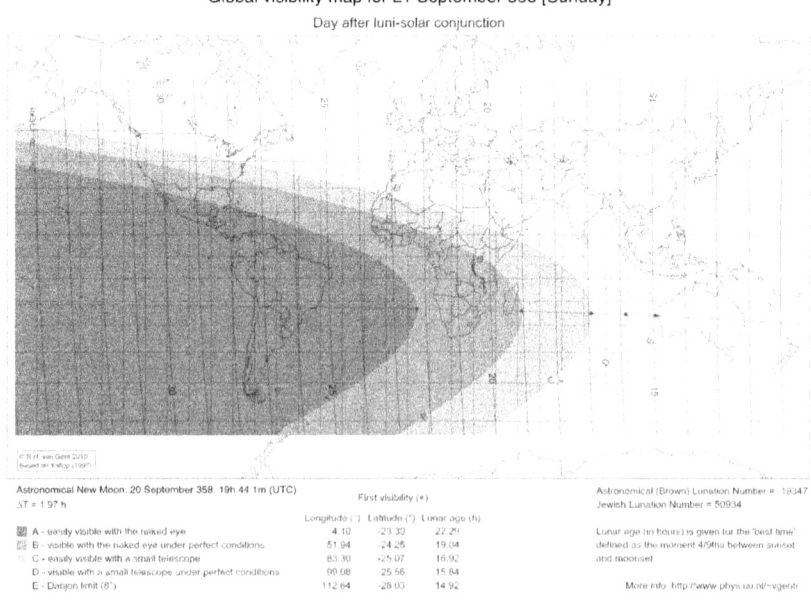

Finally, the map for Monday, September 22nd, marking 44½ hours after the Conjunction, shows the New Moon actually sighted in Eretz Yisrael.

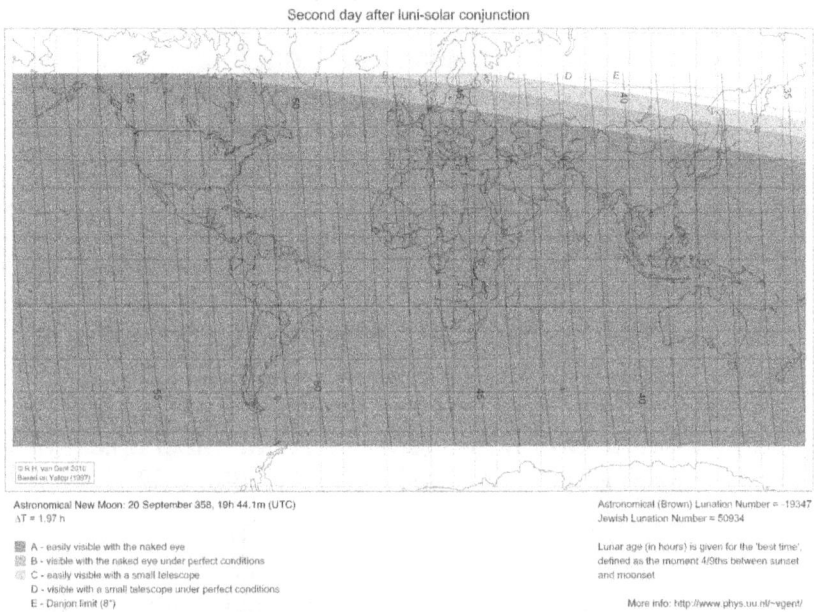

It was upon this calculation that the final entry in the Sky View "Moon of Hillel II – 358 CE" table on page 25 was based. From the point when the moon was last seen on Friday morning until the point when the moon was first seen on Monday, three 3 days 12 hours and 13 minutes had passed – certainly a long path indeed.

No Launch in 358 CE

Bearing in mind all of this new information about Rosh HaShanah 358 CE, we can now confidently propose that a year in which this rare three-day discrepancy occurred is clearly not the year in which to officially launch the fixed calendar! No one would understand what was going on (Old Moon in the morning, followed by official Molad in the evening, and then no sighting of New Moon for three days!). Chaos would ensue. To put it bluntly: 358 CE was the least ideal year in the entire century for such a launch.

Certainly, had the Ramban known the lunar reality of 358 CE, he would never have claimed that Hillel II had inaugurated the Fixed Hebrew Calendar at that date. We cannot fault him for his understanding, formulated based on what he knew – after all, it must be unsettling to the Rabbis not to know when our calendar changed from a witness-based to calculation-based one. To paraphrase what we will hear Abba, R' Simlai's father, declaring in a coming chapter: "If you don't know the Sod Ha'ibur ('Secret of the Intercalation') what else don't you know?"

At this point, if the reader has fully grasped my line of reasoning, he or she should be thoroughly astonished. I remember my own reaction when I first perceived the correlation between modern Celestial Mechanics and a source from Hai Gaon referencing the year 358 CE.

NASA, the National Aeronautics and Space Administration, established its catalog *Six Millennium Catalog of Phases of the Moon* to aid historians who required eclipse data for their research. I have been able to take advantage of it in a way unintended by its authors, by drawing on its conjunction data to discuss the Fixed Hebrew Calendar!

Let us return to the source quote:

> עד ימי הלל בר' יהודה בשנת תר'ע לשטרות, שמאותה שנה לא הקדימו ולא אחרו, אלא אחזו הסדר הזה אשר היה בידם ...

> ... until the days of Hillel ben R' Yehuda, in the year 670 of the Seleucid era, from which year they did not bring forward or postpone, but kept to this cycle which was at hand ...

As I have already explained, the widely held interpretation of this short statement is that Hillel ben R' Yehuda – who of course must have been a Patriarch, else whence the authority to do this? – replaced the unpredictable witnessed calendar with a known calendar. Thus, the fixed the month of Elul was henceforth always 29 days, whereas previously it could, like any lunar month, have lasted 29 or 30 days. The implication of this statement is that the court would no longer bring "forward" an Elul with 30 days or postpone an Elul with 29 days to suit its desire as to when Rosh HaShanah (and ipso facto Yom Kippur) would fall, but rather now "keep to the cycle at hand."

But this interpretation violates what I like to call the Schlimazel Principle. That principle asks: how could Hillel have chosen such a spectacularly unpropitious time for the launch? One would have to be a real schlimazel to pick a year on which a very bright Old Moon would be seen on Erev Rosh HaShanah, since there is only a 4% probability of doing so. Much more likely is the scenario whereby Hillel ben R' Yehuda (presuming that he was indeed the Patriarch), knew the Sod Ha'ibur i.e. that the Patriarchs had long been secretly using the Molad to set up the calendar, while maintaining a façade of a witness-based system.

I therefore offer the following theory of what happened in 358 CE: someone was upset by the sighting of the Old Moon on Erev Rosh HaShanah – which should be a lunar impossibility – and had to be placated by the alleged evocation of a new system, as if the calculated system had just been launched. In fact, the calendar was, unbeknownst to most, *already in use*. The specific problem for this year had been caused by this pesky three-day discrepancy that had, albeit infrequently, plagued the calendar for centuries already – dating at least back to the 1st-2nd century Patriarch, Rabban Gamliel, over 200 years earlier, as we will soon elaborate.

Presumably Hillel ben R' Yehuda documented this evocation in a note, which he then discarded into the geniza, only to have it reappear cited in the early 11th century in the responsum of R' Hai Gaon, wide open to all sorts of speculative interpretations. Ramban correctly realized that the note meant that a fixed calendar had replaced the testimony of witnesses. He could not know that the note was written purely to placate those who were upset that Rosh HaShanah was clearly established much too early. Many have followed the Ramban's lead in this matter.

It is a common assumption in this line of thinking that Hillel must have been the Nasi, otherwise he could not have had the power to launch the Fixed Hebrew Calendar. However, according to the new theory we are building here, this does not necessarily follow. From the note we do not know if Hillel was the Patriarch who was in the know, or simply another person who had witnessed or been informed of the Old Moon and approached the Patriarch of the time. More on this later.

Why the Secrecy?

It is important to insert here an observation that lies at the core of this book. Why "*Sod* Ha'ibur"? What is the rationale of the secret? What is the hidden tension in this subject?

Many, including scholars, do not even realize how secret it actually is. Rabbis I have spoken to often presume that we can find everything we need to know about the Fixed Hebrew Calendar in the Talmud. I remember a delightful Shabbat meal in Boca Raton where a friend who is a rabbi expressed his certainty that he would find all the necessary sources right there, and would easily be able to give me the references after Shabbat. He is by far not the only one who under this illusion. (The reader is invited to recall all his/her assumptions before reading this book!)

R' Yitzchak Yisraeli, a disciple of the Rosh, provides a reason why the calendar system was not clearly delineated in the Gemara. We find in his book *Yesod Olam* (4:14):

> If it were known and people would be aware of it ... they would challenge Beit Din and argue [with] them and would oppose them with claims and logical arguments. This would lead to great dispute and ruining the festivals, as that event of Rabban Gamliel and R. Yehoshua, where Rabban Gamliel ruled according to

the tradition that he had received and R. Yehoshua argued with him because he relied on his logic.[18]

Summary

We have suggested here that the universally held belief that the Patriarch Hillel II initiated the Hebrew Calendar as we know it today is untenable in the light of lunar reality.

No one would replace a system based on an actual sighting of the Crescent New Moon with a Calculated Fixed Calendar System so inconsistent with its precursor. On that so-called inaugural date, this new system set Rosh HaShanah to be three days before the New Moon could be sighted. This flew right in the face of the dictum that one cannot see the Old Moon in the morning and the New Moon that night, cited by R' Yohanan ben Nuri but known to all.

The fact that the note cited by Hai Gaon contained such a statistically significant date testifies to this not being a chance happening but rather a bug in the Calculated Fixed Calendar System, a system already operational for years, characterized by an infrequent yet niggling moon-discrepant Rosh HaShanah being established.

In subsequent chapters I will show that the period of Rabban Gamliel/R' Yehoshua, and also that of R' Hiyya, contained similarly exceptional years. The Talmudic sections discussing these personalities will be better understood with the realization that at that time, too, the very same calendar we use today, sans Dehiyyot, was being employed by the Nasi to pick the witnesses and establish the date of Rosh HaShanah.

---

[18] From a translated shiur given by Rabbi Shai Walter, uploaded March 2007 to http://www.kby.org/english/torat-yavneh/view.asp?id=4009.

The Moon and Lunar Visibility

When we begin a discussion of Lunar Visibility we need to recognize right from the start the tension between traditional sources (i.e. the oral and written law) and science (i.e. both mathematically deduced and actual observation).

Lunar Visibility in the Traditional Sources

The first commandment given to Israel as a nation (as opposed to the individual patriarchs) was that of sanctifying the New Moon/month:

> החדש הזה לכם ראש חדשים ראשון הוא לכם לחדשי השנה.
>
> This month shall be for you the beginning of the months, it shall be for you the first of the months of the year.[19]

To paraphrase a famous saying: As much as we have kept its appointed days, the Hebrew Calendar has kept us as a people.

The first and second halves of the verse appear to be saying the same thing. Rashi, apparently sensing the redundancy in this verse, elaborates here:[20]

> החדש הזה - (מכילתא ש"ר) הראהו לבנה בחידושה ואמר לו כשהירח מתחדש יהי' לך ראש חודש.
>
> *This month*: (Mechilta Shemot Rabbah) God showed Moshe the moon in its renewal and said to him: "When the moon renews itself, it will be the beginning of the month for you."

The key word here is הראהו, "God showed him," indicating that the moon was seen. Rashi also goes on in his next words to emphasize the word הזה in the verse as being

---

[19] Exodus 12:2.

[20] Rashi to Exodus 12:2.

something that is pointed at with a finger, declaring "This!" Both of these words indicate something visible to the eye. They are clearly not referring to the Conjunction, when the moon is not seen, but rather to the first appearance of the thin crescent of the New Moon.

Rav Yitzchak Zev Soloveitchik explains that Moshe's question to God was, in fact, "What is the precise definition of the new month?" In reply, God showed Moshe the crescent of the New Moon. He instructed Moshe: "See this and then sanctify the new month." In other words, the Almighty explained that the Conjunction of the sun and moon does not create a new month; only the actual appearance of the new crescent creates the new month.[21]

So far so good; this moon is actually seen. But the spotting of the New Moon by any individual does not a new month make. It was decided that there would be one Jewish calendar for all the people and that should be established by a court in Eretz Yisrael. Witnesses would be examined by the calendrical court and the court would sanctify the month.

The problem arises when the witness system breaks down:

> משנה. מעשה שבאו שנים, ואמרו: ראינוהו שחרית במזרח וערבית במערב. אמר רבי יוחנן בן נורי: עדי שקר הם.

> Two witnesses came and said: "We saw the Old Moon in the Morning and the New Moon in the Evening." R' Yohanan ben Nuri said: "They are false witnesses!"[22]

In the Yerushalmi, R' Simlai explains R' Yohanan's premise for rejecting this claim:

> א"ר שמלאי טעמיה דר' יוחנן בן נורי כל חדש שנולד קודם לשש שעות אין כח בעין לראות את הישן ותני כן נראה ישן בשחרית לא נראה חדש בין הערבים נראה חדש בין הערבים לא נראה ישן בשחרית.

---

[21] Rav Yitzchak Zev Soloveitchik, *Hiddushei MaRran Riz Ha-levi* on the Torah, Parashat Bo.

[22] Rosh HaShanah 24b-25a.

R' Simlai gives the reasoning of R' Yohanan ben Nuri as follows: In every case of a Molad New Moon earlier than six hours, the eye cannot see the Old Moon [of the previous month]. And it is taught thus: if the Old Moon appears in the morning, the New Moon cannot appear in the evening; if the New Moon appears in the evening, the Old Moon could not have appeared in the morning.[23]

In other words, the span from the morning to the evening equals 12 hours. If "שנולד" – *shenolad*, i.e., the Molad – happened one hour after sunrise, then it certainly is not possible to see the Old Moon before sunrise, occurring just one hour previously, for the moon is too dim at that point. The only moon possibly visible on such a day would be the New Moon, after sunset.

Likewise, if the "שנולד" happened one hour before sunset then it certainly will not be possible to see the New Moon after sunset, occurring just one hour later, for the moon is too dim at that point. The only moon possibly visible on such a day would be the Old Moon, before sunrise. "שנולד" therefore means here the turnaround point, at which the dimming process changes into the brightening process.

R' Simlai is showing considerable lunar knowledge here. He understands that the moon never really disappears but rather it is a problem with the human eye. The eye cannot discern a dim moon when it is in the proximity of a bright sun.

So much for the Yerushalmi. In the Bavli we find the father of R' Simlai quoted, bringing a similar expression to refute a statement of Shmuel's. This expression has caused many rabbis to err in their understanding of lunar visibility.

אמר ליה אבא אבוה דרבי שמלאי לשמואל ידע מר האי מילתא
דתניא בסוד העיבור נולד קודם חצות או נולד אחר חצות?

---

[23] Yerushalmi Rosh HaShanah 2:6.

R' Simlai's father, Abba, said to Shmuel: "Do you know the meaning of what was taught in the Baraita of Sod Ha'ibur [the Secret of the Intercalation]? Molad before noon or Molad after noon?"[24]

We will discuss Shmuel and this important sugya, mentioning as it does the Baraita of Sod Ha'ibur (a Baraita we have never seen firsthand, only in citations) in a later chapter. For now we will turn to R' Zeira's interpretation, appearing a few lines further along in the Talmud, in order that we may refute it:

כי סליק רבי זירא שלח להו: צריך שיהא לילה ויום מן החדש, וזו שאמר אבא אבוה דרבי שמלאי: מחשבין את תולדתו, נולד קודם חצות - בידוע שנראה סמוך לשקיעת החמה, לא נולד קודם חצות - בידוע שלא נראה סמוך לשקיעת החמה.

When R' Zeira went up [to Palestine], he sent back word to them [in Babylon]: It is necessary that there should be [on New Moon] a night and a day of the New Moon. This is what Abba, R' Simlai's father, meant: "We calculate [according to] the New Moon's birth. If it is born before midday, then certainly it will have been seen shortly before sunset. If it was not born before midday, certainly it will not have been seen shortly before sunset."[25]

For R' Zeira, the night is a very important part of the discussion, as will be shown from his next quote. Here R' Zeira apparently believed that the calculation of the Molad, which is the subject of the next chapter, does determine that point when the moon stops getting dimmer and starts getting brighter; and that once it has attained six hours of brightness, the moon can be seen. The purpose of calculating the Molad, according to Rav Ashi as cited on the same page of Talmud, is to refute false witnesses.

---

[24] Rosh HaShanah 20b. We will provide a different answer to this question in the chapter on the Dehiyyah Molad Zaqen.

[25] ibid.

However, in one special case R' Zeira's reasoning would contradict R' Yohanan ben Nuri's position that it is impossible to see the Old Moon in the morning and the New Moon that same night: in the case when the Molad calculates to be exactly at noon. Here, just before sunrise would be over six hours and just after sunset would be over six hours, and hence both moons can be visible according to R' Zeira. To resolve this, R' Zeira brings an explanation of the path of the moon according to the science of his day:

אמר רבי זירא אמר רב נחמן עשרים וארבעה שעי מכסי סיהרא לדידן שית מעתיקא ותמני סרי מחדתא לדידהו שית מחדתא ותמני סרי מעתיקא.

R' Zeira said in the name of R' Nahman: The moon is hidden for 24 hours. To us [in Bavel], six of these hours belong to the Old Moon and 18 to the New Moon. For them [in Eretz Yisrael], six belong to the New Moon and 18 to the Old Moon.[26]

Now we can understand the importance of the night. Celestial objects rise in the East and set in the West. Then comes night, a period when celestial objects reset themselves. R' Zeira has tacked on another 12 hours before the New Moon can be seen in Bavel; and 12 hours before the Old Moon can fully disappear in Eretz Yisrael.

Where does he get these extra 12 hours? The answer, I believe, is from the "Flat Earth" rabbinic model. In this model, 12 hours is the time it takes for the sun after passing to the West of Israel to enter the Rakia (sky) and reappear in the East in Bavel. As we learn:

חכמי ישראל אומרים ביום חמה מהלכת למטה מן הרקיע ובלילה למעלה מן הרקיע וחכמי אומות העולם אומרים ביום חמה מהלכת למטה מן הרקיע ובלילה למטה מן הקרקע אמר רבי ונראין דבריהן מדברינו.

The Sages of Israel maintain: The sun travels beneath the sky by day and above the sky at night; while the

---

[26] ibid.

> Sages of the nations of the world maintain: It travels beneath the sky by day and below the earth at night. Said Rebbi: And their view is preferable to ours.[27]

Dr. Zvi Shkedi elaborates on this statement:

> In Psachim p. 94b, the Jewish scholars of the Talmud admitted that their theory for the movement of the sun was wrong. (By day the sun moves from east to west under the sky and at night the sun moves back from west to east above the opaque sky.) This same theory is also presented in Baba Batra p. 25b. In a debate with the gentile scientists, the Jewish scholars accepted the gentiles' theory as being more correct. (The sun moves in a continuous circle above the earth by day and under the earth at night.) From here we learn that the Jewish scholars did not mind the possibility that their theories in the field of science could be wrong – they were always open to learning from the wisdom of the gentiles. This dispute is also mentioned in Midrash Rabbah, Bereshit 6:8. Rabbi Shimon Bar Yochai concludes that: "We do not know whether they [the stars] fly through the air, glide in the heaven, or travel in their usual manner. It is a very difficult matter, and people cannot understand it."
> A similar dispute is mentioned in Midrash HaGadol, Bereshit 1:17, regarding the movement of the stars in the sky. The Midrash concludes that "the gentile scholars defeated the scholars of Israel."[28]

Its decisive tone notwithstanding, the Midrash does not accurately represent the prevailing Jewish view taught today. This is still as per R' Zeira above, namely that the moon is invisible for 24 hours, a period from the last sighting of the Old Moon to the sighting of the New Moon. This contradicts the "wisdom of the gentiles" i.e. current astronomical science, according to which we know that at a

---

[27] Pesachim 94b.

[28] http://torah-science.blogspot.co.il/2008/12/torah-science-and-greek-philosophy.html.

minimum the moon must be invisible for 36 hours, and more commonly for 60 hours (while on rare occasion it even extends to 84 hours). It is unfortunate and unnecessary that this 24-hour view has prevailed, for this contemporary "Torah" view of lunar visibility does not dovetail, as will be shown later, with the views held by many important Sages including R' Simlai, Shmuel, Rabban Gamliel and R' Hiyya.

Lunar Visibility from a Scientific Point of View

To better understand, here is a chart[29] of the month of September 120 CE, the very month in which, as I will show in a later chapter, the conflict between Rabban Gamliel and R' Yehoshua occurred:

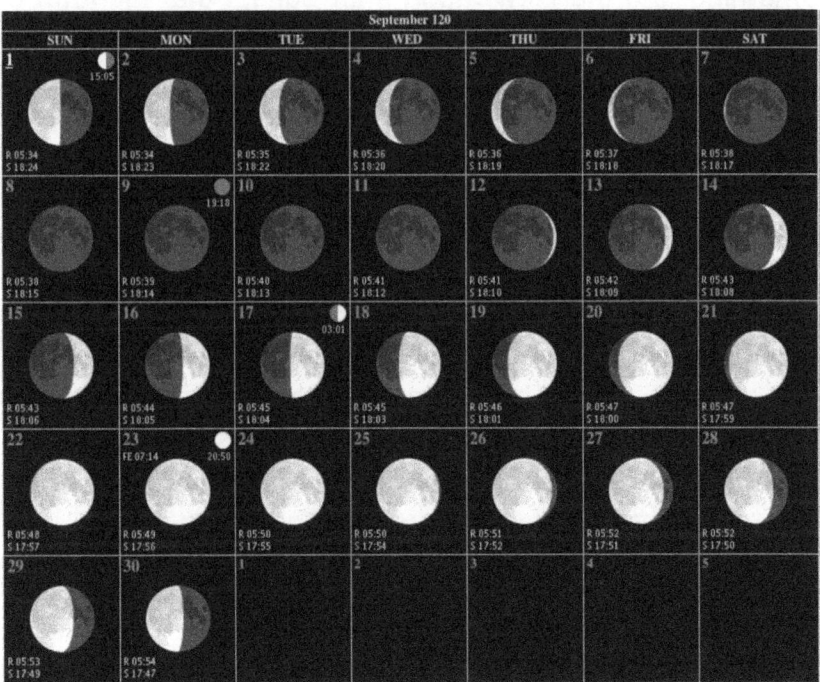

---

[29] http://www.sodhaibur.com/moon-chart.pdf

The chart documents the appearance of the moon during the course of the Gregorian calendar month of September, 120 CE. The month begins with the moon in the last quarter. At the start of the first week, the moon will be seen in the morning both before and after sunrise. As we move toward the end of the first week in September, the moon becomes dimmer and will ultimately only be seen before sunrise. On Sunday, September 8, the moon will rise at 4:13 AM at a brightness of 2.7%. The chart shows black for this day because the algorithm of the program, which drew this chart, considered the 12 hours and 12 minutes that the moon was invisible (its light obliterated by the sun) as more significant than the 1 hour and 26 minutes before sunrise that the moon was actually visible. This is the day on which witnesses claimed to have seen the Old Moon in the morning and the New Moon after sunset that night, in the source we already cited (Rosh HaShanah 24b).

Let us examine how the scientific world views the sighting of a New Moon. The US Naval Website discusses the challenges of an early sighting of the moon:

> In the first two days after Lunar Conjunction, the young crescent Moon appears very low in the western sky after sunset, and must be viewed through bright twilight. It sets shortly after sunset. The sighting of the lunar crescent within one day of the Lunar Conjunction is usually difficult. The crescent at this time is quite thin, has a low surface brightness, and can easily be lost in the twilight. Generally, the lunar crescent will become visible to suitably located, experienced observers with good sky conditions about one day after the Lunar Conjunction. However, the time that the crescent actually becomes visible varies quite a bit from one month to another. The record for an early sighting of a lunar crescent, with a telescope, is 12.1 hours after the Lunar Conjunction; for naked-eye sightings, the record is 15.5 hours from the Lunar Conjunction. These are exceptional observations, and crescent sightings this

early in the lunar month should not be expected as the norm.

Using Global Visibility Maps from R. H. van Gent, the Dutch Astronomer we mentioned in previous chapters, we have determined "Re'iyah Age" – the timing of the first possible sighting of the New Moon for the month of Tishrei, relative to the Lunar Conjunction – for the years 1999 through 2018 CE (Hebrew years 5760-5759). The following chart outlines the results:

HY Year	Molad	Conjunction	Diff	Re'ah Age
5760	Sep 10, 1999 3:44 PM	Sep 10, 1999 0:02	15h 42m	42h
5761	Sep 28, 2000 1:17 PM	Sep 27, 2000 21:53	15h 24m	20h
5762	Sep 17, 2001 10:05 PM	Sep 17, 2001 12:27	9h 38m	29h
5763	Sep 7, 2002 6:54 AM	Sep 7, 2002 5:10	1h 44m	36h
5764	Sep 26, 2003 4:27 AM	Sep 26, 2003 5:09	-42m	36h
5765	Sep 14, 2004 1:15 PM	Sep 14, 2004 16:29	-3h 14m	25h
5766	Oct 3, 2005 10:48 AM	Oct 3, 2005 12:28	-1h 40m	53h
5767	Sep 22, 2006 7:37 PM	Sep 22, 2006 13:45	5h 52m	52h
5768	Sep 12, 2007 4:26 AM	Sep 11, 2007 14:44	13h 42m	51h
5769	Sep 30, 2008 1:58 AM	Sep 29, 2008 10:12	15h 46m	55h
5770	Sep 19, 2009 10:47 AM	Sep 18, 2009 20:44	14h 3m	45h
5771	Sep 8, 2010 7:36 PM	Sep 8, 2010 12:30	7h 6m	53h
5772	Sep 27, 2011 5:08 PM	Sep 27, 2011 13:09	3h 59m	52h
5773	Sep 16, 2012 1:57 AM	Sep 16, 2012 4:11	-2h 14m	37h
5774	Sep 5, 2013 10:46 AM	Sep 5, 2013 13:36	-2h 50m	52h
5775	Sep 24, 2014 8:18 AM	Sep 24, 2014 8:14	4m	33h
5776	Sep 13, 2015 5:07 PM	Sep 13, 2015 8:41	8h 26m	33h
5777	Oct 1, 2016 2:40 PM	Oct 1, 2016 2:12	12h 28m	39h
5778	Sep 20, 2017 11:28 PM	Sep 20, 2017 7:30	15h 58m	34h
5779	Sep 10, 2018 8:17 AM	Sep 9, 2018 20:01	12h 16m	22h

The above chart covering 20 years is a fair representation of the Molad of Tishrei. If Re'iyah is the term referring to the first "sighting" (i.e. the sunset when the New Moon can actually be seen), then the average age of the moon at Re'iyah – in other words, the time span from the Lunar Conjunction to actual visibility – is 40 hours. This shows that it takes more time to actually see the New Moon after the Conjunction than even the 24 hours that the Rambam thought.

As we previously explained, for modern (scientific) man, the term "New Moon" means the instant in time when the sun, moon, and earth are closely aligned, but we have chosen to call this instead the "Lunar Conjunction", using the term in a looser and non-technical sense than is usual (it usually refers to exact alignments) because for us the term "New Moon" needs to refer to something else.

In this book, "New Moon" is used as ancient man used it, to denote the first thin crescent of the moon, visible within a time span ranging from a minimum of 15.5 hours to a maximum of over 55 hours after the Lunar Conjunction, after the sun has set and before the moon has set (the moon sets fairly quickly at the beginning and end of the month).

Now, a Lunar Conjunction occurs at one moment for the entire earth, but the witnessing of a New Moon is very localized. Much depends on its trajectory, as becomes apparent when studying van Gent's diagrams. In September, the month we used for our findings, the orbit of the moon might bring it well into the southern hemisphere. It is therefore possible that the New Moon may be visible at sunset in Sharm el-Sheikh, which falls within its trajectory, and yet not visible in Jerusalem, just slightly further north, until another full day has passed, at the next sunset, despite the geographical proximity of the two cities. Thus, tiny differences in latitude can create a 24-hour delay in the sighting of the New Moon.

Summary

Two elements of lunar visibility are presented here, each according to both traditional and scientific sources. The first is the time from the Molad/Conjunction (respectively) until the sighting of the New Moon. Traditional sources believe this to be a minimum of six hours. However my study from 1999 through 2018 CE, making an accurate determination from the van Gent charts, shows an average of 40 hours.

Secondly, the Talmud states that the time from when the Old Moon is last seen until the time of sighting of the New Moon is 24 hours. The Rambam states approximately two days. The reader who invests a little thought into the matter should realize that the Old Moon is always seen just before sunrise and the New Moon just after sunset, implying that these days will not be complete ones, but will contain a half day. This confirms my tables, which show a minimum of 1½ days, normally 2½ days, and occasionally 3½ days (i.e. 36, 60 and 84 hours respectively).

The Molad

In the second chapter, the widespread but false belief that the calculated Fixed Calendar originated with Hillel the Patriarch in 358 CE was discussed. Now, I hope to make the reader better understand the calendar's inner workings. The Fixed Hebrew Calendar is substantially based on the Molad of Tishrei.

Etymologically the word "molad" is about birth. The moon is reborn each month after its disappearance at the end of the previous month. Presumably, in the days of Moshe Rabbeinu the Molad referred to the actual sighting of the New Moon, which occurred each month, weather permitting. With the onset of the Fixed Hebrew Calendar, however, the Molad diverged from the reality of the moon and became purely a function of the calculated calendar.

The date on which the calendrical court started using the Molad to establish the new month as opposed to actual sightings of witnesses – albeit not necessarily informing the public of the change – is a question of overarching significance for this book.

Rabban Gamliel, who lived 1st–2nd century CE, knew the value of the Moladic interval [Synodic Month]. This is clearly stated in Talmud Rosh HaShanah 25a:

> אמר להם רבן גמליאל: כך מקובלני מבית אבי אבא: אין חדושה של לבנה פחותה מעשרים ותשעה יום ומחצה ושני שלישי שעה ושבעים ושלשה חלקים.

> Rabban Gamliel said to them: Such I have received as a tradition from the house of my fathers: the New Moon is not seen less than 29 days 12 hours and 793 halakim [have passed].

This statement appears in the Talmud immediately after the famous story of the disagreement between Rabban Gamliel and R' Yehoshua over the issue of witnesses who supposedly saw the Old and New Moon on the same day.

What does this statement add? Well, the Synodic month is the basis of the fixed calendar; so my contention is that Rabban Gamliel is here signaling to the maven that the calculated Molad is involved in his acceptance of the "false" witnesses.

At some point in the history of the Jewish people, we stopped using an actual sighting of the moon and started using a calculated calendar based on the Molad of Tishrei. Many of our rabbis have held that 358 CE was that point in time. The previous chapter should have sown considerable doubt with respect to that assertion. Perhaps it was already in use to some degree in the time of Rabban Gamliel, over 200 years earlier? If the discussion in the Talmud of the conflict between Rabban Gamliel and R' Yehoshua is read with the realization that Rabban Gamliel was using the calculated Molad as his primary criterion for the acceptance of witnesses, some important mysteries are cleared up. This will be discussed further in a later chapter.

Twelve Lunar Months Do Not a Year Make

שמור את חדש האביב ועשית פסח ליקוק אלהיך כי בחדש האביב הוציאך יקוק אלהיך ממצרים לילה.

Keep the month of spring, and make the Passover offering to the Lord, your God, for in the month of spring, the Lord, your God, brought you out of Egypt at night.

This verse from Deuteronomy 16 mandates us to keep the Passover holiday in the spring season.

We are accustomed to assume this to be unique to the Jewish People, particularly because Islam's calendar is maintained at a steady 12 months and thus Ramadan is constantly changing its season. The roots of Islam lie with a nomadic people who were not focused on agriculture; but other land-based people were subject to a much greater extent to the changing seasons. Their holidays had an agricultural aspect, and they needed to keep their lunar calendar in sync with the sun.

This problem was shared with the ancient Babylonians and other peoples who used a lunar calendar and wanted to keep their festivals in the proper season. Meton of Athens was credited with providing the solution, but it has now been shown that it should be more properly attributed to work done by the Chaldeans.

In their monograph *Babylonian Chronology 626 BC.-A.D. 75*, Professors Richard Anthony Parker and Waldo H. Dubberstein write:

> It may have been in the reign of Nabonassar, 747 BC that Babylonian astronomers began to recognize, as the result of centuries of observation of the heavens, that 235 lunar months have almost exactly the same number of days as nineteen solar years.

To see the equivalence:

    235 lunar months are:

        = 235 X (29 days 12 hours and 793 halakim)

        = 6939 days, 16 hours and 33 minutes

    19 Solar Years are:

        =19 X (365 days and 6 hours)

        = 6939 days and 18 hours

Now years contain a whole number of months. Hence, it needed to be decided which years would have 13 months. Below we present what could be described as the first 19 years of the Hebrew Calendar starting from Creation. The very first entry comes from the acronym, בהר"ד, 2-5-204, BaHaRaD, the Molad of Tohu, standing at 2 days, 5 hours and 204 halakim.

Under the column "Meton Mns" we show how mathematics would distribute these months under what I would call the natural distribution. In the second column we have the

Year		Day	Hours	Parts	Molad of Tishrei		Meton Cycle	Meton Mns
1		Mon	5	204	Sun, Sep 6, 3761 BCE	23:11:19	12.3684	12
2		Fri	14	0	Fri, Aug 27, 3760 BCE	7:59:59	24.7368	12
3	ג	Tue	22	876	Tue, Aug 16, 3759 BCE	16:48:39	37.1053	13
4		Mon	20	385	Mon, Sep 4, 3758 BCE	14:21:23	49.4737	12
5		Sat	5	181	Fri, Aug 23, 3757 BCE	23:10:03	61.8421	12
6	ו	Wed	13	1057	Wed, Aug 13, 3756 BCE	7:58:43	74.2105	13
7		Tue	11	566	Tue, Sep 1, 3755 BCE	5:31:26	86.5789	12
8	ח	Sat	20	362	Sat, Aug 21, 3754 BCE	14:20:06	98.9474	12
9		Fri	17	951	Fri, Sep 8, 3753 BCE	11:52:49	111.3158	13
10		Wed	2	747	Tue, Aug 28, 3752 BCE	20:41:29	123.6842	12
11	א	Sun	11	543	Sun, Aug 18, 3751 BCE	5:30:09	136.0526	13
12		Sat	9	52	Sat, Sep 6, 3750 BCE	3:02:53	148.4211	12
13		Wed	17	928	Wed, Aug 25, 3749 BCE	11:51:33	160.7895	12
14	ד	Mon	2	724	Sun, Aug 14, 3748 BCE	20:40:13	173.1579	13
15		Sun	0	233	Sat, Sep 2, 3747 BCE	18:12:56	185.5263	12
16		Thu	9	29	Thu, Aug 23, 3746 BCE	3:01:36	197.8947	12
17	ז	Mon	17	905	Mon, Aug 11, 3745 BCE	11:50:16	210.2632	13
18		Sun	15	414	Sun, Aug 30, 3744 BCE	9:22:59	222.6316	12
19	ט	Fri	0	210	Thu, Aug 19, 3743 BCE	18:11:39	235.0000	13

distribution according to the mnemonic, GUHADZaT, (גוחאדזט).

Each of the rows with a Hebrew letter shows where Jewish tradition calls for a year with 13 months. These years coincide with the natural distribution, except for the GUHADZaT cycle's choice of 8th year, while the natural distribution opts for the 9th.

There are 19 different series where the years containing 13 months are separated from each other by one or two years of 12 months. The reasons for different starting points is obscure. The series we call GUHADZaT is 3-6-8-11-14-17-19.

The Fix is In

What is fixed about the Fixed Hebrew Calendar? There are ten months of fixed length, two months of variable length, and one month, Adar I, that "reincarnates" periodically in order to meet the needs of the Meton Cycle, i.e. for seven out of the 19 years to contain 13 months each.

#	English	Hebrew	Length
1	Nisan	נִיסָן	30 days
2	Iyyar	אִיָּר / אייר	29 days
3	Sivan	סִיוָן / סיוון	30 days
4	Tammuz	תַּמּוּז	29 days
5	Av	אָב	30 days
6	Elul	אֱלוּל	29 days
7	Tishrei	תִּשְׁרֵי	30 days
8	Marḥeshvann	מַרְחֶשְׁוָן / מרחשוון	29 or 30 days
9	Kislev	כִּסְלֵו / כסליו	29 or 30 days
10	Tevet	טֵבֵת	29 days
11	Shvat	שְׁבָט	30 days
12L*	Adar I*	אֲדָר א׳	30 days
12	Adar / Adar II*	אֲדָר / אֲדָר ב׳	29 days

Normally months alternate between 29 days and 30 days, which would make a year length of 354. But because the length of the average month is, in fact, slightly over 29 and a half days, in practice some years will contain five months of 29 days and seven months of 30 days, totaling a year length of 355. Marheshvan can increase by one day and Kislev can reduce by one day. Adding a 13th month of 30 days results in year lengths of 354, 355, 383, or 384 days. (Other lengths become possible once the Dehiyyot are introduced, as we will see later.)

By knowing the days until the coming Rosh HaShanah, we can properly set up the calendar. Thus, there is considerable smarts in this setup. A traveler can depart in Tevet with 17 months before he faces a problem as to the date of the start of Nisan, without having to keep track of the Molad.

What is most important here is Tishrei. The Molad of Tishrei is the main determining factor in the Fixed Hebrew Calendar. In the days prior to the establishment of the Dehiyyot, you needed to know only the Molad of Tishrei in order to know when to fast on Yom Kippur. If you were also cognizant of the length of that particular year (by knowing the Molad of Tishrei of the next year), you then had that year's entire calendar at your fingertips.

In fact I would maintain that this ease of calculation was the reason for Jerusalem's reluctance to adopt the Dehiyyot. Babylonia felt pressure from the Karaites, but Jerusalem knew that the simple system (i.e. sans Dehiyyot) allowed the entire Diaspora to observe Yom Kippur on the proper day.

Doing the Math

Unfortunately, education has not served us well when it comes to our confidence in basic math skills. In a later chapter we will discuss Shmuel of Nehardea who provided mathematical tables that could be used in the Diaspora to know the Fixed Hebrew Calendar.

But I believe that before the age of the calculator, there were some and perhaps many who could do the math.

What you needed to know was actually very little indeed, just math skills of addition under the system of day, hours, and halakim – or, even more simply, to bear in mind the following three items:

I. That each month is one day, 12 hours, and 793 halakim more than the previous month.

II. The Molad of the previous month.

III. GUHADZaT, the 19 year cycle, 3-6-8-11-14-17-19, and which year of that cycle was in force.

And that was it! With these in place, you could be confident of fasting on Yom Kippur on the exact same day as in Jerusalem. If you were sophisticated enough to calculate the length of the coming year, you could even pinpoint Passover and Shavuot; otherwise, you would have to keep two days of each yom tov.

Here is an example, to illustrate the ease of this process. In June 2014, we were in year 17 of the 19-year cycle. This called for a 13-month year.

Given that Rosh Hodesh Tammuz was Saturday, 0 hours, and 120 halakim, Rosh Hodesh Av must be Sunday, 12 hours, and 913 halakim.

Elul is a little trickier, because the total will push us past the one day mark, leading us to skip to Tuesday:

12 hours and 913 halakim +

1 day, 12 hours + 793 halakim =

2 days, 1 hour + 626 halakim.

So Rosh Hodesh Elul is Tuesday, 1 hour, and 626 halakim

Tishrei's halakim count also overshoots the full hour:

1 hour + 626 halakim +

1 day, 12 hours + 793 halakim =

1 day, 14 hours + 339 halakim

So Tishrei's Molad is Wednesday, 14 hours, and 339 halakim.

Now we know exactly when to fast on Yom Kippur.

From Tishrei, we move into cycle year 18, which has 12 months, and we can keep on calculating in similar vein to the above. (I will save the discussion as to how we establish the non-fixed months for a later chapter.)

BaHaRaD

It is commonly thought that positioning of the Molad of Tishrei was mandated by BaHaRad, an acronym given to the time of the mythical Molad shel Tohu.

The usefulness of BaHaRaD lies in giving us a memorable reference point with a known Molad. To calculate the Molad for any lunar month, I need to know a previous Molad and the number of lunar months intervening. In this case if I know the Hebrew Year, and I know that every 19 years equals 235 lunar months, I can calculate any Molad going all the way back to BaHaRaD (though it might take a bit of time!).

Of course, as demonstrated, the easiest way to calculate a Molad is to know the Molad of the previous month and add 1 day, 12 hours, and 793 halakim.

Summary

The Molad of Tishrei is the key point around which our calendar pivots.

Each Molad is part of a series, calculated based on the average length of a lunar month. The interval between Molads is 29 days, 12 hours and 793 halakim. Like all Hebrew months, Tishrei begins after sunset on whatever Hebrew day the Molad falls. However, with Tishrei being the start of the year, the day of the Molad is highly significant, and hence Tishrei alone is subject to later-enacted rabbinical postponements (this will be discussed below).

19 solar years is equivalent to 235 lunar months. 235 is not a multiple of 19; hence, if we are to create 19 lunar years, seven of them must contain not 12 but 13 lunar months. But which seven? In the Hebrew calendar, GUHADZaT is the mnemonic for 3-6-8-11-14-17-19, the specific years in the 19-year-cycle which take an intercalcuary month (Adar I).

The importance of BaHaRaD is not so much the question of the precise, real time of the Molad of Tohu, but rather the relationship of the Hebrew Year to the Molad. If we ever lose our count of the Molad, we can reestablish it knowing simply the Hebrew Year.

What's the Old Moon Got to Do With It?

R' Hiyya and the Old Moon

The Talmud Bavli in tractate Rosh HaShanah relates the experience of R' Hiyya with the Old Moon:

רבי חייא חזייא לסיהרא דהוה קאי בצפרא דעשרים ותשעה, שקל קלא פתק ביה, אמר: לאורתא בעינן לקדושי בך, ואת קיימת הכא? זיל איכסי!

R' Hiyya once saw the [Old] Moon in the heavens on the morning of the 29th day. He took a clod of earth and threw it at it, saying, "Tonight we want to sanctify you, and you are still here! Go and hide yourself!"[30]

Professor Isaiah M. Gafni of the Hebrew University of Jerusalem, in his book *Land, Center and Diaspora*, refers to "a particular sage scolding the [outgoing] moon (of the previous month) for having the temerity to continue its appearance an extra day, contrary to rabbinic calculations ... the moon is forced to acquiesce to the authority of the rabbinic court, and forthwith disappears."[31]

Gafni has painted R' Hiyya as a buffoon chasing the moon from the sky with a clod of dirt. However, setting aside such flippancy, there is a surprising implication in the text of the Talmud to the effect that the rabbinical court established the New Month before witnesses had actually seen the New Moon! Additionally, the text implies, albeit in a somewhat comical or magical fashion, that the moon can be controlled (by the Rabbis).

Another version of this story appears in the Talmud Yerushalmi:

---

[30] Rosh HaShanah 25a.

[31] This text appears on page 104 with a footnote attributing it to the Talmud in Rosh HaShanah, 25a, though strictly speaking the "forthwith disappears" part does not occur there, but rather in the similar citation in the Yerushalmi.

רבי חייה רבה היליך לאורו של ישן ארבעת מיל רבי אבון משדי עלוי צררין ואמר לה לא תבהית בני מריך ברמשא אנן בעיין תיתחמי מיכא ואת מיתחמי מיכא מיד איתבלע מן קומוי.

R' Hiyya the Great walked by the light of the Old Moon for four miles. Rabbi Abun threw pebbles at [the Old Moon] and said to it: "Do not upset the children of your Master, tonight we have to see you from this side [i.e. the New Moon], but you are seen from here [the Old Moon is still visible]." Immediately it disappeared.[32]

Now what we have here, in the Bavli and Yerushalmi, is clearly two different versions of the same incident; an incident that we are about to confirm with a precise date and correspondence with lunar reality.

Unlike Gafni, and consistent with some commentators such as the Ritva, I am going to reject the reality of the colorful talk of pebbles or clods of earth thrown at the moon and consider them simply literary manifestations of the negative thoughts around the inconvenient processes that had unfolded. Furthermore, the fact that the moon disappeared was not in response to rabbinical ravings or invocations of magic. It is the nature of the Old Moon to be obliterated by the rising sun.

What is noteworthy here is R' Hiyya's four-mile walk and the question of how R' Hiyya knew that the court was going to sanctify the moon that night. Also it seems clear here that Rashi, intentionally or not, with his mention of Rebbi's being "concerned that the local people would protest" is associating this incident with the earlier conflict involving Rabban Gamliel, who was Rebbi's grandfather, and R' Yehoshua. In both cases, the Nasi was aware of the visible Old Moon and took active steps to try to hide the fact.

Back in the chapter entitled "Hillel the Patriarch" it was shown that the moon of Hillel ben R' Yehuda rose at 4:11 AM on September 19, 358 CE, Erev Rosh HaShanah. The

---

[32] Yerushalmi Rosh HaShanah 2:4.

sunrise was 5:45 AM, a difference of one hour and 34 minutes, adequate for a walk of four miles (though in Hillel's case we do not hear of him taking such a walk). Thus, the lunar event experienced by R' Hiyya resembled the lunar event of Hillel ben R' Yehuda, a couple of centuries later.

Whereas neither Talmudic source provides us with a date to accompany the text of R' Hiyya,[33] it is possible to deduce it. R' Hiyya was an Eretz Yisrael amora of priestly descent, living approximately 180-240 CE. Although he moved at an early age from Bavel to Eretz Yisrael, before he left he might well have come under the influence of the Babylonian sage Shmuel of Nehardea.[34] The Molad study provides a date that is consistent with both these biographical facts and, moreover, with an exceptional lunar occurrence: September 17, 198 CE. An inspection of the data in the Molad of Tishrei study finds this date to be the most likely in describing the event documented in the Talmud above. According to the Fixed Hebrew Calendar, Rosh HaShanah of 198 CE would have started Sunday night, September 16. On Sunday morning, a very bright Old Moon would have risen at 4:03 AM and would disappeared with the rise of the sun at 5:44 AM – giving Hiyya over an hour and a half to walk four miles by its light, as mentioned.

On the next page we have the Sky View Café table of the moon as seen by R' Hiyya in September of 198 CE. From the information in this table, and the van Gent Global Visibility Map[35] which follows it, we can deduce that the New Moon could only be seen a full two days after it was assumed to be seen – i.e. after sunset on Tuesday, September 18; and this, only by an expert viewer with

---

[33] Although more than one Sage named Hiyya exists, it is a reasonable assumption, based on the very similar nature of the narrative, that R' Hiyya the great was actually R' Hiyya of the Babylonian Talmud's narrative. He is also known as Hiyya bar Abba.

[34] *Jewish Encyclopedia* 1906, citing Isaac Hirsch Weiss, *Dor Dor ve-Dorshav*, iii. 94.

[35] http://www.sodhaibur.com/van-gent-maps/lunvis_3959.pdf

The Moon of R' Hiyya – 198 CE

Molad of Tishrei Mon, Sep 17, 16:07
Conjunction Mon, Sep 17, 18:30

Moonrise	Illum %	Age	Sunrise	Sunset	Moonset	Illum %	Age	Note
Sat, Sep 15, 2:56	9.2%	2d 16h	Sat, Sep 15, 5:43					Old Moon still bright enough to be seen after sunrise.
Sun, Sep 16, 4:03	3.6%	1d 14h	Sun, Sep 16, 5:44	Sun, Sep 16, 18:05				Old Moon seen only before dawn for 1 hour and 40 minutes. Possible to walk 4 miles as per Yerushalmi. Calculated day of Molad starts after sunset so moon is sanctified that evening.
Mon, Sep 17, 5:11	0.6%	0d 13h	Mon, Sep 17, 5:45	Mon, Sep 17, 18:04	Mon, Sep 17, 18:14		-0d 0h	Moon very close to sun and hidden by its brightness.
				Tue, Sep 18, 18:02	Tue, Sep 18, 18:46	1.5%	1d 0h	According to van Gent charts expert viewer could see moon but without contemporary science would not know where to look.
				Wed, Sep 19, 18:01	Wed, Sep 19, 19:18	5.8%	2d 1h	Moon seen by all viewers per van Gent chart.

Moon invisible for (total of) 3d 12h 17m
Sky View Café 5.8

62 What's the Old Moon Got to Do With It?

access to the knowledge of when and where to look. This knowledge was not available in R' Hiyya's day. It stands to reason, therefore, that the first time the New Moon would be seen by everyone would be after sunset, September 19, 198 CE – a three-day discrepancy.

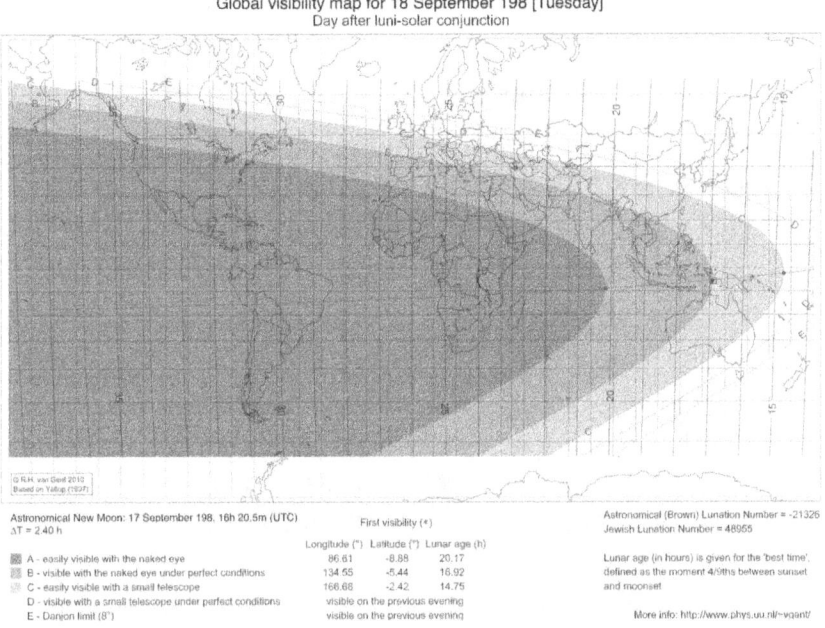

The question remains with regard to both Talmudic stories: How did R' Hiyya know that the calendrical court would sanctify Rosh HaShanah that evening? The answer is that Shmuel taught him.

Shmuel of Nehardea

Shmuel was a teacher of Halacha, as well as a judge, physician, and astronomer. He was born circa 165 CE at Nehardea, in Babylonia, and died there about 257 CE. He was knowledgeable in astronomy, declaring: "I am as familiar with the paths of heaven as with the streets of Nehardea."[36]

---

[36] Berachot 58b.

The Talmud reports Shmuel's ambitious claim:

אמר שמואל: יכילנא לתקוני לכולה גולה.

I can establish the Hebrew Calendar for all the Diaspora.[37]

Elsewhere (Hulin 95b) we hear:

כתב שדר ליה עיבורא דשיתין שני.

He sent [R' Yohanan] the calendar for the next 60 years.

But R' Yohanan's reply was rather curt:

אמר: השתא, חושבנא בעלמא ידע.

He only knows mere calculations.[38]

Shmuel wanted honor for his ability to predict what the calendrical court would establish as Rosh Hodesh over a 60-year period. R' Yohanan replied that honor is bestowed for Torah knowledge, not for the ability to calculate. Note that R' Yohanan did not, however, disprove Shmuel or demonstrate that the calculations disagreed with what the court did in practice.

Clearly, Shmuel could not do what he claimed unless there was a calculated calendar being used by the Nasi, and witnesses being picked artificially to remain consistent with its dates. I am not sure why the commentators are so oblivious to this fact – perhaps it is due to the Sages' dismissal here of Shmuel's endeavors.

Furthermore, there is every reason to think that the calendar used by the Nasi of Shmuel's day was the very same Fixed Hebrew Calendar we use today, minus the Dehiyyot. In other words, we have evidence here that the calculated calendar we use today did not begin with Hillel II in 358 CE, but at some earlier time, such that it was already in effect at the time of Shmuel. Further evidence for

---

[37] Rosh HaShanah 20b.

[38] Hulin 95b.

this is found in the fact that the very same Old Moon calendrical issue that we have demonstrated as arising at the time of Hillel II occurred also for R' Hiyya, Shmuel's younger contemporary (and student)?

I do not believe that Shmuel was privy to the Nasi's secrets. Rather, his prediction of future dates was predicated on his gathering data on the court's behavior, systematically assembling data from the reports of the messengers that Eretz Yisrael sent to Bavel, and on his knowledge about the Molad gleaned from the Babylonian astronomers amongst whom he lived. He thus gained a coherent mathematical picture, something impossible when working with the vicissitudes of witnessed testimony, which contains an inherent random factor. Thus, he was able to write up 60 years' worth of the future Hebrew Calendar.

We have already come across Abba, R' Simlai's father, in a previous chapter. In the Talmud in Rosh HaShanah, we find him apparently implying that Shmuel does not fully understand lunar science:

אמר ליה אבא אבוה דרבי שמלאי לשמואל: ידע מר האי מילתא דתניא בסוד העיבור: נולד קודם חצות או נולד אחר חצות? - אמר ליה: לא. - אמר ליה: מדהא לא ידע מר - איכא מילי אחרנייתא דלא ידע מר.

R' Simlai's father, Abba, said to Shmuel: Do you know the meaning of what was taught in the Baraita of Sod Ha'ibur [the Secret of the Intercalation]? Molad before noon or Molad after noon? Shmuel answered no. [He said to him]: Then there may be other things you do not know too.[39]

Does this conversation prove Shmuel's calculations erroneous? Once more, the answer is no. Again, all that was needed to be done was to show where Shmuel's calculations indicated that Rosh HaShanah would start on a certain day while the calendrical court actually sanctified

---

[39] Rosh HaShanah 20b.

a different day. Just as in the case of R' Yohanan, this is not done. No one is able to refute Shmuel's findings.

But Abba is not like R' Yohanan, who said, "He knows mere calculations." Rather, Abba begins an interesting discussion that, far from dismissing calculations, actually enters into the thick of them. What Abba is discussing here is an issue we have already touched upon at length. He is offering the solution to the very same problem with the calendar revealed by both Hillel ben R' Yehuda (Hillel II) and R' Hiyya – the problem of a highly visible Old Moon before the sunrise that precedes Rosh HaShanah.

In asking "Molad before noon or Molad after noon?", Abba was highlighting the issue of Moladot in the last quarter of the day. All cases in the Molad of Tishrei Study with a three-day discrepancy have Moladot in the last quarter of the day i.e. after 12 noon.[40] Shmuel could not have known about this because he was in Bavel, not in Eretz Yisrael, and did not physically see this problem occurring. The moon in Bavel is not exactly the same as the moon in Eretz Yisrael. If Rebbi assumed that the Old Moon could not be seen in Ein Tav, how much more so Shmuel would not relate the Old Moon in Bavel to that of Eretz Yisrael.

The editors of the Bavli insertion dealing with Abba might have, at face value, been aiming to obscure the significance of Shmuel's marvelous ability to calculate the calendar. This may have been necessary at that time. Yet perhaps they have another purpose targeting us later generations – to assure us that they were quite well aware of the problem of a highly visible Old Moon before sunrise of the morning determined as Erev Rosh HaShanah, an impossible occurrence when using witnesses. They are conveying to us the message: "We know the problem, and we know the solution: the Dehiyyah Molad Zaqen." (This

---

[40] See the three-day discrepancy table in the appendix of this book. This fact is not true in reverse: not every Molad in the last quarter of the day has a three-day discrepancy; only 16% of them do.

Dehiyyah involves postponing the Molad by one day when it falls in the last quarter of the day. More on this soon).

It is in the very nature of the Molad calculation itself that in 4% of cases, a very bright Old Moon appears 3½ days before the New Moon. This would be an impossible result in a witness-based system. An error by witnesses could at most mean that one would mistakenly see the moon on the evening of the 29th day instead of the evening of the 30th day when it was actually visible – a deviation of one day. Such an error would have had to occur for three consecutive months to create such a three-day gap – and this is unlikely in the extreme.

How the Fixed Hebrew Calendar Became Skewed

By now I would hope that the reader is coming to realize that it was the calculation itself of the Fixed Hebrew Calendar which occasionally – 4% of the time – skewed the start of Rosh HaShanah to three days before it would be possible to see the New Moon. Some of the factors creating this skew are as follows:

1) The effect of the Molad of Tohu. As the reader will recall, the Molad of Tohu was a construct of the first Molad, calculated by extrapolating backwards to before Creation. This Molad was set at 2 days, 5 hours and 204 halakim; that was the first Rosh Hodesh of year "0", which of course, does not exist. The subsequent passage of 12 lunar months marks the start of year 1.

From the Molad of Tishrei study we recall that for 70% of the time, the day defined as the Molad falls two days before the New Moon. Thus, simply by dint of adding two days to the Molad of Tohu, 70% of the time the New Moon could have appeared more or less on schedule, instead of two days off target. Furthermore, no sighting of the Old Moon the morning before Rosh HaShanah begins would have been possible. Let me clarify that this is not to say that this calculation was set up in error, but rather that the purpose of the calculation was *not* to simulate and replace witnesses. The likely purpose of the calculation, and the reason for the inbuilt discrepancy, will be discussed in a coming chapter.

2) The effect of the rollback of the Molad to the previous sunset. Had this rollback been changed to a roll forward, to the next sunset, it would have eliminated almost any possibility of a sighting of an Old Moon. This is in fact the basis of the Dehiyyah Molad Zaqen, the topic of the next chapter. Again, this was done deliberately; precisely why will be discussed soon.

3) The effect of the path of the moon. As was seen by looking at the van Gent chart for 358 CE, the path of the moon can make quite a difference – for example, if its orbit creates an angle that does not cover Eretz Yisrael.

Though these factors resulted in a calendar that pointed to neither the sighting of the New Moon nor the Conjunction, this was not the result of error nor incompetence. We will develop a rationale as we continue.

Rosh HaShanah 2013

The effect of the path of the moon can be illustrated by the very year in which I am writing this chapter, 2013. The Molad of Tishrei this year will be Thursday, September 5 at 10:46 AM, which is 16 hours and 830 halakim. This Molad will not be subject to any Dehiyyot. Its claim to fame is an extremely unusual path, passing under the entire African continent. On the next page I have documented this path on a van Gent chart[41]. This results in a three-day discrepancy that is not subject to the Dehiyyah Molad Zaqen.

The Old Moon will rise at 5:10 AM Wednesday morning with a brightness of 2.2% until the sun rising at 6:16 AM obliterates it. So this year, residents of Israel who are early

---

[41] http://www.sodhaibur.com/van-gent-maps/1434g.pdf

risers will be treated to one of the few cases of seeing the Old Moon in the morning of Erev Rosh HaShanah.

I took pictures of this moon. One is on the back cover of this book. The first photo[42] demonstrates how at 5:44 the Old Moon could be seen without too much difficulty – it appears clearly in the center of the photo. In the second photo, taken a few minutes later at 5:53:30, the Old Moon can only now be seen with great difficulty[43].

It should be noted that these photos show a moon that is a fraction of the brightness of the moon of Rabban Gamliel.

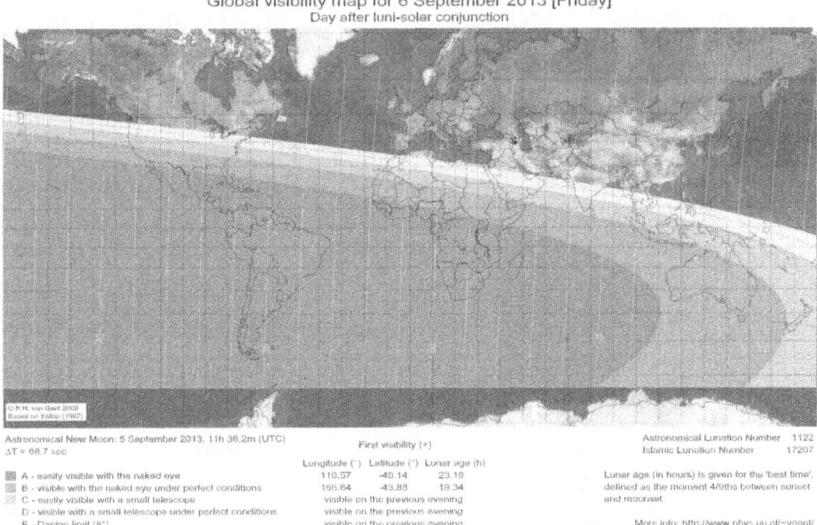

Old Moon Sighting Not Deliberate

It makes no sense that the Fixed Hebrew Calendar was designed to violate R' Yohanan ben Nuri's dictum, that it is impossible to see the moon both in the morning and the evening – i.e. that this was an intended effect. To the contrary, the text citing Abba, R' Simlai's father, shows that the Talmudic Rabbis viewed it as a problem. Remember,

---

[42] http://www.sodhaibur.com/old-moon/img_0771.pdf

[43] http://www.sodhaibur.com/old-moon/img_0774.pdf

Rebbi sent R' Hiyya to Ein Tav hoping to hide this very problem.

אמר ליה רבי לרבי חייא: זיל לעין טב וקדשיה לירחא.

Rebbi then said to R' Hiyya: "Go to Ein Tav and sanctify the month!"[44]

(Rebbi is the abbreviated title given to Judah the Prince, who was the Nasi at that time.)

The solution concealed in the statement provided by Abba in the Yerushalmi[45] was that if the Molad occurred after midday, then we defer Rosh HaShanah by one day. Thus we can avoid the Moladot in the last quarter of the day, that are leading to the three-day discrepancies, and ipso facto, to the Old Moon sightings.

But knowing the solution and implementing a solution are two different things. Although we do not know exactly who was responsible, it no doubt took great rabbinical leadership to supplant a calendar determined by actual lunar witnesses to one based – albeit secretly – on a calculation. It would take great rabbinical leadership to modify that calculation. This would not be fully implemented until the conflict between Saadia, in Bavel, and Aaron Ben Meir, in Eretz Yisrael, in 922 CE. At that point, the Dehiyyah Molad Zaqen would be adopted as a formal factor in the Fixed Hebrew Calendar and the calendrical bug of discrepancies and Old Moon sightings would, for the most part be eliminated.

---

[44] Rosh HaShanah 25a.

[45] To recap: "In every case of a Molad New Moon earlier than six hours, the eye cannot see the Old Moon [of the previous month]. And it is taught thus: if the Old Moon appears in the morning, the New Moon cannot appear in the evening; if the New Moon appears in the evening, the Old Moon could not have appeared in the morning" (Yerushalmi Rosh HaShanah 2:6).

Summary

Why was the sighting of the Old Moon significant?

As we noted previously, according to the Rambam, astronomically speaking, the last sighting of the Old Moon and the first sighting of the New Moon are approximately two days apart. It contravenes nature to witness both in the same day.

When we do "see" both on the same day, it can only be by virtue of a virtual sighting like the calculated Molad and not by real sightings. This virtual sighting is being mandated by the Molad calculation, secretly being used by the Nasi.

The Nasi is, of course, aware that the witnesses did not really see the moon. The witnesses, on the other hand, though they know that they did not actually see the moon, presume it was viewable, and proceed to report it, for the honor and the reward.

72 What's the Old Moon Got to Do With It?

The Rabban Gamliel/R' Yehoshua

We have finally arrived at one of the incidents central to our thesis.

There are few better-known Mishnayot than the story of the conflict between Rabban Gamliel and R' Yehoshua, portions of which we have already cited. Here it is in full:

> משנה. מעשה שבאו שנים, ואמרו: ראינוהו שחרית במזרח וערבית במערב. אמר רבי יוחנן בן נורי: עדי שקר הם. כשבאו ליבנה קיבלן רבן גמליאל. ועוד באו שנים ואמרו: ראינוהו בזמנו, ובליל עיבורו לא נראה. וקיבלן רבן גמליאל. אמר רבי דוסא בן הורכינס: עדי שקר הן; היאך מעידים על האשה שילדה, ולמחר כריסה בין שיניה? אמר לו רבי יהושע: רואה אני את דבריך. שלח לו רבן גמליאל: גוזרני עליך שתבא אצלי במקלך ובמעותיך ביום הכפורים שחל להיות בחשבונך.

Mishnah: Two witnesses came and said: "We saw the Old Moon in the morning and the New Moon in the evening." R' Yohanan ben Nuri said: "They are false witnesses!" When, however, they came to Yavneh, Rabban Gamliel accepted them. And more[46], two witnesses came and said: "We saw [the Molad] at its proper time." The next night it was not seen. Rabban Gamliel accepted them, but R' Dosa ben Horkynos said: "They are false witnesses! How can men testify that a woman has born a child when on the next day we see her belly still swollen?"

Said R' Yehoshua to him: "I see [the force of] your argument." Thereupon Rabban Gamliel sent to him to say, "I enjoin upon you to appear before me with your staff and your money on the day which according to your reckoning should be Yom Kippur."[47]

---

[46] Commonly this "ועוד" is translated as "on another occasion." I would argue that, on the contrary, "ועוד" means "moreover, on the same occasion." Taken together, both Mishnayot simply describe what occurs when we have a three-day discrepancy.

[47] Rosh HaShanah 24b-25a.

The stage is set for a conflict. Both tradition and logic seem to be on the side of R' Yehoshua, with authority on the side of Rabban Gamliel. This conflict can be understood on multiple levels, from the most sophisticated – as laid out, for example, in *The Social Structure of the Rabbinic Movement in Roman Palestine* by Catherine Hezser – to a classroom role-play, with the students identifying with the underdog R' Yehoshua against the teacher Rabban Gamliel, who forces him to bend to his will.

On the face of it, what flaw can be found in the arguments of R' Yohanan ben Nuri and R' Dosa ben Horkynos, and in R' Yehoshua's acceptance of them? Is it not obvious that when witnesses lie, even partially, their testimony ceases to be acceptable? As long as this argument is viewed as one predicated on witnessed testimony, Rabban Gamliel is undoubtedly in the wrong.

Yet, although rabbinical misconduct is not rare, neither in the Talmud nor (sadly enough) today, I am very bothered by the facile judgment that seems to dominate the discussion of this event: namely, that Rabban Gamliel abused R' Yehoshua. Was not Rabban Gamliel the ultimate expert on the moon, after all? We are even told that he had diagrams of the moon's phases in his upper chamber![48] Moreover, Rabban Gamliel was not simply the Nasi, he was the Nasi at a crucial time in our survival, when we had just lost our Temple and needed to reorientate our practices toward the synagogue. How could this great Jewish personality be on the weak side of this argument?

Why Is R' Yehoshua Comforted?

At the point at which we interrupted the unfolding of events in the Mishnah, R' Yehoshua is distraught. Rabban Gamliel is forcing him in public to violate what he considers to be Yom Kippur.

---

[48] Mishnah Rosh HaShanah 2:8.

The Gemara goes on to recount that he seeks counsel from R' Akiva, who gives him a drasha (hermeneutical sermon) about the nature of sanctifying the moon:

אמר לו: [רבי,] מפני מה אתה מיצר? אמר לו: (רבי) עקיבא, ראוי לו שיפול למטה שנים עשר חדש ואל יגזור עליו גזירה זו. אמר לו: רבי, תרשיני לומר לפניך דבר אחד שלמדתני. - אמר לו: אמור. - אמר לו: הרי הוא אומר אתם, אתם, אתם, שלש פעמים, אתם - אפילו שוגגין, אתם - אפילו מזידין, אתם - אפילו מוטעין. בלשון הזה אמר לו: עקיבא, נחמתני, נחמתני.

He said to him, "Master, why are you in distress?" He replied: "Akiva, it were better for a man to be on a sick-bed for twelve months than that such an injunction should be laid on him."

He said to him, "[Master], will you allow me to tell you something which you yourself have taught me?" He said to him, "Speak." He then said to him: "'*Atem*' [you, plural] is written three times,[49] to imply 'you' [may fix the festivals] even if you err inadvertently; 'you' even if you err deliberately; 'you' even if you are misled."[50]

Yehoshua then replies to him in these words:

Akiva, you have comforted me, you have comforted me.

But the question is – why was R' Yehoshua comforted?

Recall that R' Yehoshua was forced to humiliate himself on what he knew for a fact to be Yom Kippur. If there was truly an error here on Rabban Gamliel's part, one of accepting false witnesses, what is comforting about it being deemed somehow legitimate, with no one willing to listen to R' Yehoshua's rightful (in his own eyes) attempt at repair? What is comforting about the casual disregard for the truth? True, God gave to the Jewish People – and through them the Nasi – the power to establish the new month in accordance with whatever they decide; but it is still not

---

[49] The reference is to Leviticus 22:31, 23:2, and 23:4.

[50] Rosh HaShanah 25a.

comforting if one knows the "real and true" answer and is ignored.

I wish to argue here that it was not in "*you, even if you err inadvertently*" that R' Yehoshua found comfort. Rather, it was "*you, even if you err deliberately*" that was the source of R' Yehoshua's solace. His acceptance following R' Akiva's words lay in the dawning realization that Rabban Gamliel knew perfectly well that these witnesses were false but *accepted them anyway* because he was governed by the dictates of a fixed calendar.

R' Yehoshua realized, or perhaps was informed explicitly by R' Akiva, that Rabban Gamliel's actions were dictated by the masoret, the tradition passed down through Rabban Gamliel's family, the very same masoret that is at the basis of the calendar we use today. Understanding this did serve to allay R' Yehoshua's fears, for now he understood Rabban Gamliel's rationale. What had appeared to be an error was, in fact, entirely intentional.

"Preposterous!" the naysayers might declare. "There was no fixed calendar in the 2nd century. The fixed calendar will not be established for another couple of centuries, in 358 CE!"

On the contrary, I believe this has been well addressed in my chapter on Hillel the Patriarch. It was noted in that chapter that on the morning of Friday, September 19, 358, Erev Rosh HaShanah, a bright (3.6%) Old Moon was visible for over an hour and a half. This event is so unusual it is self-verifying. Does one really imagine that Hillel II would create a new calendar system that particular year, thus defying R' Yohanan ben Nuri's edict that it is impossible to see the Old Moon in the morning of Erev Rosh HaShanah? The sighting of the Old Moon is the signature of Fixed Hebrew Calendar. It signals that the month was not established by witness but by some other methodology.

An Argument over Masoret

From the above, it would seem that Rabban Gamliel had a different masoret from R' Yehoshua, one that was a very well-kept secret. I believe this masoret is what gave rise to the term Sod Ha'ibur.

R' Yehoshua, like the vast majority of his peers, only knew of the biblically based masoret – namely, actual witnesses testifying to lunar sightings. Rabban Gamliel's masoret, on the other hand, is much more familiar to us: it is essentially our present-day masoret minus the rabbinical postponements.

The basis for my bold proposition is threefold: firstly, astronomical facts; secondly, correlation with our texts; and thirdly, the explicit words of Saadia Gaon. Rabbi Yitzchak Yisraeli, *Yesod Olam*, part 4, chap. 6, cites R' Saadia Gaon as follows:

דע כי הגאון ר' סעדיה זצ"ל ואחרים שהודו לו ונמשכו אחרי סברתו, הודו ואמרו כי מעולם, ואפילו כשהיה בית המקדש קיים, וכן משחרב ואילך, לא קדשו בית דין ראשי חודשים, ולא קבעו המועדים לישראל על פי ראיית הלבנה החדשה, ולא סמכו עליה כלל בשום זמן מהזמנים שעברו. אלא לעולם משנתנה תורה, וכל ימי בית ראשון ושני וזמן הגלות, לא היו קבוע ראשי חודשים והמועדים אלא על פי חשבון המתוקן הזה המסור בידינו מקדמונינו ז"ל, וכפי משפטיו והלכותיו הנוהגות בזמן הזה מעיבור השנים... ולא היו בית דין בזמן הראשון נזקקים לראייה אלא כדי לגלות הדבר ולהראות איך הוא העיון מעיד על אמיתת החשבון הנכון המתוקן הזה המסור בידינו מהם.

Know that Rabbeinu Saadia Gaon of blessed memory, and others who agreed with him and were drawn to his position, confirmed that never – not even when the Temple stood, and certainly not following its destruction – did the court sanctify the New Moon or establish the festivals for Israel on the basis of the sighting of the [actual] New Moon. Nor at any time did they ever rely on such a sighting. Rather, from the time that the Torah was given, throughout the entirety of the first and second Temple periods, and during the period of the exile, the New Moons and festivals were always established on the basis of this calculation handed down to us from our ancient authorities, and in accordance with the laws and halachot that apply today regarding the intercalation of the years … And in the initial period, the court used the sighting of the moon solely in order to make the matter known and to demonstrate how it attests to the truth of the calculations handed down to us from them.

To be fair we should note from Hai Gaon:

זה שאמרתם שכתב רבינו סעדיה גאון פיומי ז"ל, קנה הוא שדחה בו את אפיקורוס.

That which you cite in the name of Rabbeinu Saadia Gaon of blessed memory is a reed with which he pushed aside the heretics.[51]

How true this is, or what heretical opinions might have been floated on the subject, we do not know. Ironically though, standing in direct contrast to Hai Gaon's supposition here about Saadia is Rabban Gamliel. Where Saadia supposedly cited a calculated calendar to rebuff the heretics, R' Gamliel – I suggest – hid it to placate the pious.

A Marvelous "Coincidence"

In light of the above, let us reconsider our Mishnah and the events of 2013, that paralleled it closely.

- *Two witnesses came and said: "We saw the Old Moon in the morning and the New Moon in the evening."* This is an accurate description of events in 2013, as was related at the end of the last chapter. Certainly the Old Moon was visible to skywatchers before sunrise on Wednesday, September 4, Erev Rosh HaShanah. That night, being Rosh HaShanah, implicitly indicated a sighting of a New

---

[51] Hai Ga'on, *Otzar ha-Geonim*, Yom Tov, Responsa, p. 4.

Moon (for now, we will ignore the fact that this is a virtual sighting only, as we know). And that night, I found myself at the Kotel, marking the start of a "three-day yom tov" experience, unusual for those of us who live in Israel. We certainly acted as if the lunar month had begun. In this we echoed the Talmudic witnesses, reporting a New Moon where there was none:

- *"We saw [the Molad] at its proper time."*

The Mishnah continues:

- *The next night it was not seen.*

Right again – no moon to be seen on Thursday night, September 5. Thus, the experience of Rabban Gamliel and R' Yehoshua was essentially repeated in Rosh HaShanah 2013.

How is that for a Bat Kol? During the time I am writing this book, HaShem displays the moon of Rabban Gamliel!

Old Moon Sighting Indicative of a Fixed Calendar

The Fixed Calendar, aka the Calculated Hebrew Calendar, was accompanied by two undesirable consequences. These consequences were intrinsic, not in the formulation of the calculation, but in its parameters. The parameters of the calculation established Rosh HaShanah on average several days before the appearance of the New Moon,

The first consequence, occurring less than 4% of the time, was a very visible Old Moon.

The second consequence, according to the Molad of Tishrei Study, occurred in 75% of all the years under the study. Here, one would not see the New Moon even after sunset of the second day of the month, violating R' Dosa ben Horkynos's edict in our Mishnah. Even under the Dehiyyot rules in use today, this remains true 25% of the time.

Yet the second problem goes unnoticed. Why? Because we look to the New Moon to establish the lunar month. Afterwards it is already established and the moon becomes of no interest.

Returning to the first consequence, associated with a visible Old Moon on the day of the Molad of Tishrei, this problem has been countered by the Dehiyyah Molad Zaqen. This will be discussed in the next chapter. This rule, though known much earlier, was not routinely implemented until the days of Saadia Gaon.

In fact, logically, a sighting of an Old Moon had an important function for observers of a lunar calendar. This is because when one saw the Old Moon before dawn in the morning sky, of one thing we could be certain: that the New Moon would not be seen that evening under any circumstances.

And this, in fact, is what prompted the conflict between Rabban Gamliel and R' Yehoshua.

Rabban Gamliel Was Using the Molad

Could the Gemara give any greater hint to the fact that Rabban Gamliel was using a fixed Molad system than by its next statement?

> אמר להם רבן גמליאל: כך מקובלני מבית אבי אבא: אין חדושה של לבנה פחותה מעשרים ותשעה יום ומחצה ושני שלישי שעה ושבעים ושלשה חלקים.

> Rabban Gamliel said to them: Such I have received as a tradition from the house of my fathers: the New Moon is not seen [until] less than 29 days, 12 hours and 793 halakim [have passed].

Why did Rabban Gamliel note "not less"? The answer can be found in a reference by Azariah De' Rossi to a book by Rabbi Abraham Bar Hiyya Hanasi, Sefer ha'Ibur, where the latter remarks that according to Ptolemy, the Egyptian sages originally held that there were only 792 halakim (rather than the 1080 held by the fixed calendar).[52]

This knowledge, as well as the knowledge of the fact that 235 lunar months equal 19 solar years, was discussed in the previous chapter. From R' Akiva we learned that Rabban Gamliel had the right to sanctify as he saw fit.

So what is more logical – that Rabban Gamliel was abusing R' Yehoshua, accepting impossible witness accounts, and, most serious of all, establishing Yom Kippur on the wrong day, simply to pull rank? Or that Rabban Gamliel was forced to accept these witnesses who reported the New Moon at the right time for the purposes of the fixed calendar (though unfortunately also adding the unwanted information that they had seen the Old Moon too), in order to preserve his responsibility to those afar, such as those in Bavel who were counting on him to make Elul always 29 days?

This responsibility seems implicit in the following statement of R' Hisda:

חשין לצומא רבה תרין יומין אמר לון רב חסדא למה אתם מכניסין עצמכם למספק הזה חזקה שאין ב"ד מתעצלין בו.

> They thought because of the uncertainty they needed to fast two days of Yom Kippur. R' Hisda said, "Why have you immersed yourself in doubt? We can count on the court not to be remiss."[53]

In sum: just as Rosh HaShanah 2013 was determined by the calculation of the Molad, so too was the Rosh HaShanah of the conflict of Rabban Gamliel and R' Yehoshua. We will soon demonstrate that the events of that conflict are consistent with the lunar facts of 120 CE.

---

[52] *The Light of The Eyes* (translated and annotated by Dr. Joanna Weinberg), pp. 511-512.

[53] Yerushalmi Rosh HaShanah 1:4.

How It Was Actually Done

The Rambam, in Hilchot Kiddush HaHodesh 1:6, provides a clue as to how Rabban Gamliel succeeded in using a Fixed Hebrew Calendar with the appearance of accepting actual witnesses:

בית דין מחשבין בחשבונות...אם ידעו שאפשר שיראה יושבין ומצפין לעדים כל היום כולו שהוא יום שלשים, ... ואם ידעו בחשבון שאי אפשר שיראה אין יושבים יום שלשים.

The court calculated the path of the moon… If it was possible to see the moon [after sunset of the 29th day] the court would be open to receive witnesses the entire 30th day… If it was not possible to receive witnesses, the court would not receive witnesses on the 30th day [thus that previous month would have 30 days].

What was the calculation they used? None other than the very same calculation we use today for the Molad, and, stemming from that, for allocating the fixed months of the year. Rosh HaShanah, before the use of the Dehiyyot, was always synchronous with the Molad of Tishrei. The other months were still determined according to their fixed lengths as will be discussed shortly.

But we have another question on the table. As I explained in my very first chapter, the New Moon could never actually be seen on the Molad of Tishrei. So why would witnesses ever come? How could the façade of witness-based testimonies on astronomically moonless nights be maintained for many years?

This is a good question and I am not sure I have the ultimate answer. My first answer lies in the power of suggestion. They presumed it was viewable, since Elul was always 29 days, as it says in the Talmud:

מימות עזרא ואילך לא מצינו אלול מעובר.

From the time of Ezra, Elul was always 29 days long.[54]

---

[54] Rosh HaShanah 19b.

The court was only open when witnesses were expected. Witnesses would testify with confidence that they would not be refuted because, as the Rambam has told us, the calendrical court would not be open unless they expected that witnesses would see the moon (or, according to our historical explanation of events, unless the calendrical court wished witnesses to testify on that particular day).

Additionally, the witnesses might also have been lured by the thrill of the chase, the honor, or perhaps the free dinner, per Rosh HaShanah 23b:

משנה. חצר גדולה היתה בירושלים. ובית יעזק היתה נקראת, ולשם כל העדים מתכנסין, ובית דין בודקין אותם שם. וסעודות גדולות עושין להם, בשביל שיהו רגילין לבא.

There was a large court in Jerusalem called Beit Ya'zek. There all the witnesses would assemble and the rabbinical court examined them. They would entertain them lavishly there so that they should have an inducement to come.

Perhaps, though, there were times when no one came. Then the court would be forced to intimidate someone to say he saw the moon, per Rosh HaShanah 20a:

הוו יודעין שכל ימיו של רבי יוחנן היה מלמדנו: מאיימין על העדים על החדש שלא נראה בזמנו לקדשו, אף על פי שלא ראוהו - יאמרו ראינו!

Know that when R' Yohanan was alive, he taught that witnesses may be intimidated to testify on a moon that was not seen in its time, in order that it be sanctified in its right time. And even though it was not seen, they should say they saw it!

Failing even this strategy, the calendrical court would have some of their own judges bear witness to the moon, per Rosh HaShanah 25b:

משנה... ראוהו בית דין בלבד - יעמדו שנים ויעידו בפניהם, ויאמרו מקודש מקודש.

> If the judges [of the calendrical court] were the only ones who saw the New Moon,[55] two of the judges should stand before the court and give testimony, and [the court] will say, "Sanctified, Sanctified."

All of above (luring the witnesses, intimidating the witnesses, judges testifying etc.) only took place on the 30th day, as the calendrical court only accepted witnesses when it needed to establish that the previous month was 29 days in length. If their calculation had established that the previous month should be 30 days in length, then such a month would be automatically sanctified, without the testimony of witnesses, because Hebrew months can only be 29 or 30 days in length.

So, by hook or crook the moon of Tishrei would officially be sanctified on the Molad of Tishrei, in spite of the fact that, as my study shows, according to the calculated calendar the moon is never visible at sunset before the Molad of Tishrei. The ordinary people, for their part, would presume that though they did not see the moon, someone else, perhaps more expert, did see it, though the truth is that the New Moon is generally easily viewable to anyone with a view of the western horizon. Only in a small percentage of cases is it viewable exclusively by those of superior location or greater expertise.

As a final note we should add, for the sake of rounding out the Talmudic story, that the witnesses were certainly not asked questions about the Old Moon – indeed, this information was inconvenient and awkward to know! However, in the story that led to the Rabban Gamliel/R' Yehoshua conflict, they volunteered the report because they had indeed seen the Old Moon and thought they should mention it.

Rabban Gamliel had no choice but to press on and accept this testimony as he needed to sanctify the date. But the

---

[55] As I explain it, they did not really see it, but they had an imperative to make Elul 29 days.

report was now out, having been said in the hearing of the court, and this was what got R' Yehoshua all riled up.

The Astronomical Facts behind the Story

Using the Molad of Tishrei Study I presented in the first chapter, I sought a date that was consistent with the life of Rabban Gamliel.

The study I made of the Molad of Tishrei lists three years in which a three-day Tishrei Molad discrepancy might conceivably have occurred during the reign of Rabban Gamliel as Nasi – 74, 83 and 120 CE – as shown in the following table:

Heb Year	Hrs	Pts	Molad	Conjunction Jerusalem ST	Difference	Skew
3835	23	824	Fri, Sep 7, 0074 17:45	Fri, Sep 7, 0074 20:35	-2h 49m	3d
3844	21	287	Sun, Aug 29, 0083 15:15	Sun, Aug 29, 0083 19:23	-4h 7m	3d
3881	21	601	Mon, Sep 9, 0120 15:33	Mon, Sep 9, 0120 19:04	-3h 31m	3d

Christian sources distilled from Josephus put the death of Rabban Gamliel at approximately 117 CE.

> Ripe in years, full in honors, and beloved by all, Gamaliel died about A. D. 117.[56]

Wikipedia, without citing precise sources, lists Rabban Gamliel's service as Nasi:

> **Nasi**
> 80 (Est.) – 118 (Est.)

In light of these dates, both 74 CE and 83 CE appear too early in Rabban Gamliel's tenure for him to be provoking others, and certainly for his retirement! However, an exact scientific date putting him in charge at Tishrei 120 CE seems reasonable.

---

[56] *A Dictionary of Christian Biography, Literature, Sects and Doctrines*, Volume 2, p. 608.

The preference for 120 CE is dramatically strengthened by the astronomical data that we have already seen with reference to 358 CE and that we will see later concerning 835 CE. The visibility of an Old Moon is not mentioned in any sources in connection with either of these years; but we learn of that fact from lunar science.

Lunar science lines up for 120 CE too. That year's Tishrei Molad, like that of 358 and 835 CE, had a skew of three days, implying the likelihood of the visible Old Moon that plays such a pivotal role in the conflict. Moreover, the Gemara informs us that following the altercation with R' Yehoshua, Rabban Gamliel departs from the scene. This too is a reasonable possibility in 120 CE, assuming that the above approximations of his death year are a little off.

Now for the lunar science provided by the Sky View Café table, on the facing page. The Molad of Tishrei for 120 CE was Monday, September 9 at 3:33 PM, which is 21 hours and 601 halakim. The Old Moon rose on Sunday at 4:15 AM, and sunrise was at 5:38 AM. It was at an illumination of 2.7%, not quite as bright as the Old Moons of R' Hiyya and Hillel ben R' Yehuda, but bright enough to be able to surprise the witnesses and cause them to make note of it. Who knows, perhaps even R' Yehoshua himself saw it!

The left-hand bottom corner of the table states that the moon disappeared for 3 days, 12 hours and 34 minutes. This represents the total time of the moon's invisibility, from the disappearance of the Old Moon to the first appearance of the New Moon. This is consistent with Rabban Gamliel's statement in Rosh HaShanah 25a:

אמר להם רבן גמליאל לחכמים: כך מקובלני מבית אבי אבא: פעמים שבא בארוכה, ופעמים שבא בקצרה.

Rabban Gamliel said to the Sages, "This I have received from the house of my father's fathers – [The moon] sometimes takes a long path and sometimes takes a short path."

The Moon of Rabban Gamliel - 120 CE

Molad of Tishrei	Mon, Sep 9, 15:33
Conjunction	Mon, Sep 9, 19:18

Moonrise	Illum %	Age	Sunrise	Sunset	Moonset	Illum %	Age	Note
Sat, Sep 7, 3:17	6.8%	2d 16h	Sat, Sep 7, 5:38					Old Moon still bright enough to be seen after sunrise.
Sun, Sep 8, 4:13	2.7%	1d 15h	Sun, Sep 8, 5:38	Sun, Sep 8, 18:15				Old Moon seen only before dawn for 1 hour and a half. Possible to walk 4 miles as per R' Hiyya in the Yerushalmi. Calculated day of Molad starts after sunset so moon is sanctified that evening.
Mon, Sep 9, 5:09	0.5%	0d 14h	Mon, Sep 9, 5:39	Mon, Sep 9, 18:14	Mon, Sep 9, 18:24		−0d 1h	Moon very close to sun and hidden by its brightness.
				Tue, Sep 10, 18:13	Tue, Sep 10, 18:57	1.2%	1d 0h	According to van Gent charts no possibility of seeing moon on Sunday after sunset.
				Wed, Sep 11, 18:12	Wed, Sep 11, 19:29	4.4%	2d 0h	Moon seen by all viewers per van Gent chart.

Moon invisible for (total c 3d 12h 34m
Sky View Café 5.8

Here is the van Gent map for September 10, 120 CE. I encourage you to use the link at the footnote and see the series of van Gent maps for 120 CE.[57] The van Gent charts for the year 120 CE do not exhibit quite as much skew as the data for R' Hiyya – i.e., the discrepancy is not as large. But they do fit in with the Rabban Gamliel and R' Yehoshua narrative. Certainly, it would have been likely that many could have seen the Old Moon in the morning of the same day that Rabban Gamliel sanctified as Rosh Hodesh; and hence, two of them reported it.

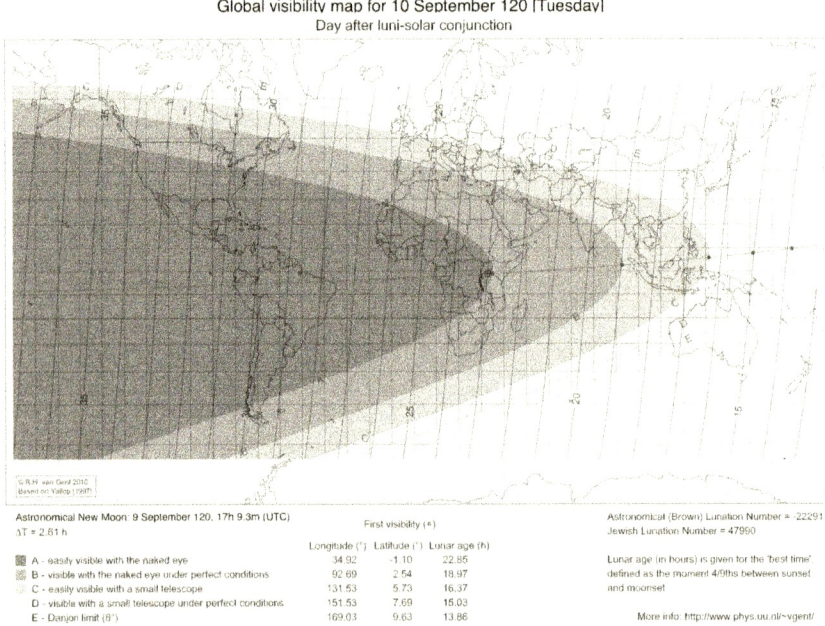

Looking closely at the Global Visibility Map, one should be able to see that the "B" parabola (representing expert viewers) only just covers Israel, whereas the "A" parabola (moon is easily viewable with the naked eye) misses Israel completely. One should make note that after sunset, Friday, September 8, 120, the night after the 29th of Elul, it would be expected that expert witnesses would be searching the

---

[57] http://www.sodhaibur.com/van-gent-maps/lunvis_3881.pdf

skies for the New Moon. But two nights later, on the 10th of September, there is no reason for an expert search because the court would not be hearing testimony; so it is likely that only after three days was the moon actually seen, as was the case with 198 CE, 358 CE, and 835 CE.

Rabban Gamliel sanctified the month of Tishrei on Monday, September 9, effectively starting Rosh HaShanah after sunset, Sunday night. R' Yehoshua, ignorant of the calculated calendar and fixing of the witnesses taking place, claimed that the moon should have been sanctified Tuesday morning, September 10. Rabban Gamliel could not allow this opinion any credence and had to quash it. The story becomes simple to understand as soon as we know the lunar facts and deduce the existence of a fixed calendar being used behind the scenes.

Back to 358 CE

And now, armed with this information, we can return to examine the incident in 358 CE, and present a reasoned alternative scenario to the claim that Hillel II established the Fixed Hebrew Calendar in that year. The sequence of events would have been as follows:

1) Someone was upset by the witnessing of the Old Moon on Erev Rosh Hashanah. That person might have been Hillel ben R' Yehuda himself, or perhaps he simply was informed of it. This individual, Hillel ben R' Yehuda, was not, as common wisdom has it, the Nasi.

2) Believing an error to have been made, Hillel approached the Nasi, who was then compelled to admit to him that he was selecting the witnesses on the basis of a fixed calendar, handed down to him through the line of Rabban Gamliel's family.

The Nasi may well have known that under this system, the anomaly of a viewable Old Moon on Erev Rosh Hashanah did occasionally happen, and that this was simply to be accepted.

3) Hillel ben R' Yehuda misunderstood the Nasi (or was misled), presumed that it was a *new* system, created and launched in that year, and wrote a note to that effect.

4) This note was later found cited in the responsum of Hai Gaon cited by R' Avraham ben Hiyya, in the early 11th century; and it shaped the understanding (or misunderstanding) of most of the great rabbis who followed, from Ramban down.

Summary

I have presented here an entirely new approach toward the problematic but universally accepted understanding of the conflict between Rabban Gamliel and R' Yehoshua.

Support for my argument lies in the simple fact that a significant sighting of an Old Moon at the end of Elul is impossible under a witnessed lunar calendar. It is only a calculated Molad that can occasionally produce the phenomenon of a substantial visible Old Moon on the morning before Rosh HaShanah.

Hence, I deduced that Rabban Gamliel was not on an ego-trip of authority. In fact he was preserving a very important and necessary tradition, well-supported in the Talmud, that Elul was always 29 days. The calendar was being set not according to live testimony but something else altogether. This something else was the masoret received in Rabban Gamliel's family. For Rabban Gamliel, this and this alone was the true calendar according to which all of Israel must function, and hence he could not brook R' Yehoshua's divergence from it. Yet he could also not tell him explicitly what was happening, as it was kept secret from the vast majority of the people. In this way, the conflict ensued.

The masoret continued to be a secret up to the year 358 CE and beyond, but in that year, Hillel noticed that something strange was up, and so the calendar "came out of the closet," leading to the false notion that it was created in that year.

The Dehiyyah Molad Zaqen

A Rule Shrouded in Mystery

The Dehiyyah Molad Zaqen is one of four rabbinical rules of postponement ("Dehiyyot"). It calls for postponing Rosh HaShanah for one day whenever the Molad falls in the last quarter of the day; i.e. at or after 12 noon. Due to a different rule, Dehiyyah Lo ADU Rosh, this sometimes becomes a two-day postponement.[58]

The term "Zaqen" (literally "old") is commonly understood as referring to the last quarter of the "Moladic" day. But if the word "Molad," meaning "birth," refers to the birth of the *New* Moon, then Molad Zaqen might make subtle reference to the mirror image of that moon, the last visibility of the previous month's moon – what we call the *Old* Moon.

In Sacha Stern's book *Calendar and Community*, he makes a brief statement about the Molad Zaqen rule:

> The origins of the rule of molad zaqen ... are as obscure as is its rationale. However, we know that its introduction into the rabbinic calendar was relatively late.[59]

Dr. Irv Bromberg, of the University of Toronto, states:

> Traditionally, this postponement was considered necessary to ensure the visibility of the New Moon on the first day of Rosh HaShanah. *In reality, it doesn't ensure that.*[60]

---

[58] If the Dehiyyah Molad Zaqen postpones Rosh HaShanah to a Sunday, Wednesday or Friday, then the Lo ADU Rosh rule will kick in to postpone it another day.

[59] p. 195.

[60] http://individual.utoronto.ca/kalendis/hebrew/postpone.htm#zakein. Italics mine, R.F.

Remy Landau, on his website *Hebrew Calendar Science and Myths*[61], likewise points to its implementation but not its purpose.

Wikipedia, on its page for the Hebrew Calendar states:

> "Dehiyyah Molad Zaqen," meaning an "old conjunction," is thought to be a relic of when the calendar was established empirically (although there is some doubt).

In terms of its date of establishment, there appears to be a contradiction between Stern's supposition that it is a relatively late rule, and that of Wikipedia, that it is an ancient rule dating back to the witness-based calendar. It is possible that the rule existed but was not implemented. We see that as late as 835 CE in the Exilarch's letter it is mentioned but not implemented.

The True Purpose of the Rule

It is amazing that no one seems to know the purpose of the Molad Zaqen rule, yet everyone knows that it was important enough to spawn a major conflict between Saadia Gaon and Ben Meir in 922 CE, which actually resulted in different dates for Yom Kippur in Eretz Yisrael and Bavel.

One obvious conclusion of the Molad of Tishrei Study is that the problematic three-day discrepancy, giving rise to a visible Old Moon Erev Rosh HaShanah, is something that occurs periodically, if infrequently, under the Fixed Hebrew calendar. Hence, a reasonable hypothesis regarding the Dehiyyah Molad Zaqen is that it was created to prevent the appearance of a significantly visible Old Moon on the morning of Erev Rosh HaShanah.

This was necessary for two reasons:

1) People *did not* know that a calculation had supplanted witnesses.

---

[61] http://hebrewcalendar.tripod.com/

2) People *did* know that if one sighted the Old Moon before sunrise, it would not be possible to see the New Moon that night.

When we experimentally apply the Molad Zaqen rule on the data in the Molad of Tishrei study, we find that the three-day discrepancies disappear.

Consider Hillel's Year, 358 CE. A bright 3.6% Old Moon was visible Friday morning, but the Molad dictated that Rosh HaShanah should start that night. Had he lived at that time, R' Yohanan ben Nuri would surely have protested its impossibility. The brightness of the Old Moon related to the fact that the actual New Moon would not be seen until Monday night, a three-day discrepancy.

Had the Molad Zaqen rule already been in place at that time, in 358 CE, Rosh HaShanah would have been postponed for one day after the calculated Molad, beginning after sunset on Saturday night. It would not have begun immediately following a bright Old Moon and there would have been much less confusion in the minds of people. In fact, and significantly, all 78 cases of three-day discrepancies found in the Molad of Tishrei study, spanning more than 2000 years, disappear under the rule of the Molad Zaqen.

I believe that the Sages who lived before the Common Era experienced this problem, and realized its solution. We see this in the Talmud when Abba, R' Simlai's father, mentions the Baraita of Sod Ha'ibur to Shmuel and asks: Molad before noon or Molad after noon? This is the criterion for applying the Dehiyyah Molad Zaqen. The fact that it existed in the Baraita is good indication that the ancient Sages who established the Fixed Hebrew Calendar were aware of this undesired complication and knew that the rule of the Molad Zaqen would correct the problem.

As we explained in the previous chapter, this problem was the source of the conflict between Rabban Gamliel and R' Yehoshua. The witnesses saw the Old Moon in the morning and purported to have seen the New Moon in the evening. It was indeed quite a phenomenon, that Erev Rosh HaShanah Old Moon! The previous occasion on which such a sighting would have been likely was on Erev Rosh HaShanah 83 CE, 37 years earlier. As you may recall from page 57, in 198 CE R' Hiyya was indeed concerned that such a sighting might be upsetting to people, because it was indicative that Rosh HaShanah should not, in actuality, begin that evening. No wonder they reported it.

For this reason I argue that this story took place in September 120 CE, since that year was similar to the year discussed by R' Hiyya, 198 CE. These dates with a three-day discrepancy are consistent with the facts described in the Talmud.

Molad Zaqen and Lunar Science

Here is the table of all the years with three-day discrepancies from the 2nd through the 4th century:

Year	Day	Hrs	Pts	Molad of Tishrei	Conjunction	Skew
3881	Mon	21	601	Sep 9, 0120 15:33	Sep 9, 0120 19:04	3d
3897	Wed	22	1015	Sep 12, 0136 16:56	Sep 12, 0136 19:31	3d
3906	Fri	20	478	Sep 3, 0145 14:26	Sep 3, 0145 18:08	3d
3934	Thu	23	249	Sep 23, 0173 17:13	Sep 23, 0173 22:00	3d
3943	Sat	20	792	Sep 14, 0182 14:44	Sep 14, 0182 18:13	3d
3959	Mon	22	126	Sep 17, 0198 16:07	Sep 17, 0198 18:16	3d
4004	Fri	22	394	Sep 1, 0243 16:21	Sep 1, 0243 21:07	3d
4066	Wed	21	585	Sep 6, 0305 15:32	Sep 6, 0305 20:29	3d
4119	Sat	23	233	Sep 20, 0358 17:12	Sep 20, 0358 21:41	3d
4128	Mon	20	776	Sep 11, 0367 14:43	Sep 11, 0367 19:15	3d

In each of the above cases, a very visible Old Moon would be seen before sunrise when Rosh HaShanah was due to begin after sunset that evening. Such was the case for all 78 years of the Molad of Tishrei study with three-day discrepancies. Yet, as we have already mentioned, when the Dehiyyah Molad Zaqen rule is implemented, all three-day discrepancies disappear – because all have Moladot in the last quarter of the day. How telling it is that three of the ten cases are actually important in our sources.

It thus seems clear to me that the Dehiyyah Molad Zaqen is intended to prevent the sighting of the Old Moon in proximity to the Molad. I find it strange that no one has yet made this association, especially since its name could be translated literally as "the postponement [to prevent the seeing] of the Old Moon."

Note that the Dehiyyah Molad Zaqen not only alters the three-day discrepancies, but also many entries that were two-day discrepancies as well and also have a last-quarter Molad. Some, although not all, of these two-day discrepancies will have a visible Old Moon, though not as visible as in the case of a three-day discrepancy. (There are no one-day discrepancies with a Molad in the last quarter of the day.)

Of the 2020 years in the Molad of Tishrei study, 522 of the Moladot fell in the last quarter of the day and would therefore have been subject to the Molad Zaqen rule after it was implemented. As mentioned, 78 of these years contain three-day discrepancies. The other 405 years contained two-day discrepancies, which under the rule would become one-day discrepancies.

(It must be noted that in the previous chapter, we drew attention to a very unusual Molad of Tishrei situation occurring by chance in 2013, as this book was being compiled. This year is subject neither to the Molad Zaqen rule nor any other Dehiyyot; but it *is* affected by the orbit of the moon. The method by which I determined the 74 three-day discrepancies did not take into account the effect of the moon's orbit; the number of times such an extreme orbit could occur is even more infrequent than regular three-day discrepancies.)

The time is fast approaching to reveal why all this chaos ensued in the Fixed Hebrew Calendar – why one possible purpose of this calendar was to deliberately prevent seeing the New Moon at the start of Rosh HaShanah. Whatever this purpose was, the Dehiyyot served to thwart it; but these rules were implemented more than a millennium after the Fixed Hebrew Calendar itself was born, by which time the mystery purpose may have lost its urgency. We shall soon find out if this is the case.

Summary

The Dehiyyah Molad Zaqen is a rabbinical postponement rule whose rationale has been obscured. Here we offer a logical reason for this rule: to prevent a very visible Old Moon showing up on Erev Rosh HaShanah.

The Molad of Tishrei study has pinpointed 78 out of the 2020 years of the study in which the Molad sets a date for Rosh HaShanah three days before the New Moon could actually be seen. Since each of these cases fell in the last quarter of the day, all of them have been deferred under the Dehiyyah Molad Zaqen, converting three-day discrepancies to at most a two-day discrepancy.

The Dehiyyot and Calendar Setup

In this chapter I will expand on the nature of the calculated calendar and explain the Dehiyyot in greater depth. This will involve more extensive calculations than in the previous parts of the book. The reader who is not desirous of following these calculations should skip to the summary at the end of the chapter.

Back on page 75 we observed that God is deemed to have given the Jewish people the power to establish the months as they saw fit, declaring, "You, even if you err deliberately." Thus were made the original calendar rules; and likewise, later, were implemented the Dehiyyot.

We had survived for a great many centuries without Dehiyyot, and in fact, there were definite advantages to the pre-Dehiyyot calendar. In "Doing the Math" on page 54 I showed how simple it was to properly know the dates of Rosh HaShanah, Yom Kippur, and Sukkot by maintaining the Molad. With a little more effort one could even determine the dates of Passover and Shavuot.

Although there were certainly good reasons for them, the Dehiyyot complicated the calendar process such that few could now set up their own calendar. The reliance on the rabbinic authorities thus only increased.

Lunar and Solar Calendars

Prior to the implementation of Dehiyyot, the length of Hebrew years was defined based on a relatively simple system. A year might be 354, 355, 383, or 384 days long.[62]

---

[62] One adjustment the rabbis made to the original year was to shorten or lengthen it by a day, so that Rosh HaShanah would fall on the right day. Following this, some years might now also be 353 or 355 days in length (or in a leap year, 383 or 385 days). The months used to adjust the length are Cheshvan and Kislev, which can take either 29 or 30 days. See the table on page 97, which displays the lengths of Cheshvan and Kislev in each type of year.

Since the lunar month lasts approximately 29 and a half days, the normal rule was that each lunar month of 30 days was followed by one of 29 days, so as to average out at 29 and a half. A regular year contains 12 months, therefore the length of a regular year is 12 x 29 ½ = 354 days.

This would be the entire story if lunar months were exactly 29 and a half days long. But we know from the chapter on the Molad that they actually last for 29 days, 12 hours and 793 halakim. These 793 halakim add 44 minutes and 3 $1/3$ seconds a month, which over a 12-month year totals at 8 hours, 48 minutes and 40 seconds. This additional amount accumulates to a full day every three years, leading to a need for an extra day by the end of the 3rd year.

A separate issue is the synchronization of the lunar period with the solar period. By a fortunate coincidence, 235 lunar months are approximately equal to 19 solar years. In order to keep in step with the solar calendar (so that the festivals would continue to fall in the right seasons), in every cycle of 19 years, seven of the years need to be "leap years" and contain 13 months. As mentioned in a previous chapter, the mnemonic GUHADZaT represents which specific seven years take the added month, Adar I (30 days long).

Days in a year are rounded down to the nearest whole day. Thirteen lunar months equals 383 days, 21 hours and 33 minutes. When the previous year had remainder of 3 hours and 26 minutes or less then the year will have 383 days, a greater remainder will mean the year will have 384 days.

All this means that before the implementation of the Dehiyyot we had year lengths of 354, 355, 383,and 384 days. But with the implementation of Dehiyyot, Rosh HaShanah is postponed, adding a day to the previous year and shortening the coming year. So with Dehiyyot we can have year lengths of 353, 354, 355, 383, 384, 385 days.

What follows is a chart showing how we establish the calendar with different year lengths:

Month Length Chart

	353 Days	354 Days	355 Days	383 Days	384 Days	385 Days
Tishrei	30	30	30	30	30	30
Cheshvan	29	29	30	29	29	30
Kislev	29	30	30	29	30	30
Tevet	29	29	29	29	29	29
Shvat	30	30	30	30	30	30
Adar I	NA	NA	NA	30	30	30
Adar	29	29	29	29	29	29
Nisan	30	30	30	30	30	30
Iyyar	29	29	29	29	29	29
Sivan	30	30	30	30	30	30
Tammuz	29	29	29	29	29	29
Av	30	30	30	30	30	30
Elul	29	29	29	29	29	29
	353	354	355	383	384	385

The Dehiyyot

In my opinion, the first Dehiyyah to be permanently implemented was the Molad Zaqen. This happened with the conflict between Saadia [Gaon] and Ben Meir in 922 CE. It eliminates nearly all of the problematic appearances of the Old Moon on the morning of Erev Rosh HaShanah. The importance of this Dehiyyah was underscored by R' Hiyya previously when he noted how disturbing the appearance of the Old Moon would be. The implementation is very subtle, causing a day to be added to the preceding Cheshvan. Cheshvan becomes 30 days in length instead of 29, thereby postponing Rosh HaShanah by one day. If the Old Moon was previously visible on the day of the Molad, it is now no longer visible, one day later. Problem solved! It also has the added positive effect of reducing the disparity between when Rosh HaShanah is observed and when the New Moon can actually be seen.

When it comes to another Dehiyyah, Lo ADU Rosh, again we find that the exact point in history at which it was implemented is uncertain. Its advocacy begins in the Gemara and it is mentioned in the Exilarch's letter of 835/6 CE, which will be cited in our next chapter; but this might be a theoretical discussion, since Molad Zaqen is also mentioned but not implemented.

It seems to me that only after Hai Gaon did the knowledge that the calendar was based on calculation, rather than witnessed testimony, become widespread. It was then that Lo ADU Rosh become formally enacted. This rule requires that whenever the Molad of Tishrei occurs either on a Sunday, Wednesday or Friday (mnemonic – אד"ו ADU), the first day of Tishrei be postponed to the following day. Its purpose is to ensure that Rosh HaShanah falls out on the right days and no rituals are compromised.[63]

Since the implementation of the Molad Zaqen would, if it postpones the Molad to a Sunday, Wednesday, or Friday, require in turn a further postponement under Lo ADU Rosh, this would create some additional year lengths. For example if a normal 354-day year were subject to the Molad Zaqen rule followed by the Lo ADU Rosh rule, the length of that year would now be 356 days. This cannot be compensated for solely by changes to the lengths of Cheshvan and Kislev, so the Rabbis adopted two sub-rules,

---

[63] Dr. Irv Bromberg summarizes for us the Talmudic explanations of the Lo ADU Rosh rule. He notes that the exclusion of Wednesday and Friday serves to prevent Yom Kippur from occurring on either side of Shabbat, which would be ritually inconvenient with regard to the burial of a corpse (Rosh HaShanah 20a). Moreover, the exclusion of Sunday serves to prevent Hoshanah Rabbah from occurring on Shabbat, which would render the traditionally beaten willow branches muktze i.e. prohibited from moving on Shabbat (Sukkah 43a; Yerushalmi Sukkah 4:5). http://individual.utoronto.ca/kalendis/hebrew/postpone.htm.

Dehiyyah GaTaRaD and Dehiyyah BeTU'TeKaPoT,[64] to eliminate invalid year lengths 356 and 382 by preventing the Molad Zaqen rule from creating the need for another Lo ADU Rosh postponement. We do this by a postponement in the year previous to that of the problematic Molad Zaqen, which now starts one day later, making the Molad of Tishrei no longer fall on a day subject to Lo ADU Rosh.

Need an Advil? A Review

By now your head is spinning and you wish you had skipped to the summary of this chapter. But it is not as complicated as you think. Simply put, there are two main Dehiyyot:

Dehiyyah Molad Zaqen: Used when the Tishrei Molad is in the last quarter of the day

Dehiyyah Lo ADU Rosh: Used when the Tishrei Molad falls on Sunday, Wednesday, or Friday

If you have a year length that is not in the chart, no need to call the doctor, just apply GaTaRaD or BeTU'TeKaPoT to return it to a valid length. That's it!

---

[64] Dehiyyah GaTaRaD, which is not found in the Talmud, eliminates all of the 356-day Hebrew years that resulted from the introduction of Dehiyyah Lo ADU Rosh. Dehiyyah GaTaRaD requires that Tishrei 1st be postponed to Thursday whenever the Molad of Tishrei for a 12-month year is on Tuesday at 9 hours and 204 parts or later. This shortens the year, returning it to a valid length. The name GaTaRaD is the acronym formed from the Hebrew letters gimel (=3 for Tuesday), tet (=9), resh (=200), and daled (=4).
Dehiyyah BeTU'TeKaPoT, which is not found in the Talmud, eliminates all of the 382-day Hebrew years that resulted from the introduction of Dehiyyah Lo ADU Rosh. Dehiyyah BeTU'TeKaPoT requires that Tishrei 1st be postponed to Tuesday whenever the Molad of Tishrei following a 13-month year is on Monday at 15 hours and 589 parts or later. This lengthens the year, returning it to a valid length. The name BeTU'TeKaPoT is the acronym formed from the Hebrew letters bet (=2 for Monday), tet (=9), vav (=6), taf (=400), kuf (=100), peh (=80), and tet (=9). Quoted from http://hebrewcalendar.tripod.com.

Rambam and Dehiyyot

Now, there is a fascinating conflict between the Rambam and the Ravad on the Dehiyyot. Rambam writes:[65]

ועיקר שאר הארבע דחיות האלו הוא זה העיקר שאמרנו שהחשבון הזה במהלך אמצעי, וראיה לדבר שהרי המולד יהיה בליל שלישי וידחה לחמישי ופעמים רבות לא יראה ירח בליל חמישי ולא עוד אלא ולא בליל ששי מכלל שלא נתקבצו השמש והירח קבוץ אמתי אלא בחמישי.

The primary reason for these four Dehiyyot is the same as the one we previously referred to: that the Molad is based on the average length of a lunar month [Synodic period of the moon]. As proof, there are times when the Molad falls on Tuesday and is postponed until Thursday,[66] and yet the moon is still not seen in the evening on which Thursday begins [Wednesday night], nor do we see the moon in the evening on which Friday begins [Thursday night], thus showing that the true Conjunction actually occurred on Thursday.

So that the reader can understand exactly what the Rambam is saying let us look at a specific example from years 5745 and 5746.

We start without implementation of any Dehiyyot:

Heb Year	Months in Year	Days Year	Hrs	Pts	Molad	Rosh HaShanah After Sunset	Dehiyyot
5745	12	355	17	976	Tue, Sep 25, 1984 11:54	Mon, Sep 24, 1984	
5746	13	384	2	772	Sat, Sep 14, 1985 20:42	Fri, Sep 13, 1985	

We implement Lo ADU Rosh, postponing 5746 by one day, but this adds a day to 5745.

Heb Year	Months in Year	Days Year	Hrs	Pts	Molad	Rosh HaShanah After Sunset	Dehiyyot
5745	12	356	17	976	Tue, Sep 25, 1984 11:54	Mon, Sep 24, 1984	
5746	13	383	2	772	Sat, Sep 14, 1985 20:42	Sat, Sep 14, 1985	Lo ADU

---

[65] Hilchot Kiddush HaHodesh 7:8.
[66] This is a Dehiyyah GaTaRaD followed by a Lo ADU Rosh.

This makes Hebrew Year 5745 a 356-day long year, a unacceptable year length. The Dehiyyah GaTaRaD is implemented to repair this problem, pushing the start of 5745 later, to Wednesday after sunset:

Heb Year	Months in Year	Days Year	Hrs	Pts	Molad	Rosh HaShanah After Sunset	Dehiyyot
5745	12	354	17	976	Tue, Sep 25, 1984 11:54	Wed, Sep 26, 1984	GaTaRaD
5746	13	383	2	772	Sat, Sep 14, 1985 20:42	Fri, Sep 13, 1985	Lo ADU

What is critical here is that we have deferred the start of Rosh HaShanah 5745 from Monday after sunset (i.e. onset of Tuesday – since Hebrew days begin after sunset the day before), to Tuesday after sunset (i.e. onset of Wednesday). This is subject to Lo ADU Rosh and in turn gets pushed off to Wednesday after sunset (i.e. onset of Thursday). This reduces the length of Hebrew Year 5745 to 354 days, which our month allocation procedure handles.

Now we can get to the point of the Rambam's Halacha mentioned above. The Rambam postulates that we do not see the moon on Wednesday night, nor on Thursday night, Thus, a moon that was expected to be seen on Monday night after sunset because of the Molad is actually not seen until Friday night after sunset – which makes this a four-day discrepancy.[67] I am unsure if a four-day discrepancy is even possible. Perhaps there was a girsa (textual variant) problem and the moon was seen three days after the Molad on Thursday night.

In any event – WOW! The Rambam just described a three-day-plus discrepancy. He is holding on to his principle that Re'iyah happens 24 hours after the real Conjunction; but he believes that the purpose of the Dehiyyot was to correct for a real Conjunction occurring, as in the case of his example, two days after the Molad.

The Ravad criticizes the Rambam for ignoring the Talmudic position as to why Lo ADU Rosh was created – not in order to correct for Conjunctions but rather so that there would

---

[67] The Rambam is talking hypothetically here. None of the van Gent charts seem to indicate that a four-day discrepancy is possible.

not be two holy days in a row: so that the dead need not wait two days for burial, so that there be fresh vegetables for a Shabbat after Yom Kippur, and so that Hoshanah Rabbah not be compromised by Shabbat.[68] The Rambam, for his part, could reply that we know that these Dehiyyot were implemented late in the calendar's existence. The problems solved by the Dehiyyot were tolerated for centuries upon centuries. We could make an argument that the earlier Talmudic rationales were really advocacy for the establishment of the rules, with the actual underlying purpose to bring the Fixed Hebrew Calendar more in line with lunar reality. Some similar logic will be shown in the next chapter.

The greatness of the Rambam lies in the fact that he was willing to learn from the science of the day. It is not even such complicated science – the moon presents itself for all to see; but most of us just don't look. I myself never noticed that the New Moon is absent from the Erev Rosh HaShanah sky until I actively searched for it. Here in Halacha 8 of Hilchot Kiddush HaHodesh chapter 7, the Rambam is stating that the calculation produces the Molad early, and the Dehiyyot serve to correct it.

There is no question that the Dehiyyot do bring the calendar closer to reality as the Rambam has written, but I believe the Ravad is correct in arguing that this was not the purpose of the Dehiyyot per se. In a short while, I am going to suggest a purpose that even the Ravad did not think of.

Close Counts Only in Horseshoes

In a nutshell, the problem facing us is that our calculated calendar gives a Tishrei Molad about 1 day and 19 hours on average too early over the 2020 years of the study. With all due respect to the Rambam and his suggestion that the Dehiyyot bring the calendar back in line with reality, we find

---

[68] Based on the Talmudic positions outlined in footnote 63.

that when we apply the Dehiyyot, this discrepancy is reduced to slightly less than 1 day and 2 hours – the problem remains unremedied.

The following chart outlines the distribution of Dehiyyot applying to all 2020 Rosh HaShanahs from the Molad of Tishrei Study:

From the chart one can see the effect and lack of effect of the Dehiyyot:

On the one hand, 570 three-day and two-day discrepancies remain even after application of the Dehiyyot. This means that 29% of the time, the New Moon will not be visible after the sunsets inaugurating both the first and second day of Rosh HaShanah. Rosh HaShanah 2002 was one of the years in this classification. It was the year that prompted me to investigate and author this book.

On the other hand, in 60% of the years, the disparity between when Rosh HaShanah is observed and the visible New Moon has been reduced.

Interestingly, Dehiyyah GaTaRaD, a postponement that causes a two-day jump, displays three occurrences which convert one-day discrepancies before the New Moon into Moladot that fall one day after the New Moon, a situation which guarantees a visible New Moon on the first night of Rosh HaShanah.

Summary

In this chapter I went into greater detail regarding the intricate workings of the lunar calendar, demonstrating why there was a need for Dehiyyot and how they work. An extensive analysis of the Rambam's views on Dehiyyot was presented.

If the purpose of the Dehiyyot was to reduce or eliminate the discrepancy between when Rosh HaShanah starts and when the New Moon is actually first seen, this could have been achieved much more simply by adding 1 day, 18 hours and 41 minutes to the Molad shel Tohu!

The Dehiyyot have a logical basis. They were discussed in the Gemara though not implemented. Not to have Yom Kippur fall directly before or after Shabbat made sense. Once Saadia Gaon forced acceptance of the Dehiyyah Molad Zaqen, out of concern to correct the problems the sighting of the Old Moon was causing with the Karaites, the other Dehiyyot were inserted into the Fixed Calendar as well.

The Exilarch's Letter of 835 CE

Prof. Sacha Stern, widely regarded as a leading expert in Jewish Calendars, has aggregated an encyclopedia of sources pertaining to the Hebrew Calendar, spanning the 12 centuries between the 2nd century BCE and the 10th century CE. This quote is from pages 184-5 of his book *Calendar and Community*:

> Of far greater importance, however, is a much later document from the Cairo Geniza: a letter of a Babylonian Exilarch – one of the main leaders of the Rabbanite community – with detailed calendrical instructions for the year 835/6 CE. The letter reveals that Passover (15 Nisan) in that year was due to occur on a Tuesday; whilst according to the present-day rabbinic calendar, it should have occurred on Thursday. According to the Exilarch, the setting of Passover on Tuesday was dictated by a concern to avoid visibility of the new moon before the first day of the month. This concern does not exist in the present-day rabbinic calendar.
>
> Once discovered and published in 1922, the Exilarch's letter proved beyond doubt that almost five hundred years after R' Yose and 'Hillel the Patriarch', the fixed calendar in its present-day form had still not been instituted.[69]

Here, Stern has thrown a monkey wrench into the accepted notion that the basics of the calendar as understood today could have been established in 358 CE, for according to Stern, they were not even established in 835 CE!

In Stern's view, the "setting of Passover [836 CE] on Tuesday" (presumably by the court in Eretz Yisrael) "was

---

[69] Stern's translation exhibits differences from Mann's translation, publicly available on WikiSource. https://en.wikisource.org/wiki/The_Exilarch's_Letter

dictated by a concern to avoid visibility of the New Moon before the first day of the month." This "rule," that we can move the date of Rosh Hodesh earlier so that it is not preceded by a visible New Moon, is not something we have ever encountered before. It is important to realize that the only source for this rule is this interpretation of the Exilarch's letter by Stern.

The letter, written by Babylonian Exilarch David ben Yehuda, and discovered, as Stern notes, in the Cairo Geniza, was sent to the community in Eretz Yisrael. The Exilarch takes care to begin it with a message of unity:

> Whereas all of us, and all those of Israel, might be of one partnership in the [fixation of all of the lunar] months and in all of the feasts, in accordance with this custom that our fathers and the academies have made a rule of practice [amongst us] until now…

Following this, he struggles with the difficult question of when the moon of Nisan should fall in order to make everything come out correctly. And he ends:

> So it is that we rely upon them always (i.e. the court in the land of Israel), so that Israel might not be broken-up into vying factions. Wherefore, I and the heads of the academy, as well as the Rabbis, and all of Israel, rely upon this calendar …[70]

As one can see on the next page from the photos of the source documents, providing an accurate translation of the documents is not exactly simple and straightforward. But the issue goes beyond translation. Based on evidence from the actual lunar facts of 835 CE, it is my belief that Stern's analysis is very flawed.

---

[70] For the full text in English and Aramaic, see https://en.wikisource.org/wiki/The_Exilarch's_Letter.

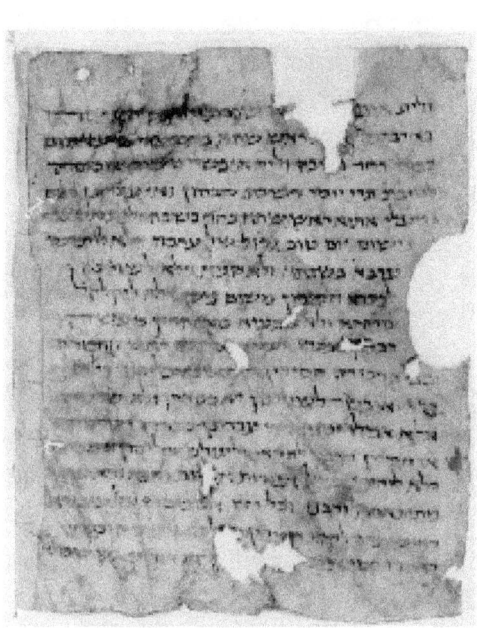

Now let us examine the calendar facts and see how they might impact our understanding of the Exilarch's letter. We need to ascertain whether indeed there were Dehiyyot already in use at the time. The Molad of Tishrei for 835 CE was Friday, August 31, at 22 hours and 660 halakim (4:36 PM). The year 835 CE, Hebrew year 4596, was the 17th year of the 19-year cycle and thus a leap year. The Molad for Tishrei 836 CE was Thursday, September 18, at 20 hours and 169 halakim (2:09 PM). According to present rules, both days are subject to the Dehiyyah Molad Zaqen. 835 CE would begin on a Saturday. 836 CE, now due to begin on a Friday, would then receive a further Dehiyyah due to the rule Lo ADU Rosh. This would lengthen the previous year to 385 days.

The basic apportionments of days for a 385-day year up to the month of Nisan are listed in this chart.

Month	Length (in Days)	Days to Nisan
Tishrei	30	30
Cheshvan	30	30
Kislev	30	30
Tevet	29	29
Shvat	30	30
Adar I	30	30
Adar	29	29
Nisan	30	
Iyyar	29	
Sivan	30	
Tammuz	29	
Av	30	
Elul	29	
	385	208

Since the Molad of Tishrei 835 CE was in the last quarter, under the Molad Zaqen rule it gets deferred one day to Saturday, August 28, and thus the year begins with Rosh Hashanah on Friday night at sunset.

Adding 208 days to Saturday, August 28, we find that Rosh Hodesh Nisan comes out on Thursday, March 27, 836 CE.

But the letter stated that Passover was expected on Tuesday, which would also put Rosh Hodesh Nisan on Tuesday, proving that the Molad Zaqen rule was not used.

In his understanding of the letter, Stern presumes that mention by the Exilarch of the other Dehiyyot means that they were implemented as opposed to advocated. Yet Stern's own analysis states that Nisan was established two days earlier "dictated by a concern to avoid visibility of the New Moon before the first day of the month." This rule, or concern, was heretofore unknown and indicated to Stern that the methodology of the calculated calendar had yet to be established. Thus he contradicts himself. But stranger yet, Stern presumes a heretofore unknown calendar rule.

A Whole New Rule? Not Likely

To complicate the discussion by the presumption of a whole new rule for calculating the calendar seems to me to be unrealistic and unnecessary, especially in light of the fact that within 87 years, Saadia Gaon will force acceptance of the Dehiyyot more or less as we use them today. This will come to pass via the Saadia-Ben Meir controversy – whose pivotal concern was whether or not the Molad Zaqen was used.

Now, in the Exilarch's letter, mention is made of the Dehiyyot, prompting Stern to assume that the Dehiyyot were implemented. But even Stern notes in his book, citing another letter:

> However, the polemical character of this letter should not be overlooked. Although a meeting between Palestinians and Babylonians is not historically impossible, this story – for which we have no other

record – could equally have been a piece of fictitious Babylonian self-legitimization.[71]

In line with this thinking, I want to argue that this Babylonian self-legitimization was in force here as well. In other words, the mention of Dehiyyot stemmed not, as Stern assumes, from their actual implementation, but rather from the Exilarch's desire to convince the calendrical court in Eretz Yisrael to implement all of the Dehiyyot, in order to make Rosh HaShanah more consistent with lunar reality.

What happens if we redo the calendar for that year without Dehiyyot? The Molad of Tishrei for 835 CE was Friday, August 31, at 22 hours and 660 halakim (4:36 PM). The year 835 CE, Hebrew year 4596, was the 17th year of the cycle and thus a leap year. The Molad of Tishrei for 836 CE was Thursday, September 18, at 20 hours and 169 halakim (2:09 PM). If we do not implement Dehiyyot, we have a normal 384-day year length. Rosh HaShanah 835 CE was not deferred and started at sunset Thursday Night.

Here is the chart for a 384-day year, up to Nisan:

Month	Length (in Days)	Days to Nisan
Tishrei	30	30
Cheshvan	29	29
Kislev	30	30
Tevet	29	29
Shvat	30	30
Adar I	30	30
Adar	29	29
Nisan	30	
Iyyar	29	
Sivan	30	
Tammuz	29	
Av	30	
Elul	29	
	384	207

---

[71] *Calendar and Community*, page 268.

Here the days to Nisan are 207 days (Cheshvan is not full).

Without Dehiyyot, Tishrei 835 CE starts on Friday, August 31, 835 (as opposed to Saturday with Dehiyyot). Adding 207 days, Rosh Hodesh Nisan falls out Tuesday, March 25, 836 CE. This is indeed what happened, as Stern states. He, however, claims the court was using Dehiyyot but that some heretofore-unknown rule made it fall two days early; whereas my argument is that the court simply did not implement any Dehiyyot that year. This is not to say that the court never implemented Dehiyyot, but that if Dehiyyot were implemented, it would be *an individual decision by an individual court*. Though the principles of Dehiyyot were discussed in the Talmud, this was never stated as a mandate or set in stone.

Why then did the letter mention the sighting of the moon – a mention which so excited Stern? The answer is that it was, in fact, a sighting of the *Old Moon* back at the start of the year that put the Exilarch in such a panic.

It was without surprise, but still with great amazement, that looking in the Molad of Tishrei study I discovered that Friday, August 31, 835 CE was indeed another of those pesky three-day discrepancies. This explains the Exilarch's worry about the moon; he was concerned about the fact that Rosh HaShanah 835 CE was undeniably too early. This was nothing more than common sense on the part of the Exilarch. An Old Moon clearly visible Erev Rosh HaShanah, plus two following days with no New Moon to be seen, would undoubtedly embarrass the Rabbanite establishment at a critical time in its history, as will be discussed shortly. The Exilarch was worried, since the year starting too early might well force Nisan to arrive too early also.

Here is the van Gent chart[72], which unequivocally shows that the moon would not be seen until three days after the Molad – namely, Sunday after sunset.

---

[72] http://www.sodhaibur.com/van-gent-maps/lunvis-4596.pdf

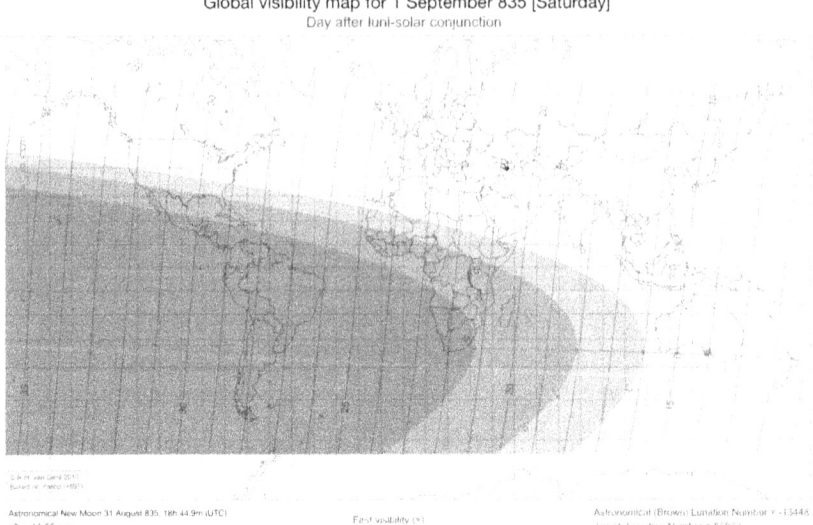

In a pattern that is becoming all too familiar to us by now, we have here an hour and 40 minutes of Old Moon visible on the morning of Erev Rosh HaShanah. This fact is the source of Stern's error in understanding the Exilarch's letter. The explanation lies in the lunar facts.

The Lunar Conjunction for Tishrei was Friday, August 31 at 9:01 PM in Eretz Yisrael. The Old Moon would rise 41 hours before the Conjunction, at 3:51 AM, Thursday morning, Erev Rosh HaShanah at a brightness of 3.6% – a highly visible Old Moon!

The Exilarch had good reason to be concerned as to how this would play out at Passover. This is because Tishrei is the keystone of the year. If Tishrei started early, then all following months could be expected to be early too.

We know from the Exilarch's letter that he was deferring to Eretz Yisrael in calendar matters. This supports the assertion that the calculated calendar had yet to be publicly established and implemented; for had it been so, the Exilarch could have run the calculation for himself and been confident that Yom Kippur would fall on exactly the same day in both Eretz Yisrael and Bavel. His not doing so implies his ignorance of the existence of calculations. It stands to reason that the people, and perhaps many rabbis too (including, it seems, the Exilarch), had every reason to think that witnessed testimony still lay at the core of the calendar.

Yet our data clearly shows that Rosh HaShanah 835 CE, according to the court in Eretz Yisrael and accepted by the Exilarch, began a day before the Conjunction. Obviously, honest witnesses could not have produced such a result; calculations were being used, whether the Exilarch knew it or not.

How did this all play out at Passover? Well, since this was a leap year, in fact the Exilarch had no need to worry, for the extra month, Adar I, of 30 days was inserted before the regular Adar, that takes 29 days. This served to push the New Moon of Nisan back one day and solved the Old Moon issue.

There are several interesting things to note in the Global visibility map for Tuesday 25 March 836 (not reproduced here) – the day Rosh Hodesh Nisan should have fallen out in Bavel. The New Moon will not be seen until Wednesday night after sunset, but that is in fact only a two-day discrepancy and not so noticeable. The Old Moon can be seen Monday morning. It will be at only 1.1% visibility, for just 38 minutes, after which it will be washed out by the rising sun.

Rabbinical Malfeasance

Now it is time to explain what we meant by speaking above of "a critical time" in the Rabbanite establishment's history.

According to Rabbi Avraham ben David in his *Sefer Ha-Qabbalah*, the Karaite movement crystallized in Baghdad in the Gaonic period (circa 7th-9th centuries CE), under the Abbasid Caliphate, in what is present-day Iraq. This is the view universally accepted among Rabbinic Jews.[73]

Now, Karaites certainly would not accept the idea of the rabbinical substitution of a calculated calendar for a witnessed one. The Karaites believe that the Torah mandated witnesses to establish the new month. Any confusion experienced by the Rabbanite Exilarch surrounding calendrical issues would doubtless have provided grist to the mill of Karaite polemics; hence the Exilarch's great desire to avoid all semblance of confusion.

Whether they believed that the Rabbis had simply erred in 835 CE, or they concluded that the Rabbis were using a calculated calendar in defiance of the Torah, either way the situation was helpful to the Karaites and not at all helpful to the Exilarch. This, I believe, would have prompted tremendous concern in Baghdad regarding discrepancies between how Eretz Yisrael established the calendar and how the moon was actually seen. The Exilarch would not want a repeat of what had taken place on Rosh HaShanah 835 CE to occur at Nisan time in 836 CE. This concern was not shared by the Rabbis in Eretz Yisrael, whose Karaite population was much smaller and not causing them the same trouble.

The Exilarch's concern was about a visible Old Moon, not the New Moon. The potential problem was Monday morning March 24, where he feared a repeat of what had just happened at Rosh HaShanah. A visible Old Moon might rise in Baghdad before sunrise, and then that evening Nisan would begin, according to the counting since Rosh HaShanah. Should that happen, such a sighting would aid the Karaites in proving that the Rabbis were not properly observing Passover at the correct time.

With our access to lunar science we know that in the end, the moon only rose at 5:58 AM for 38 minutes, at 1.1% visibility, which meant that it was not likely to be noticed.

---

[73] Wikipedia

But the Exilarch could not know that and – I believe – real damage had already been done the previous Rosh HaShanah, damage that would have been mitigated had the court in Eretz Yisrael utilized the Dehiyyah Molad Zaqen.

In sum: The Exilarch's calculation challenges, namely to ensure that all festivals fall out on the appropriate day, were exacerbated by the fact that he was dealing with the Karaites. The Karaites, very active at the time with their own Torah interpretations, did not believe the Rabbinic oral law to be divinely inspired. This group would welcome the fact that the rabbinical leader's calendar appeared to be so obviously wrong. More than just a thorny calendrical problem, this was a battle for the hearts and minds of the Jews of Bavel!

922 CE: Battle Royale

We remain concerned with Bavel and Eretz Yisrael, but move forward almost a century in time.

The year 922 CE saw a major dispute between Saadia Gaon, prominent rabbi and exegete, in Bavel, and Rabbi Aaron ben Meir, the Nasi in Eretz Yisrael, over the "Dehiyyah Molad Zaqen" postponement rule. Though a significant historical conflict, our knowledge of this "Battle Royale" derives exclusively from finds in the Cairo Geniza at the end of the 19th century. It is very likely that it was kept deliberately under wraps, so as not to play into the hands of gloating Karaites.

As mentioned above, in 835 CE, just 87 years previously, the Molad Zaqen rule was not implemented, causing the Exilarch much angst. However, by this time the leadership in Bavel seemed bent upon implementing the Molad Zaqen rule, in order to work out the calendrical kinks that were causing so much trouble.

The bone of contention was Passover 922. According to the court in Eretz Yisrael, with Ben Meir at the helm, the first day of Passover would fall on Sunday. Bavel however had already worked out that it would fall on Tuesday.[74]

Saadia (he had yet to be named Gaon) was brought in to wrest away control of the calendar from Ben Meir. Saadia's motivation is easy to understand. The Karaites – a thorn in Babylonian Jewry's side – would have a field day following any breakdown in the Rabbanites' system of calculation; any inconsistency between Rosh Hodesh and the actual moon was grist for their polemical mill.

Ben Meir's reasoning is less transparent, and it is commonly thought this was purely a political conflict, with Eretz Yisrael jealously protecting its control of the Hebrew Calendar. Moreover, Dehiyyot add another layer of complexity to the calculation of the calendar. But it is also possible that a noble purpose lay behind Ben Meir's actions. Jews at the time lived scattered, not all of them in Bavel or Eretz Yisrael. It stands to reason that Jewish communities in Italy or Spain or other locations would not know that Dehiyyot had been implemented, leading to chaos and inconsistency.

I, however, believe that it was a psychological conflict, with Eretz Yisrael implementing a system with which it had been entrusted, a system in which Dehiyyot had not been included. A change to the system would imply that Rabban Gamliel got it wrong. It could well be that although there might have been discussions about it in Eretz Yisrael, there was considerable resistance to implementing any Dehiyyot.

It is true that Ben Meir did not directly oppose the Dehiyyah Molad Zaqen rule; rather he was suggesting different parameters for it. But I believe this was a delaying tactic on his part against an opponent with whom it was difficult to argue; and that, in fact, he did not actually want the rule implemented at all. Ben Meir was claiming that the Dehiyyah Molad Zaqen should be applied when the Molad falls at 18 hours and 642 halakim or later – as opposed to

---

[74] Stern, *Calendar and Community*, p. 266.

the simple 18 hours rule by which Saadia held and that we now observe (i.e. last quarter of the day).

Looking at the chart below, a possible rationale for Ben Meir's unusual suggestion emerges. This chart shows that had he successfully defended his position, the Dehiyyah Molad Zaqen would only have been implemented 12 years later, in 934 CE – this appears on the next to last line of the table.

934 CE would be the first year since the dispute whose Molad fell later than 18 hours and 642 halakim. Hence, Ben Meir's position postpones the conflict with Saadia until 934 CE, by which time the fight might be forgotten or different protagonists might have emerged. Had he acceded to Saadia's position, however, the years 923 CE and 927 CE would have required application of the Molad Zaqen rule – meaning that the decision would have had to be made immediately.

Heb Year	Hrs	Pts	Molad	Conjunction Jerusalem ST	Difference	Skew
4680	5	547	Sat, Sep 2, 0919 23:30	Sat, Sep 2, 0919 9:34	13h 56m	1d
4681	3	56	Fri, Sep 20, 0920 21:03	Fri, Sep 20, 0920 6:29	14h 34m	1d
4682	11	932	Wed, Sep 10, 0921 5:51	Tue, Sep 9, 0921 19:04	10h 48m	2d
4683	9	441	Tue, Sep 29, 0922 3:24	Mon, Sep 28, 0922 19:49	7h 36m	2d
4684	**18**	**237**	**Sat, Sep 18, 0923 12:13**	**Sat, Sep 18, 0923 12:06**	**0h 7m**	**2d**
4685	3	33	Wed, Sep 6, 0924 21:01	Thu, Sep 7, 0924 1:27	-4h 25m	2d
4686	0	622	Tue, Sep 25, 0925 18:34	Tue, Sep 25, 0925 22:56	-4h 21m	2d
4687	9	418	Sun, Sep 15, 0926 3:23	Sun, Sep 15, 0926 2:04	1h 19m	2d
4688	**18**	**214**	**Thu, Sep 4, 0927 12:11**	**Thu, Sep 4, 0927 2:08**	**10h 4m**	**2d**
4689	15	803	Wed, Sep 22, 0928 9:44	Tue, Sep 21, 0928 20:42	13h 3m	2d
4690	0	599	Sun, Sep 11, 0929 18:33	Sun, Sep 11, 0929 4:27	14h 6m	1d
4691	9	395	Fri, Sep 1, 0930 3:21	Thu, Aug 31, 0930 18:44	8h 38m	2d
4692	6	984	Thu, Sep 20, 0931 0:54	Wed, Sep 19, 0931 19:37	5h 18m	2d
4693	15	780	Mon, Sep 8, 0932 9:43	Mon, Sep 8, 0932 11:34	-1h 51m	2d
4694	13	289	Sun, Sep 27, 0933 7:16	Sun, Sep 27, 0933 11:08	-3h 52m	2d
4695	**22**	**85**	**Thu, Sep 16, 0934 16:04**	**Thu, Sep 16, 0934 19:22**	**-3h 17m**	**3d**
4696	6	961	Tue, Sep 6, 0935 0:53	Mon, Sep 5, 0935 21:01	3h 52m	2d

In the end, Ben Meir withstood the pressure from Bavel and refused to listen to Saadia. This conflict resulted in different calendars being observed by the Jews in Eretz Yisrael and Babylon (and other countries) for several years. However, until the death of Hai Gaon in 1038, Babylonia was still the center of Jewish learning, and it prevailed.

This 10th-century incident represents the crossroads when the basic Moladic Fixed Hebrew Calendar, which we have shown was being used at least from the time of Rabban Gamliel, was changed through the adoption of the Dehiyyot to more closely reflect the actual lunar experience.

Summary

Tishrei 835 CE seems to have brought an unpleasant surprise for the Exilarch. Something very odd was up with the moon, and he was probably rather taken aback. No science existed then to be able to forecast a three-day discrepancy, and the Molad Zaqen rule that would eventually eliminate the problem was yet to be adopted. In writing to Eretz Yisrael, the Exilarch hoped to ward off a repeat of this problem at Passover time, (justifiably) fearing that the Old Moon would once again be seen before sunrise on the very day that, after sunset, would be declared Rosh Hodesh Nisan.

The core of this problem is the three-day discrepancy. Its most unfortunate iteration was in 358 CE, when it caused almost the entire Jewish world to erroneously assume the initiation of the calendar system itself in that year. This same Jewish world (i.e., rabbis and commentators) wronged Rabban Gamliel, interpreting his strictness towards R' Yehoshua in 120 CE as an ego problem; and similarly failed to understand the significance of R' Hiyya's actions in 198 CE.

We are about to enter into the final chapters, where I present what I believe was the real origin of the Fixed Hebrew Calendar.

Setting the Scene

The fact that we don't know exactly when the Hebrew Calendar changed from witness based to calculation based would seem at first to be very strange. Why would a calendar be produced and not published? After all, the very purpose of the calendar is to make it easy for Jews worldwide to make their observance of Yom Tov correspond with the observance of Yom Tov in Eretz Yisrael.

Under Islam, the New Moon is observed according to the locale one finds oneself. It is conceivable that a Muslim could observe Ramadan in Mecca a day before it is observed in Istanbul. Furthermore, there are no adjustments for the seasons. But for the Jews, it was the sighting of the moon in Jerusalem that was the determinant of the calendar and all of its festivals worldwide.

All the festivals are important, but none is stricter or more awe inspiring than the 10th of Tishrei, Yom Kippur. It is of supreme importance that the Day of Atonement be observed on the correct date. But if one were living in Babylon or Rome or Seville, how would it be possible to learn in time when the month of Tishrei was sanctified, and thus mark Yom Kippur correctly? Would the messengers arrive in time?

The Power of the Calendrical Court

The Talmud in Rosh HaShanah attests to the tremendous halachic power vested in the calendrical court. As we saw, following his conflict with Rabban Gamliel, R' Yehoshua was in great distress. He had been ordered unequivocally to violate Yom Kippur, as far as he knew it! The Talmud narrates that R' Akiva, one of the greatest rabbinical leaders of the time, comforted him by convincing him that Rabban Gamliel was within his rights. The halachic power granted to the Nasi meant that he alone determined when Yom Kippur fell – whether erroneously or not.

This power of the calendrical court is embodied in the blessing we make in Musaf for Rosh Hodesh:

כי בעמך ישראל בחרת מכל האמות, וחקי ראשי חדשים להם קבעת.

You chose Israel from all the nations and empowered them to establish the months.

So whatever the calendrical court did and for whatever reason, with or without a sighting of the moon, it was right. Whatever day is sanctified as the start of the new month is indeed the start of the new month.

In four places in the Talmud Bavli, mention is made of the fact that:

מימות עזרא ואילך לא מצינו אלול מעובר.

From the time of Ezra, Elul was always 29 days long.[75]

The only way in which Elul could always be 29 days long was if the calendrical court sanctified the month on the morning of the 30th day. This was obviously not a witness-based sanctification, for that would inevitably lead to more varied results.

As we mentioned previously, R' Hisda confirms that this was a responsibility of the calendrical court:

חשין לצומא רבה תרין יומין אמר לון רב חסדא למה אתם מכניסין עצמכם למספק הזה חזקה שאין ב"ד מתעצלין בו.

They thought because of the uncertainty they needed to fast two days of Yom Kippur. R' Hisda said, "Why have you immersed yourself in doubt? We can count on the court not to be remiss."[76]

Saying that Elul was always 29 days might not be quite the same thing as saying a fixed calendar was being employed, but actually ends up the same thing for all intents and purposes. For when you establish Elul as 29

---

[75] Rosh HaShanah 19b.

[76] Yerushalmi Rosh HaShanah 1:4.

days, the months adjacent need to be 30 days, simply due to the length of a Synodic month. Two adjacent months of 29 days cannot occur. The only surefire way to avoid this is to pre-set the calendar.

What We Have Learned

There is a central point I wish to extract from our previous discussions.

We have shown that 358 CE was not the inauguration of the Fixed Hebrew Calendar, as the Ramban claims and as is accepted by the vast majority of scholars. In 358 CE, the Fixed Hebrew Calendar must have been already in effect. Proof: the three-day discrepancy, present in 358 CE, is not a natural occurrence but rather is an infrequent byproduct of the use of the Fixed Hebrew Calendar.

Under a witnessed calendar one could perhaps make a mistaken sighting of the New Moon, confusing a cloud illuminated by the setting sun. But this error could at most lead to a one-day discrepancy. A two-day or three-day discrepancy is precluded by the fact that we are counting 29 days from the previous month's sighting.[77]

R' Hiyya's encounter with the Old Moon, documented in the Talmud Rosh HaShanah 25a, would not have occurred as described had the Fixed Hebrew Calendar not been in effect in his day. His firm expectation of the onset of Rosh HaShanah that same night clearly points to this.

Moreover, the celebrated conflict between Rabban Gamliel and R' Yehoshua would also not have taken place had Rabban Gamliel not been using the Fixed Hebrew Calendar.

Many rabbis, both past and present, have been wrong in their understanding of the calendar. I state this as a matter of fact and not as criticism. Even the Rambam, who

---

[77] Under a Fixed Hebrew Calendar, the Crescent New Moon is never actually seen on Rosh Hodesh.

demonstrates knowledge of many aspects of lunar science, could not know the laws of Celestial Mechanics and could not recreate the skies that caused the conflict between Rabban Gamliel and R' Yehoshua.

The Fixed Hebrew Calendar was not forged out of Kabbalah or magic. It was not created by Hillel, the Patriarch, but evolved out of the labors of the Chaldeans, who amassed copious lunar data and made insightful conclusions from it. This we have learned from modern-day scholars who have studied the cuneiform tablets the Chaldeans left behind.

In this book, I have been employing modern mathematics and Celestial Mechanics in order to ferret out lunar reality at key dates in our available sources. Johannes Kepler, Isaac Newton, Joseph-Louis Lagrange, Simon Newcomb and Albert Einstein, to name only some of the great recent scientists, provided the basis for our ability to know the lunar facts from 120 CE.

But it is important to note that such calculations were not part of the system that enabled the creation of the Fixed Hebrew Calendar, and it has no need for them. As will be shown in the final chapter, all the science that was needed was available as far back as during the reign of Nabonassar, who ascended the throne in 747 BCE.

What also seems evident, borne out by the fact that we know there was a Baraita called Sod Ha'ibur and by the reaction of R' Yehoshua, is that there was information that was being kept not only from the people but also from the Rabbis. It was provided only to those who needed to know.

In the final chapter we will give two very valid reasons for the necessity of a Fixed Hebrew Calendar as a base for the decisions of the calendrical court, rather than true lunar witnesses. But for now we will discuss why they hid the fact.

Need for Secrecy

Religious communities are an amalgamation of a variety of souls. Some of these souls are very practical and some very fundamentalistic. In the last chapter we mentioned the Karaites; but, no doubt, earlier individuals and groups existed who believed that the Torah mandated an actual sighting of the New Moon determining Rosh HaShanah and ipso facto Yom Kippur.

In my chapter on Hillel the Patriarch, this idea of the need for secrecy was strengthened by a quote from R' Yitzchak Yisraeli, a disciple of the Rosh, who writes about this in his book *Yesod Olam* (4:14):

> "If it were known and people would be aware of it ... they would challenge Beit Din and argue [with] them and would oppose them with claims and logical arguments. This would lead to great dispute and ruining the festivals, as that event of Rabban Gamliel and R. Yehoshua, where Rabban Gamliel ruled according to the tradition that he had received and R. Yehoshua argued with him because he relied on his logic."[78]

In addition, as Dr. Irv Bromberg suggests, once known about, it could well be argued that the calculation could be improved.[79]

But there is another rationale, pointed out to me by my hevruta Rav Shuki Reich, namely that the witnessing of the moon was a process centered upon the importance of the participation of the ordinary Jew. To take away his participation by the employment of a calculation could have negative consequences.

---

[78] From a translated shiur given by Rabbi Dr. Shai Walter (director of the Drazin Institute for Kiddush HaHodesh and Ibur HaShanah Studies at Yeshivat Kerem B'Yavneh), uploaded March 2007 to http://www.kby.org/english/torat-yavneh/view.asp?id=4009.

[79] http://calendars.wikia.com/wiki/Rectified_Hebrew_calendar

Reviewing the Evidence

Consistent with all of the above, throughout this book I have been theorizing, based on the very emphatic mathematical evidence, that the fact that the witnesses were being selected by virtue of their testimonies' correspondence with the Fixed Hebrew Calendar was kept hidden.

Let us momentarily look back at that evidence. Here are all nine instances of Tishrei Moladot with three-day discrepancies over the 239-year period between 120 CE (Rabban Gamliel) and 358 CE (Hillel II), with 198 CE (R' Hiyya) in between them:

Had I only the evidence from the time of Rabban Gamliel and R' Yehoshua (120 CE) and that of R' Hiyya (198 CE), it would have been sufficient to prove my point and write this book. When I studied Stern's book and got the three-day discrepancy from the Exilarch's letter in 835 CE, it gave me the ability to refute the observations of an eminent calendar scholar. But the three-day discrepancy of 358 CE gave the greatest joy, for it validated not only my theory but all my calculations.

120 CE is a date consistent with the facts that are known about Rabban Gamliel. 198 CE is a date consistent with the facts known about R' Hiyya.

358 CE is more than a date consistent with the facts, it is the date explicitly mentioned in at least one source. This is beyond coincidence. The calendar was causing these three-day discrepancies. To draw up a simile, it was like a creature submerged in a lake. When we witness the disturbances and ripples on the surface of the lake, we understand that there is a creature down there. Thus, Hillel's note, Rabban Gamliel's behavior, R' Hiyya's declarations and the Exilarch's anxiety are all ripples indicating the existence of a subterranean calendar.

Summary

To this point in my book I have established an interesting relationship between the Molad and Conjunction. It is just math, and not even such sophisticated math except for the Celestial Mechanics on which the times of the Lunar Conjunctions are based. But the way that this data is interwoven into the historical record is what is truly amazing.

As we proceed from here, our tools will be history and common sense.

The question on the table will be "Why?" Why did the Fixed Hebrew Calendar establish Rosh HaShanah so early? And to be more specific: Why does the Molad of Rosh HaShanah fall 26% of the time one day before the New Moon, 70% of the time two days before the New Moon, and 4% of the time three days before the New Moon – and, most puzzling, never actually on the New Moon itself?

This could not be an error. The Rabbis who established this system were extremely intelligent. And if the Rabbis had so desired, it would have been very easy to fix, simply by adding days to the Molad shel Tohu.

The Origin of the Hebrew Calendar

Now it is time to wrap up all the loose ends and present the final part of my theory.

Historical Evidence

Neither the Jewish people nor its calendar evolved in a vacuum. In the 6th century BCE, with the onset of the Babylonian Captivity, the Jews became immersed in a culture that had developed considerable knowledge about the lunar calendar.

The sun and the moon served as timepieces not only for the Jews but for ancient mankind in its entirety. The sun provided the measure of the day, the year, and the season. For some cultures, such as Egypt, it provided the principle object of worship.

The moon provided the month, a useful division of the year. For agricultural people, the month related to the particular agricultural needs of that period. Agriculture must be in sync with the seasons, which in turn are in sync with the sun. Thus, it became very important to keep the month-based calendar in sync with the sun. This was not true of all peoples who used the moon as a timepiece. Islam, appearing much later, in the 7th century CE, was initially adopted by desert people who were not concerned that their holidays match the seasons. Thus, their lunar calendar has just 12 months, which maintain no relationship with the sun.

Mesopotamia had many millennia of experience with measuring and predicting astronomical events. An eclipse of the sun is documented on May 3, 1375 BCE in Ugarit, Syria, on a clay tablet, just as we Israelites were about to leave our bondage in Egypt. Chaldean astronomy was focused on the moon and the seasons. From their devotion to collecting astronomical data, an important calendar science began to surface.

This science was empirically driven, as opposed to Aristotle's science which was logic driven; indeed, the sands of Iraq are littered with the remnants of the clay tablets upon which the Chaldeans recorded their data.

It was from the Babylonian astronomers that the Hebrew Calendar system derived the ability to keep the holidays in sync with the seasons. In their monograph *Babylonian Chronology 626 BC.-A.D. 75*, Professors Richard Anthony Parker and Waldo H. Dubberstein write:

> It may have been in the reign of Nabonassar, 747 BC that Babylonian astronomers began to recognize, as the result of centuries of observation of the heavens, that 235 lunar months have almost exactly the same number of days as nineteen solar years.

Another important milestone was the discovery that eclipses were cyclic. Professor Lis Brack-Bernsen of Regensburg University states that the Saros, the cyclic nature of lunar phenomena, must have been known in the 6th century BCE. A Saros is a period of 223 Synodic months (approximately 6585.3213 days, or nearly 18 years 11 days) that can be used to predict eclipses of the moon and sun. The repeat of a solar eclipse would take place in an entirely different location on the earth. But a triple Saros would effect an observable solar eclipse at the same location 669 lunations, 54 years and a month later. This facilitated very accurate measurements of the average length of the lunar month.

From Wikipedia:

> The Babylonian calendar was a lunisolar calendar with years consisting of 12 lunar months, each beginning when a new crescent moon was first sighted low on the western horizon at sunset, plus an intercalary month inserted as needed by decree.

Month name	Presiding deities	Zodiac sign	Equivalent in Hebrew calendar	Equivalent in Gregorian calendar
Araḥ Nisānu 'Month of the Sanctuary'	Anu and Bel	KU (Aries)	Nisan	March/April
Araḥ Āru 'Month of the Bull'	Ea	(Taurus)	Iyar	April/May
Araḥ Simanu	Sin	BI(KAŠ) (Gemini)	Sivan	May/June
Araḥ Dumuzu 'Month of Tammuz'	Tammuz	(Cancer)	Tammuz	June/July
Araḥ Abu		āru (Leo)	Av	July/August
Araḥ Ulūlu	Ishtar	(Virgo)	Elul	August/September
Araḥ Tišritum 'Month of Beginning' (i.e. the start of the 2nd half-year)	Shamash	(Libra)	Tishrei	September/October
Araḥ Samna 'Month of Laying Foundations'	Marduk	(Scorpio)	Cheshvan	October/November
Araḥ Kislimu	Nergal	(Sagittarius)	Kislev	November/December
Araḥ Ṭebētum 'Month of the Forthcoming of Water'	Pap-sukkal	saḥ 'ibex' (Capricorn?)	Tevet	December/January
Araḥ Šabaṭu		qā (Aquarius?)	Shevat	January/February
Araḥ Addaru ~ Araḥ Adār 'Month of Adar'	Erra	(Pisces)	Adar	February/March
Araḥ Makaruša Addari ~ Araḥ Ve-Adār	Ashur	Except in year 17 of 19-year cycle, when intercalary month was after Araḥ Ulūlu.		

The Rabbis tell us that during the Babylonian Exile, the Jews adopted the Babylonian names for the months.80 This is somewhat obvious from the preceding chart. But the similarities in the year's structure go much deeper. All lunisolar calendars must alternate between 12 and 13 months; but the Babylonian calendar uses the doubling of the month of Addaru as the mechanism to keep the lunar calendar in sync with the solar year. Evidently, we adopted this mechanism too from the Babylonians, adding the month of Adar I into the Hebrew calendar.

Of special note is the month of Tišritum (Tishrei) with its deity Shamash. Shamash was the god of justice in Babylonia and Assyria. It does not require a huge leap of imagination to perceive the dangers of assimilation present in the similarity of Jewish religious practices to those of the Babylonians. There is, in fact, archeological evidence to support the failure of many Jews to return to Eretz Yisrael when Cyrus permitted them.

A second problem facing the Jews in Babylon was that of communications with Jerusalem. As the crow flies, Babylon is 500 miles from Jerusalem. But humans are not crows, and the caravan routes are more circuitous. This was significant in light of the decision of the Sages that the Jews of Bavel should observe the holidays according to the calendrical court in Jerusalem. Whereas it is implied that messengers did carry the decisions of the calendrical court to Bavel, it is a bit of a stretch to regularly count on a messenger to travel from Jerusalem to Babylon in time to know which day is Yom Kippur. Furthermore, after reaching Babylon, the information had to be disseminated throughout the region. Prof. Sacha Stern brings many conflicting sources over the use of messengers and beacons in his book *Calendar and Community*. As we discussed previously, the fact that Shmuel felt the need to

---

80 Yerushalmi Rosh HaShanah 1:2 (page 6a).

develop calculation tables shows that obtaining the information was a problem.

The Sages had a powerful tool to solve this problem, as we saw in the quote cited above:

אתם, שלש פעמים אתם, אתם, הרי הוא אומר אתם: אמר לו - אפילו מוטעין - אתם, אפילו מזידין - אתם, אפילו שוגגין.

'*Atem*' [you, plural] is written three times, to imply 'you' [may fix the festivals] even if you err inadvertently; 'you' even if you err deliberately; 'you' even if you are misled.[81]

It says, "Even if you err deliberately!" It was within the power of the calendrical court to accept witnesses who the court knew were mistaken or lying. The calendrical court could even intimidate witnesses to testify falsely.

We know that they used these tools, for otherwise it makes no sense for the Talmud to be able to say with confidence:

מימות עזרא ואילך לא מצינו אלול מעובר.

From the time of Ezra, Elul was always 29 days long.[82]

Using these tools and fixing the calendar would ensure that the system continued to work well for distant regions too, as the date could be known in advance. That way, these regions would not need to continue to look to Jerusalem for their calendar.

Based on all of the above, we have reason to place the origin of the Fixed Hebrew Calendar in Bavel at the time of Ezra. The solution offered to the second problem – that of the timely arrival of the messengers – is evident. But what has the Fixed Calendar to do with the first problem we mentioned – that of assimilation? This will be answered in the traditional Jewish fashion, by asking another question; one that we have already asked in this book.

---

[81] Rosh HaShanah 25a.

[82] Rosh HaShanah 19b.

Why Not Better Synchronization with the Moon?

Babylonian Lunar Science at the time of Ezra was amazing. Based on many centuries of accumulating astronomical data, they had arrived at an exceptionally accurate value for the Synodic month. Aiding them in this was their discovery of the Saros Cycle, the fact that lunar eclipses repeat every 223 lunations. Completing the facts necessary to establish a calculated lunar-based calendar was the realization that 19 solar years contain very nearly 235 lunations.

One Synodic month =

- 29;31:50:08:20 days sexagesimal
- 29.53059413 ... days decimal
- 29 days, 12 hours 44 min 3⅓ sec
- 29 days, 12 hours and 793 halakim

The value attributed to the ancient Babylonians and the value from Rabban Gamliel are exactly the same.

Some rabbis have attributed this value to Hillel II (358 CE). Others recognized the source as Claudius Ptolemy (90-168 CE), while some scholars attributed Ptolemy's value to Hipparchus of Nicaea (190-120 BC). But there are scholarly papers tracing the source all the way back to the ancient Babylonians, whose accumulated data led them to conclude that the value of the Synodic month was 29;31:50:08:20 days sexagesimal.

With this information available to them from their Babylonian neighbors, surely it was possible for Ezra's rabbinical contemporaries to construct a Fixed Hebrew Calendar such that Tishrei's Molad always falls out on a day containing the actual sighting of the New Moon?! This could have been achieved by establishing a Molad of Tohu to suit these ends and fine-tuning it. Yet, it appears that, on the contrary, strenuous efforts have been made to prevent this scenario from ever manifesting! What is going on?

A Weapon in the Fight Against Assimilation

This timing suggestion, locating the calendar's origins with Ezra, is undeniably conjecture; but it is reasonable and educated conjecture. We know that the Hebrew Leadership of the day sought to fight the very present danger of the Jews assimilating into Babylonian culture. Ezra was no stranger to fighting the scourge of assimilation, as these verses from the book of Ezra demonstrate:

עזרא פרק ט פסוק א-ג
וככלות אלה נגשו אלי השרים לאמר לא נבדלו העם ישראל והכהנים והלוים מעמי הארצות כתועבתיהם לכנעני החתי הפרזי היבוסי העמני המאבי המצרי והאמרי: כי נשאו מבנתיהם להם ולבניהם והתערבו זרע הקדש בעמי הארצות ויד השרים והסגנים היתה במעל הזה ראשונה: וכשמעי את הדבר הזה קרעתי את בגדי ומעילי ואמרטה משער ראשי וזקני ואשבה משומם.

עזרא פרק י פסוק י-יא
ויקם עזרא הכהן ויאמר אלהם אתם מעלתם ותשיבו נשים נכריות להוסיף על אשמת ישראל: ועתה תנו תודה ליקוק אלהי אבתיכם ועשו רצונו והבדלו מעמי הארץ ומן הנשים הנכריות.

Chapter 9: (1) After these things had been done, the leaders came to me and said, "The people of Israel, including the priests and the Levites, have not kept themselves separate from the neighboring peoples with their detestable practices, like those of the Canaanites, Hittites, Perizzites, Jebusites, Ammonites, Moabites, Egyptians and Amorites. (2) They have taken some of their daughters as wives for themselves and their sons, and have mingled the holy race with the peoples around them. And the leaders and officials have led the way in this unfaithfulness." (3) When I heard this, I tore my tunic and cloak, pulled hair from my head and beard and sat down appalled .

Chapter 10: (10) And Ezra the priest stood up, and said to them, "You have transgressed, and have taken foreign wives, increasing the guilt of Israel. (11) And now, confess to the Lord God of your fathers, and do

His will; and separate yourselves from the people of the land, and from the foreign wives."

With this in mind, I would argue that Ezra and his Sod (sod seems to have had a meaning of secret council, hence "Sod Ha'ibur", the secret council of the intercalation), adopted a calendar that put the start of the Hebrew month *on average two days* before the start of the equivalent Babylonian month! This time lag would keep the Jews from celebrating in common with their neighboring Babylonian families who also made the beginning of the month of Tishrei (Tišritum) a special day. They would be prevented from mingling and intermarrying, and would experience themselves as separate and different several times a year. A simple explanation, yet one that fits what we know culturally, historically and astronomically!

Once we realize the underlying cause, the mystery at the core of this book suddenly makes perfect sense. It is difficult to think of any other reason why the Molad calculation of the Hebrew Calendar would alway fall so early that the actual New Moon would never be seen.

The flaw in this system, an occasional visible Old Moon, would have been difficult to detect for perhaps centuries, and was probably not foreseen by the creators of the calendar.

I propose that Ezra kept the adoption of the Fixed Hebrew Calendar a secret, because whereas he understood that it was the prerogative of the Jewish People, and their legal representatives the calendrical court, to establish the calendar, for reasons mentioned previously he did not wish to make it a cause célèbre and create a backlash of popular protest.

Ezra created the secret instructions for the calendrical court in Jerusalem to follow, which probably comprised the contents of the Baraita Sod Ha'ibur. We follow the very same instructions today except that we have added the Rabbinical Dehiyyot, which were enacted many centuries later. As was shown earlier in the chapter on Dehiyyot, the Rambam realized that our calendar was skewed to be early, and attributed the implementation of the Dehiyyot to the correction of this fact. Indeed, by that time, the decline of Babylonian culture and its calendar had subverted the original reason for making the calendar early. The more efficient solution would have been to shift the entire calendar by two days – but no one thought of that! (I imagine, too, that if anyone *did* think of it, chances are that the idea of tinkering with the traditional calendar, upon which the entire Jewish world relies for its most sacred times, would be daunting…).

Summary

So there we have it: the initial purpose of the Fixed Hebrew Calendar was to solve problems created by the Babylonian exile.

Firstly, in order to keep the Jews in Bavel from sharing a common holiday of Rosh HaShanah with their idol-worshipping neighbors, Rosh HaShanah was made to occur on average two days (but always at least one day) before the pagan holiday. This was not simply like an early version of Hanukkah and Christmas coinciding. These two festivals fell on the same day and had the same purpose: Judgement Day.

Secondly, although we take it as a given that we should look to Jerusalem for our calendar, this was not always the case. In the 5th century BC, for example, there existed a Jewish community located along the Nile River named Elephantine, with its own Temple and its own calendar.

The Babylonian Jews thought that the calendar was being established by actual witnessed testimony of a moon seen in Eretz Yisrael. This mandated that the Babylonian Diaspora community be focused on Eretz Yisrael as a necessity in their lives, in order to keep tabs on when they must observe their Yom Tovim.

It is amazing to me that neither the community in Bavel, nor Jewish commentators down the ages, equated the fact of Elul being always 29 days with the use of a Fixed Hebrew calendar. I checked, and – probably due to relative positions of the sun, moon, and Earth – Elul is slightly more often 30 days in length than 29, when determined by sightings of the moon.

Yet a *hazaka* that Elul was always 29 days made keeping in sync with Eretz Yisrael easy; and indeed, the Moladic calendar before the implementation of Dehiyyot, transformed anticipating Rosh HaShanah into a relatively simple affair.

Till the Fat Lady Sings

It was my intention to conclude this book with the previous chapter. But, almost miraculously, some events occurred that brought the thesis I presented here to a new level of veracity.

It started on Shabbat Mevorchim, June 23, 2014. Shabbat Mevorchim is the Shabbat when we announce the Molad of the coming month and bless it.

How Not to Train a Dragon

Trusting the technology but not understanding the process can lead to terrible errors.

On the Molad times of www.chabad.org, the Molad of Tammuz is shown as Friday, June 27, 2014, 6:06 PM, plus 12 halakim. This, being Friday after sunset, is considered Saturday.

At the conclusion of our minyan at the Kotel, someone from another minyan approached Ephraim Caspi, a former engineer and very knowledgeable of proper halachic times. This individual requested Caspi's support for the claim that the Molad should be announced as falling on Friday, since, even without considering the daylight saving times in effect in Jerusalem, the sun would not actually set until 6:49 PM. Yet, Caspi told him with no uncertainty that the Molad was Saturday ("leil zayin"), 0 hours and 120 halakim.

Caspi was correct; but the other's error was certainly a reasonable one. The original calendar-makers' desire to present the Molad in standard clock time and to simplify its calculation by always defining sunset as 6:00 PM is not so well known, and of course does not conform with solar or lunar reality.

This oddity comes into sharp focus on another website, www.realluach.com, whose presentation of information for the Molad of Tammuz 5774 looks as follows:

On the left side of its webpage is a box:

> Friday, 27 June 2014
> 6:06 PM + 12 Chalakim
> [18 Hours, 6 Minutes, 12 Chalakim]

Juxtaposed to this information in a box on the right it adds:

> MOLAD CODE 7-0-120
> 7: Day of Week
> 0: Hour after 6 PM previous eve
> 120: Chalakim (18 Chalakim / Minute)

Thus, the uninformed reader is likely to be very confused as to the correct day of the Molad – Friday or Saturday?! (You will note that in my table, presented on the coming pages, I include both ways of describing the Molad, the purpose of which was so that the reader could check my calculations against a standard with which he is familiar.)

Had the creators of these tables not been so lazy they would have based sunset on its actual value which does vary throughout the year. In this case it was 6:49 PM. So the Molad that should have been announced was 6 hours 55 minutes and 12 halakim.

Why do we announce the Molad?

Still a more profound question remains. For what purpose is the Molad and why should it be announced in synagogue?

This whole book's primary focus is on the one Molad we don't announce, the Molad of Tishrei. The Molad of Tishrei is the prime determinant factor of the Fixed Hebrew Calendar. Yet the Molad of Tishrei is not announced in synagogue. Furthermore, the Molad of each month has absolutely nothing to do with the length of the month, the determinant factor in the subsequent Rosh Hodesh.

If I did a good job in writing this book then the reader should understand that the Molad is not indicative of a visual sighting of the New Moon of Rosh HaShanah, such sighting being made usually 2 days after the day of the Molad[83]. This means that the only importance of the Molad is in the annual calculation of Hebrew Calendar. In that calculation what is needed is the day of the Molad of Tishrei for the start and finish of the year and the fact that the hours equal or exceed 18 hours (chatzot).

I believe the purpose of announcing the Molad each month was to disguise the fact that it was not possible for anyone to one actually witness the New Moon on the Molad of Tishrei. The announcement was the means by which the calendrical court secured witnesses.

Red Herring

In the case of Tammuz, June 27, 2014, the consequences of wrongly announcing the Molad are likely not too serious (unless there are some Kabbalistic consequences of which I am not aware). But for the Molad of Tishrei this could be disastrous, tipping the entire year out of balance – and especially since in Tishrei the sun often sets before 6:00 PM. So, for example, a Molad at 5:55 PM might be after sunset, yet still be counted as the previous day.

Announcing the Molad as a time of day is a red herring. The fact that there is a remainder of x hours and y parts is only important to the next month's calculation and the Dehiyyah Molad Zaqen. Why should we worry as to the locus of the calculation? The physical moon is never going to be seen at the time of the Molad. There is no purpose of converting halakim into minutes.

---

[83] Approximately 70% 2 days, 26% 1 day and 4% 3 days

All of this perhaps provides another reason why we don't announce the Molad on the Shabbat before Rosh HaShanah. It could lead to confusion – not of the Satan, but of the uninformed!

The Smoking Gun

Reflecting on the error described here, I started to wonder about the validity of other calculation shortcuts I had garnered off the internet, and decided to redo my Molad of Tishrei Study using only the primary definitions. One of these shortcuts had allowed me to calculate the Molad without starting with the actual Molad of Tohu.

Fortunately, Apple's spreadsheet program, Numbers, uses a single value for date and time. I don't know how far it goes back, but for my purposes it suffices, extending backwards to the traditional Jewish date of creation: Sunday, September 6, 3761 BCE at 23:11:19. Thus, I started my spreadsheet with the Molad of Tohu. GUHADZaT, the mnemonic for the lunar years that take 13 months (3-6-8-11-14-17-19), is an intrinsic part of this process, so it was uppermost in my mind. I was primed to make some astounding discoveries.

Sometimes providence can be kind – or at least take pity on our efforts. Robert H. van Gent, the Dutch astronomer whom I have mentioned throughout this book, has provided me with Global Visibility Maps which show how the orbit of the moon affects the sighting of the moon. But he has also created informative webpages on the history of astronomy. Recently, I was browsing these pages for no special reason when I saw his page about the Babylonian calendar[84], citing Parker and Dubberstein's book *Babylonian Chronology 626 B.C.-A.D. 75,* which I have mentioned elsewhere, as follows:

---

[84] http://www.staff.science.uu.nl/~gent0113/babylon/babycal.htm

In order to keep the Babylonian calendar aligned with the seasons, various intercalation schemes were employed.

Initially, the insertion of an intercalary month was probably decided by considering various non-astronomical signs, such as the weather, the flight of migratory birds, the ripening of fruits and crops, etc.

Later the insertion of an intercalary month appears to have based on the observation of the heliacal rising of certain stars such as MUL.MUL (Pleiades) or MUL.KAK.SI.SA (Sirius). Continued observations of the heliacal rising of selected stars probably led to the discovery of a regular intercalation pattern such as the 19-year cycle.

After about 590 BCE, a regular intercalation scheme was adopted, inserting seven intercalary months in every nineteen years. At first, varying schemes were used, but from about 490 BCE, counting from the first year of Nabonassar (747 BCE), the years 3, 6, 8, 11, 14, 17 and 19 were augmented by adding an extra Addāru [Addāru II = XIIb]

This elicited from me the same reaction as when I first noticed that the year 358 CE, supposedly the year when Hillel II initiated the Hebrew Calendar, contained a three-day Tishrei Molad discrepancy. WOW!

Let me explain. The significance of Parker and Dubberstein's words is that from the year 490 BCE to 312 BCE, the Babylonians were arranging the order of the seven specific years that take 13 months each, according to the series – 3-6-8-11-14-17-19. That is the very same series we term GUHADZaT.

Heretofore, it has been presumed that GUHADZaT began with Hillel II in 358 CE. Now we see that there is likelihood that this structure for the Hebrew calendar came into being a many centuries earlier, while the Jews were living amongst the Babylonians. With nineteen possible choices

Till the Fat Lady Sings 143

of combinations that preclude two consecutive 13-month years, the coincidence of the two systems is too close to be random. It carries with it the implication that the Fixed Hebrew Calendar was established during the Babylonian period, not the Amoraic period of Hillel II.

Thus, the "fingerprints" of the ancient Babylonians are all over the rabbinical calculation of the Molad, with evidence dating to the lifetime of Ezra.

But wait, the best is yet to come.

Off to See the Wizard

The degree of support offered by this GUHADZaT fact to my thesis was so significant that I decided to visit Dr. Robert H. van Gent at his office at Utrecht University, in the Netherlands. As you will soon see, it was well I did. My thesis was well received by Dr. van Gent and our discussion extended over many hours. At some point in this discussion, he inquired if I had ever looked for the zero hour zero parts nodes in the Molad Table.

With the GUHADZaT evidence now pointing to an early historical start of a calculated calendar, the question seemed very appropriate.

The Epicenter of the Hebrew Calendar

The Moladot are a simple series. The Molad of each month is 29 days, 12 hours, and 793 halakim after the previous month. Conversely we can go back in time to each previous month. Can we presume that at some month the Molad would have a value of zero hours and zero parts.

It is possible that the first Molad had an initial value, like BaHaRad, the Molad of Tohu. In Azariah de' Rossi's *The Light of the Eyes,* published in 1573, BaHaRad is precluded.

More importantly any value that may be discovered must make sense as to its time and place,

My original database had 5781 entries, one for each year from the Molad of Tishrei. I now needed to build a spreadsheet with 71493 lunar months of data, and search through them to find all those with zero hours and zero parts.

Here is a bit of how this spreadsheet, at least the beginning and the end of it, looks.

MNS Tohu	Days Tohu	Day	Hrs	Parts	Molad Date
0	2	Mon	5	204	Sep 6, 3761 BCE
1	31	Tue	17	997	Oct 6, 3761 BCE
2	61	Thu	6	710	Nov 5, 3761 BCE
3	90	Fri	19	423	Dec 4, 3761 BCE
4	120	Sun	8	136	Jan 3, 3760 BCE
5	149	Mon	20	929	Feb 1, 3760 BCE
6	179	Wed	9	642	Mar 3, 3760 BCE
7	208	Thu	22	355	Apr 1, 3760 BCE
....					
....					
71489	2111114	Thu	20	701	Sep 17, 2020 CE
71490	2111144	Sat	9	414	Oct 17, 2020 CE
71491	2111173	Sun	22	127	Nov 15, 2020 CE
71492	2111203	Tue	10	920	Dec 15, 2020 CE

Quite frankly, I had no idea what the result of this search would be. As you will recall my previous chapter concluded with the belief that a zero hour zero parts month should happen during the Babylonian Captivity.

Drum role — Results!

MNS Tohu	Days Tohu	Day	Hrs	Parts	Molad Date
10812	319287	Tue	0	0	Nov 9, 2887 BCE
36732	1084720	Sat	0	0	Jul 16, 791 BCE
62652	1850153	Wed	0	0	Mar 23, 1306 CE

Only three entries with zero hours and zero parts present themselves. Two of them, 2887 BCE and 1306 CE, are results which must be excluded, due to being much too early or much too late to mark the start of the Fixed Hebrew Calendar; leaving one sole possibility. This leads to the indisputable conclusion that the Molad-based system, the very one we use to this day, began at sunset, July 16, 791 BCE!

The historicity of date makes the result astounding!

This is, of course, an outstanding result. It places the birth of the Molad calculation in the 8th century BCE, a time when knowledge of the Saros cycle, the Meton cycle, and the accurate determination of the average Synodic month were first appearing on the scene in Bavel[85]. Chazal made use of the latest in science to achieve its ends.

---

[85] In the previous chapter we noted that Parker and Dubberstein dated the realization of the equivalence of 235 lunar months with 19 solar years [Meton cycle] in 747 BCE. It is quite possible, if not likely, that the Molad and GUHADZaT began together; in which case, we can argue that Babylonia actually adopted GUHADZaT from us during the Babylonian Captivity.

But there's more ...

If all this was not enough, as I was coming to the end of writing this book a further conjecture presented itself to my mind, when I saw the dates.

July 16, 791 BCE takes the start of the Hebrew Calendar out of the period of the Babylonian Captivity and places it back into the period of the First Temple.

The worldview of the majority of the traditional Jewish world – the view expressed by Artscroll and in the web pages of Chabad and Aish HaTorah – puts King Solomon's year of passing at 796 BCE. Shortly thereafter, the Kingdom of Israel in the North, and the Kingdom of Judah (containing Jerusalem) in the South, split.

I would like to speculate that the development of a fixed calendar in the North, asynchronous with the witnessed calendar in Jerusalem, would be consistent with 791 BCE. Why would such a calendar be cultivated? The Northern Kingdom, Israel, would use it in order to differentiate itself from the Kingdom of Judah and separate the festivals of the two kingdoms.

The academic community rejects this date, claiming that <u>if indeed there was a King Solomon</u>, then his death must have been over a century earlier than posited by the Jewish world. Academia will cite archeology (pottery shards), and Greek History to prove its point.

The Rabbi's can now cite Mathematics and Babylonian Science to prove theirs.

Final Word

Here, then, we come to the end of our detective trail. As we have been explaining all along, the Molad is not a way to accurately calculate when the New Moon will next be seen. It is a way to calculate a calendar that, while appearing to be forecasting the coming New Moon, actually served to foster observance of Rosh Hodesh at least a day (and often two) before other peoples were observing their New Moon festivals.

The Babylonians developed amazing lunar science; but the Babylonians had no need to use mathematics to "see" the moon. For the Babylonians there was only one correct day: the day that the Crescent New Moon could actually be seen by one's own eyes.

The ancient Hebrew Sages had different priorities: firstly, that the Jewish nation should share one collective common lunar experience; and secondly, that this experience be unique to the Jewish People and not shared with the pagans.

Although this reason is no longer relevant (unless you wish to argue for the prevention of a Hanukkah/Christmas collision), and, moreover, the calendar has since been adjusted with Rabbinical Dehiyyot such that the discrepancy is lessened, it is nonetheless the very same calendar that we use until this day to set our most important and sacred times.

The significance of the story of R' Hiyya and the Old Moon, in the Yerushalmi escaped the traditional commentaries.

רבי חייה רבה הילך לאורו של ישן ארבעת מיל רבי אבון משדי עלוי צרריו ואמר לה לא תבהית בני מריך ברמשא אנן בעיין תיתחמי מיכא ואת מיתחמי מיכא מיד איתבלע מן קומוי

R' Hiyya the Great walked by the light of the Old Moon for four miles. Rabbi Abun threw pebbles at [the Old Moon] and said to it: "Do not upset the children of your

Master, tonight we have to see you from this side [i.e. the New Moon], but you are seen from here [the Old Moon is still visible]." Immediately it disappeared.[86]

This theme is repeated again and again over Jewish history:

– It is the story of the cause of the conflict between Rabban Gamliel and R' Yehoshua.

– It was the reason that it was thought that a fixed calendar was inaugurated in 358 CE.

– It was the cause for concern of the Exilarch who wrote his letter in 835 CE.

– It was the rationale behind the implementation of the Dehiyyah Molad Zaqen, which, long an enigma to scholars, can now be understood as a correction created by savvy rabbis to prevent seeing an Old Moon on Erev Rosh HaShanah.

I hope that these proofs, taken together, have been enough to convince my readers that there is more to the Hebrew Fixed Calendar than we have grasped to date. The chain of my arguments, culminating in my chapter on the Origin of the Hebrew Calendar, have, I hope, persuaded the reader that the Fixed Hebrew Calendar was indeed in place at the time of Ezra.

This book started with a question as to why Rosh HaShanah 2002 began two days before the Muslims started their new month of Rajab. I have received the answer to my original question, and perhaps you, the reader, have received some answers to yours.

I still sit in wonderment at some of the discoveries contained within. Most came out of melding lunar reality with Torah reality. Nonetheless, even after all of the surprises, I was amazed to find towards the end of my

---

[86] Yerushalmi Rosh HaShanah 2:4.

research that the mathematics of the Molad placed its origin in the first Temple period, 791 BCE.

It is very Jewish to answer a question with even more questions. You are most welcome to visit my website http://www.sodhaibur.com/ and discuss these issues with me.

Thank you for staying with me until the end of my book, and please feel free to take a look at the appendices.

Richard K. Fiedler
Jerusalem, 2014

Appendix A: Molad of Tishrei Study

This study is from the period of Sun, Sep 6, 3761 BC 23:11:19, the Molad of Tohu until 2020 CE.

Dates are presented according to the Gregorian calendar commonly used by most societies today. This calendar was reformed in the 16th century, but taking this change into account would cause some confusion over the span of the data, so I have chosen to use pure Gregorian dates throughout. The times of the Conjunction (Astronomical New Moon) were taken from NASA's website. Conjunction data was only entered for the Common Era.

Dehiyyot are not included in this study. When no consideration is made of the Dehiyyot, the day on which the Molad of Tishrei is calculated is synonymous with Rosh HaShanah. It appears that the use of Dehiyyot may not have been firmly established until the time of Saadia Gaon.

Here are the columns and their significance:

Hebrew Year – in Arabic numerals, the date according to the Hebrew Calendar.

Molad – the Molad is doubly represented here. First is shown the Hours and Parts (halakim), which is the more accurate presentation, using the Hebrew time system. Following that, the Molad's date and time in western notation is recorded.

Conjunction – when the Sun, Earth, and Moon are in their closest alignment of the month, nowadays known as the Astronomical New Moon.

Difference – this is the time difference between the Molad and the Conjunction. There is a very substantial variance between the two; the Molad is not the Conjunction, contrary to the assumption made by many scholars.

Skew – this is the number of days between imputed and actual moon sighting. In more detail, it is the number of days between the start of the day of the Molad of Tishrei (i.e., the sunset at the start of Rosh HaShanah, when Rosh HaShanah is determined without Dehiyyot) and the first sunset occurring a minimum of 24 hours after the true astronomical Conjunction adjusted for Israel, which is a likely approximation of when the New Moon can actually be seen. The van Gent charts provide a much more accurate value and this can make a significant difference – for example in the case of 2013, where a value of Skew of two days was predicted, but corrected by the van Gent charts to three days.

The frequency of occurrence of the Skew provided some surprising information:

Discrepancy Skew	Count	Percentage	Conjunction Difference
1 Day	522	25.84%	11h 42m
2 Day	1420	70.30%	3h 25m
3 Day	78	3.86%	-3h 42m
	2020	100.00%	5h 10m

1 – Without the Dehiyyot there is always Skew – i.e. the moon is never seen on Rosh HaShanah.

This means that:

2 – The year 2002, which catalyzed my initial study in separating between Rosh HaShanah and the actual moon sighting, was not an anomaly but the rule.

3 – A surprising new factor becomes evident: the three-day discrepancy.

Here is the first 19 years of the study starting with the Molad of Tohu:

Year	Day	Hrs	Pts	Molad of Tishrei BCE	Conjunction	Skw
1	Mon	5	204	Sun, Sep 6, 3761 23:11		
2	Fri	14	0	Fri, Aug 27, 3760 7:59		
3	Tue	22	876	Tue, Aug 16, 3759 16:48		
4	Mon	20	385	Mon, Sep 4, 3758 14:21		
5	Sat	5	181	Fri, Aug 23, 3757 23:10		
6	Wed	13	1057	Wed, Aug 13, 3756 7:58		
7	Tue	11	566	Tue, Sep 1, 3755 5:31		
8	Sat	20	362	Sat, Aug 21, 3754 14:20		
9	Fri	17	951	Fri, Sep 8, 3753 11:52		
10	Wed	2	747	Tue, Aug 28, 3752 20:41		
11	Sun	11	543	Sun, Aug 18, 3751 5:30		
12	Sat	9	52	Sat, Sep 6, 3750 3:02		
13	Wed	17	928	Wed, Aug 25, 3749 11:51		
14	Mon	2	724	Sun, Aug 14, 3748 20:40		
15	Sun	0	233	Sat, Sep 2, 3747 18:12		
16	Thu	9	29	Thu, Aug 23, 3746 3:01		
17	Mon	17	905	Mon, Aug 11, 3745 11:50		
18	Sun	15	414	Sun, Aug 30, 3744 9:22		
19	Fri	0	210	Thu, Aug 19, 3743 18:11		

The First Millennium:

Year	Day	Hrs	Pts	Molad of Tishrei	Conjunction	Skw
3762	Tue	20	785	Tue, Sep 4, 0001 14:43	Tue, Sep 4, 0001 5:05	2d
3763	Mon	18	294	Mon, Sep 23, 0002 12:16	Mon, Sep 23, 0002 6:14	2d
3764	Sat	3	90	Fri, Sep 12, 0003 21:04	Fri, Sep 12, 0003 22:15	2d
3765	Wed	11	966	Wed, Sep 1, 0004 5:53	Wed, Sep 1, 0004 10:38	2d
3766	Tue	9	475	Tue, Sep 20, 0005 3:26	Tue, Sep 20, 0005 7:55	2d
3767	Sat	18	271	Sat, Sep 9, 0006 12:15	Sat, Sep 9, 0006 9:58	2d
3768	Thu	3	67	Wed, Aug 29, 0007 21:03	Wed, Aug 29, 0007 22:05	2d
3769	Wed	0	656	Tue, Sep 16, 0008 18:36	Tue, Sep 16, 0008 5:18	1d
3770	Sun	9	452	Sun, Sep 6, 0009 3:25	Sat, Sep 5, 0009 14:02	1d
3771	Sat	6	1041	Sat, Sep 25, 0010 0:57	Fri, Sep 24, 0010 14:01	1d
3772	Wed	15	837	Wed, Sep 14, 0011 9:46	Wed, Sep 14, 0011 5:52	2d
3773	Mon	0	633	Sun, Sep 2, 0012 18:35	Sun, Sep 2, 0012 21:20	2d
3774	Sat	22	142	Sat, Sep 21, 0013 16:07	Sat, Sep 21, 0013 20:54	3d
3775	Thu	6	1018	Thu, Sep 11, 0014 0:56	Thu, Sep 11, 0014 3:50	2d
3776	Mon	15	814	Mon, Aug 31, 0015 9:45	Mon, Aug 31, 0015 4:39	2d
3777	Sun	13	323	Sun, Sep 18, 0016 7:17	Sat, Sep 17, 0016 22:21	2d
3778	Thu	22	119	Thu, Sep 7, 0017 16:06	Thu, Sep 7, 0017 1:55	2d
3779	Tue	6	995	Tue, Aug 28, 0018 0:55	Mon, Aug 27, 0018 12:50	1d
3780	Mon	4	504	Sun, Sep 15, 0019 22:27	Sun, Sep 15, 0019 13:20	1d
3781	Fri	13	300	Fri, Sep 4, 0020 7:16	Fri, Sep 4, 0020 5:38	2d
3782	Thu	10	889	Thu, Sep 23, 0021 4:49	Thu, Sep 23, 0021 6:33	2d
3783	Mon	19	685	Mon, Sep 12, 0022 13:38	Mon, Sep 12, 0022 18:27	3d
3784	Sat	4	481	Fri, Sep 1, 0023 22:26	Fri, Sep 1, 0023 23:22	2d
3785	Fri	1	1070	Thu, Sep 19, 0024 19:59	Thu, Sep 19, 0024 17:21	1d
3786	Tue	10	866	Tue, Sep 9, 0025 4:48	Mon, Sep 8, 0025 17:28	1d
3787	Sat	19	662	Sat, Aug 29, 0026 13:36	Fri, Aug 28, 0026 23:11	2d

Year	Day	Hrs	Pts	Molad of Tishrei	Conjunction	Skw
3788	Fri	17	171	Fri, Sep 17, 0027 11:09	Thu, Sep 16, 0027 22:07	2d
3789	Wed	1	1047	Tue, Sep 5, 0028 19:58	Tue, Sep 5, 0028 12:58	1d
3790	Mon	23	556	Mon, Sep 24, 0029 17:30	Mon, Sep 24, 0029 14:17	2d
3791	Sat	8	352	Sat, Sep 14, 0030 2:19	Sat, Sep 14, 0030 5:26	2d
3792	Wed	17	148	Wed, Sep 3, 0031 11:08	Wed, Sep 3, 0031 15:32	2d
3793	Tue	14	737	Tue, Sep 21, 0032 8:40	Tue, Sep 21, 0032 11:27	2d
3794	Sat	23	533	Sat, Sep 10, 0033 17:29	Sat, Sep 10, 0033 11:55	2d
3795	Thu	8	329	Thu, Aug 31, 0034 2:18	Wed, Aug 30, 0034 13:09	1d
3796	Wed	5	918	Tue, Sep 18, 0035 23:50	Tue, Sep 18, 0035 9:44	1d
3797	Sun	14	714	Sun, Sep 7, 0036 8:39	Sat, Sep 6, 0036 20:54	2d
3798	Thu	23	510	Thu, Aug 27, 0037 17:28	Thu, Aug 27, 0037 12:47	2d
3799	Wed	21	19	Wed, Sep 15, 0038 15:01	Wed, Sep 15, 0038 13:53	2d
3800	Mon	5	895	Sun, Sep 4, 0039 23:49	Mon, Sep 5, 0039 4:03	2d
3801	Sun	3	404	Sat, Sep 22, 0040 21:22	Sun, Sep 23, 0040 2:21	2d
3802	Thu	12	200	Thu, Sep 12, 0041 6:11	Thu, Sep 12, 0041 6:44	2d
3803	Mon	20	1076	Mon, Sep 1, 0042 14:59	Mon, Sep 1, 0042 18:40	3d
3804	Sun	18	585	Sun, Sep 20, 0043 12:32	Sun, Sep 20, 0043 1:00	2d
3805	Fri	3	381	Thu, Sep 8, 0044 21:21	Thu, Sep 8, 0044 7:00	1d
3806	Tue	12	177	Tue, Aug 29, 0045 6:09	Mon, Aug 28, 0045 20:05	2d
3807	Mon	9	766	Mon, Sep 17, 0046 3:42	Sun, Sep 16, 0046 21:17	2d
3808	Fri	18	562	Fri, Sep 6, 0047 12:31	Fri, Sep 6, 0047 13:26	2d
3809	Thu	16	71	Thu, Sep 24, 0048 10:03	Thu, Sep 24, 0048 13:38	2d
3810	Tue	0	947	Mon, Sep 13, 0049 18:52	Mon, Sep 13, 0049 23:12	2d
3811	Sat	9	743	Sat, Sep 3, 0050 3:41	Sat, Sep 3, 0050 1:47	2d
3812	Fri	7	252	Fri, Sep 22, 0051 1:13	Thu, Sep 21, 0051 19:19	2d
3813	Tue	16	48	Tue, Sep 10, 0052 10:02	Mon, Sep 9, 0052 20:40	2d
3814	Sun	0	924	Sat, Aug 30, 0053 18:51	Sat, Aug 30, 0053 4:57	1d

Year	Day	Hrs	Pts	Molad of Tishrei	Conjunction	Skw
3815	Fri	22	433	Fri, Sep 18, 0054 16:24	Fri, Sep 18, 0054 5:07	2d
3816	Wed	7	229	Wed, Sep 8, 0055 1:12	Tue, Sep 7, 0055 20:59	2d
3817	Sun	16	25	Sun, Aug 27, 0056 10:01	Sun, Aug 27, 0056 12:47	2d
3818	Sat	13	614	Sat, Sep 15, 0057 7:34	Sat, Sep 15, 0057 12:03	2d
3819	Wed	22	410	Wed, Sep 4, 0058 16:22	Wed, Sep 4, 0058 19:36	3d
3820	Tue	19	999	Tue, Sep 23, 0059 13:55	Tue, Sep 23, 0059 14:15	2d
3821	Sun	4	795	Sat, Sep 11, 0060 22:44	Sat, Sep 11, 0060 13:58	1d
3822	Thu	13	591	Thu, Sep 1, 0061 7:32	Wed, Aug 31, 0061 17:03	1d
3823	Wed	11	100	Wed, Sep 20, 0062 5:05	Tue, Sep 19, 0062 15:00	1d
3824	Sun	19	976	Sun, Sep 9, 0063 13:54	Sun, Sep 9, 0063 4:14	2d
3825	Fri	4	772	Thu, Aug 28, 0064 22:42	Thu, Aug 28, 0064 20:43	2d
3826	Thu	2	281	Wed, Sep 16, 0065 20:15	Wed, Sep 16, 0065 21:40	2d
3827	Mon	11	77	Mon, Sep 6, 0066 5:04	Mon, Sep 6, 0066 10:02	2d
3828	Sun	8	666	Sun, Sep 25, 0067 2:36	Sun, Sep 25, 0067 7:00	2d
3829	Thu	17	462	Thu, Sep 13, 0068 11:25	Thu, Sep 13, 0068 9:06	2d
3830	Tue	2	258	Mon, Sep 2, 0069 20:14	Mon, Sep 2, 0069 9:06	1d
3831	Sun	23	847	Sun, Sep 21, 0070 17:47	Sun, Sep 21, 0070 4:09	2d
3832	Fri	8	643	Fri, Sep 11, 0071 2:35	Thu, Sep 10, 0071 12:43	1d
3833	Tue	17	439	Tue, Aug 30, 0072 11:24	Tue, Aug 30, 0072 3:27	2d
3834	Mon	14	1028	Mon, Sep 18, 0073 8:57	Mon, Sep 18, 0073 5:05	2d
3835	Fri	23	824	Fri, Sep 7, 0074 17:45	Fri, Sep 7, 0074 20:35	3d
3836	Wed	8	620	Wed, Aug 28, 0075 2:34	Tue, Aug 27, 0075 19:56	2d
3837	Tue	6	129	Tue, Sep 15, 0076 0:07	Tue, Sep 15, 0076 2:55	2d
3838	Sat	14	1005	Sat, Sep 4, 0077 8:55	Sat, Sep 4, 0077 3:44	2d
3839	Fri	12	514	Fri, Sep 23, 0078 6:28	Thu, Sep 22, 0078 21:14	2d
3840	Tue	21	310	Tue, Sep 12, 0079 15:17	Tue, Sep 12, 0079 0:32	2d
3841	Sun	6	106	Sun, Sep 1, 0080 0:05	Sat, Aug 31, 0080 11:15	1d

Year	Day	Hrs	Pts	Molad of Tishrei	Conjunction	Skw
3842	Sat	3	695	Fri, Sep 19, 0081 21:38	Fri, Sep 19, 0081 12:19	1d
3843	Wed	12	491	Wed, Sep 9, 0082 6:27	Wed, Sep 9, 0082 4:41	2d
3844	Sun	21	287	Sun, Aug 29, 0083 15:15	Sun, Aug 29, 0083 19:23	3d
3845	Sat	18	876	Sat, Sep 16, 0084 12:48	Sat, Sep 16, 0084 17:41	2d
3846	Thu	3	672	Wed, Sep 5, 0085 21:37	Wed, Sep 5, 0085 22:39	2d
3847	Wed	1	181	Tue, Sep 24, 0086 19:10	Tue, Sep 24, 0086 16:21	1d
3848	Sun	9	1057	Sun, Sep 14, 0087 3:58	Sat, Sep 13, 0087 16:18	1d
3849	Thu	18	853	Thu, Sep 2, 0088 12:47	Wed, Sep 1, 0088 21:43	2d
3850	Wed	16	362	Wed, Sep 21, 0089 10:20	Tue, Sep 20, 0089 20:51	2d
3851	Mon	1	158	Sun, Sep 10, 0090 19:08	Sun, Sep 10, 0090 11:40	1d
3852	Fri	9	1034	Fri, Aug 31, 0091 3:57	Fri, Aug 31, 0091 4:11	2d
3853	Thu	7	543	Thu, Sep 18, 0092 1:30	Thu, Sep 18, 0092 4:45	2d
3854	Mon	16	339	Mon, Sep 7, 0093 10:18	Mon, Sep 7, 0093 14:56	2d
3855	Sat	1	135	Fri, Aug 27, 0094 19:07	Fri, Aug 27, 0094 21:05	2d
3856	Thu	22	724	Thu, Sep 15, 0095 16:40	Thu, Sep 15, 0095 11:03	2d
3857	Tue	7	520	Tue, Sep 4, 0096 1:28	Mon, Sep 3, 0096 12:03	1d
3858	Mon	5	29	Sun, Sep 22, 0097 23:01	Sun, Sep 22, 0097 8:24	1d
3859	Fri	13	905	Fri, Sep 12, 0098 7:50	Thu, Sep 11, 0098 19:22	2d
3860	Tue	22	701	Tue, Sep 1, 0099 16:38	Tue, Sep 1, 0099 11:14	2d
3861	Mon	20	210	Mon, Sep 20, 0100 14:11	Mon, Sep 20, 0100 15:00	2d
3862	Sat	5	6	Fri, Sep 9, 0101 23:00	Sat, Sep 10, 0101 3:19	2d
3863	Wed	13	882	Wed, Aug 30, 0102 7:48	Wed, Aug 30, 0102 11:36	2d
3864	Tue	11	391	Tue, Sep 18, 0103 5:21	Tue, Sep 18, 0103 6:06	2d
3865	Sat	20	187	Sat, Sep 6, 0104 14:10	Sat, Sep 6, 0104 5:58	2d
3866	Fri	17	776	Fri, Sep 25, 0105 11:43	Thu, Sep 24, 0105 23:54	2d
3867	Wed	2	572	Tue, Sep 14, 0106 20:31	Tue, Sep 14, 0106 5:35	1d
3868	Sun	11	368	Sun, Sep 4, 0107 5:20	Sat, Sep 3, 0107 18:24	2d

Year	Day	Hrs	Pts	Molad of Tishrei	Conjunction	Skw
3869	Sat	8	957	Sat, Sep 22, 0108 2:53	Fri, Sep 21, 0108 20:01	2d
3870	Wed	17	753	Wed, Sep 11, 0109 11:41	Wed, Sep 11, 0109 12:19	2d
3871	Mon	2	549	Sun, Aug 31, 0110 20:30	Mon, Sep 1, 0110 1:24	2d
3872	Sun	0	58	Sat, Sep 19, 0111 18:03	Sat, Sep 19, 0111 22:40	2d
3873	Thu	8	934	Thu, Sep 8, 0112 2:51	Thu, Sep 8, 0112 1:19	2d
3874	Mon	17	730	Mon, Aug 28, 0113 11:40	Mon, Aug 28, 0113 1:17	2d
3875	Sun	15	239	Sun, Sep 16, 0114 9:13	Sat, Sep 15, 0114 19:38	2d
3876	Fri	0	35	Thu, Sep 5, 0115 18:01	Thu, Sep 5, 0115 3:33	1d
3877	Wed	21	624	Wed, Sep 23, 0116 15:34	Wed, Sep 23, 0116 3:37	2d
3878	Mon	6	420	Mon, Sep 13, 0117 0:23	Sun, Sep 12, 0117 19:29	2d
3879	Fri	15	216	Fri, Sep 2, 0118 9:11	Fri, Sep 2, 0118 11:26	2d
3880	Thu	12	805	Thu, Sep 21, 0119 6:44	Thu, Sep 21, 0119 11:22	2d
3881	Mon	21	601	Mon, Sep 9, 0120 15:33	Mon, Sep 9, 0120 19:04	3d
3882	Sat	6	397	Sat, Aug 30, 0121 0:22	Fri, Aug 29, 0121 20:21	2d
3883	Fri	3	986	Thu, Sep 17, 0122 21:54	Thu, Sep 17, 0122 13:20	1d
3884	Tue	12	782	Tue, Sep 7, 0123 6:43	Mon, Sep 6, 0123 16:07	1d
3885	Mon	10	291	Mon, Sep 25, 0124 4:16	Sun, Sep 24, 0124 13:37	1d
3886	Fri	19	87	Fri, Sep 14, 0125 13:04	Fri, Sep 14, 0125 2:37	2d
3887	Wed	3	963	Tue, Sep 3, 0126 21:53	Tue, Sep 3, 0126 19:03	2d
3888	Tue	1	472	Mon, Sep 22, 0127 19:26	Mon, Sep 22, 0127 20:37	2d
3889	Sat	10	268	Sat, Sep 11, 0128 4:14	Sat, Sep 11, 0128 9:13	2d
3890	Wed	19	64	Wed, Aug 31, 0129 13:03	Wed, Aug 31, 0129 14:58	2d
3891	Tue	16	653	Tue, Sep 19, 0130 10:36	Tue, Sep 19, 0130 8:43	2d
3892	Sun	1	449	Sat, Sep 8, 0131 19:24	Sat, Sep 8, 0131 8:35	1d
3893	Thu	10	245	Thu, Aug 28, 0132 4:13	Wed, Aug 27, 0132 13:25	1d
3894	Wed	7	834	Wed, Sep 16, 0133 1:46	Tue, Sep 15, 0133 11:35	1d
3895	Sun	16	630	Sun, Sep 5, 0134 10:34	Sun, Sep 5, 0134 2:03	2d

Year	Day	Hrs	Pts	Molad of Tishrei	Conjunction	Skw
3896	Sat	14	139	Sat, Sep 24, 0135 8:07	Sat, Sep 24, 0135 3:51	2d
3897	Wed	22	1015	Wed, Sep 12, 0136 16:56	Wed, Sep 12, 0136 19:31	3d
3898	Mon	7	811	Mon, Sep 2, 0137 1:45	Mon, Sep 2, 0137 6:31	2d
3899	Sun	5	320	Sat, Sep 20, 0138 23:17	Sun, Sep 21, 0138 2:42	2d
3900	Thu	14	116	Thu, Sep 10, 0139 8:06	Thu, Sep 10, 0139 3:34	2d
3901	Mon	22	992	Mon, Aug 29, 0140 16:55	Mon, Aug 29, 0140 4:20	2d
3902	Sun	20	501	Sun, Sep 17, 0141 14:27	Sat, Sep 16, 0141 23:53	2d
3903	Fri	5	297	Thu, Sep 6, 0142 23:16	Thu, Sep 6, 0142 10:14	1d
3904	Thu	2	886	Wed, Sep 25, 0143 20:49	Wed, Sep 25, 0143 10:57	1d
3905	Mon	11	682	Mon, Sep 14, 0144 5:37	Mon, Sep 14, 0144 3:17	2d
3906	Fri	20	478	Fri, Sep 3, 0145 14:26	Fri, Sep 3, 0145 18:08	3d
3907	Thu	17	1067	Thu, Sep 22, 0146 11:59	Thu, Sep 22, 0146 17:09	2d
3908	Tue	2	863	Mon, Sep 11, 0147 20:47	Mon, Sep 11, 0147 22:20	2d
3909	Sat	11	659	Sat, Aug 31, 0148 5:36	Fri, Aug 30, 0148 22:28	2d
3910	Fri	9	168	Fri, Sep 19, 0149 3:09	Thu, Sep 18, 0149 16:04	1d
3911	Tue	17	1044	Tue, Sep 8, 0150 11:57	Mon, Sep 7, 0150 21:10	2d
3912	Sun	2	840	Sat, Aug 28, 0151 20:46	Sat, Aug 28, 0151 9:29	1d
3913	Sat	0	349	Fri, Sep 15, 0152 18:19	Fri, Sep 15, 0152 10:19	1d
3914	Wed	9	145	Wed, Sep 5, 0153 3:08	Wed, Sep 5, 0153 2:44	2d
3915	Tue	6	734	Tue, Sep 24, 0154 0:40	Tue, Sep 24, 0154 3:44	2d
3916	Sat	15	530	Sat, Sep 13, 0155 9:29	Sat, Sep 13, 0155 14:11	2d
3917	Thu	0	326	Wed, Sep 1, 0156 18:18	Wed, Sep 1, 0156 17:32	1d
3918	Tue	21	915	Tue, Sep 20, 0157 15:50	Tue, Sep 20, 0157 10:56	2d
3919	Sun	6	711	Sun, Sep 10, 0158 0:39	Sat, Sep 9, 0158 11:47	1d
3920	Thu	15	507	Thu, Aug 30, 0159 9:28	Wed, Aug 29, 0159 19:10	2d
3921	Wed	13	16	Wed, Sep 17, 0160 7:00	Tue, Sep 16, 0160 18:23	2d
3922	Sun	21	892	Sun, Sep 6, 0161 15:49	Sun, Sep 6, 0161 9:59	2d

Year	Day	Hrs	Pts	Molad of Tishrei	Conjunction	Skw
3923	Sat	19	401	Sat, Sep 25, 0162 13:22	Sat, Sep 25, 0162 11:40	2d
3924	Thu	4	197	Wed, Sep 14, 0163 22:10	Thu, Sep 15, 0163 2:08	2d
3925	Mon	12	1073	Mon, Sep 3, 0164 6:59	Mon, Sep 3, 0164 10:40	2d
3926	Sun	10	582	Sun, Sep 22, 0165 4:32	Sun, Sep 22, 0165 5:51	2d
3927	Thu	19	378	Thu, Sep 11, 0166 13:20	Thu, Sep 11, 0166 5:43	2d
3928	Tue	4	174	Mon, Aug 31, 0167 22:09	Mon, Aug 31, 0167 8:09	1d
3929	Mon	1	763	Sun, Sep 18, 0168 19:42	Sun, Sep 18, 0168 5:05	1d
3930	Fri	10	559	Fri, Sep 8, 0169 4:31	Thu, Sep 7, 0169 17:35	1d
3931	Tue	19	355	Tue, Aug 28, 0170 13:19	Tue, Aug 28, 0170 9:51	2d
3932	Mon	16	944	Mon, Sep 16, 0171 10:52	Mon, Sep 16, 0171 10:56	2d
3933	Sat	1	740	Fri, Sep 4, 0172 19:41	Sat, Sep 5, 0172 0:08	2d
3934	Thu	23	249	Thu, Sep 23, 0173 17:13	Thu, Sep 23, 0173 22:00	3d
3935	Tue	8	45	Tue, Sep 13, 0174 2:02	Tue, Sep 13, 0174 0:50	2d
3936	Sat	16	921	Sat, Sep 2, 0175 10:51	Sat, Sep 2, 0175 0:45	2d
3937	Fri	14	430	Fri, Sep 20, 0176 8:23	Thu, Sep 19, 0176 19:24	2d
3938	Tue	23	226	Tue, Sep 9, 0177 17:12	Tue, Sep 9, 0177 3:05	2d
3939	Sun	8	22	Sun, Aug 30, 0178 2:01	Sat, Aug 29, 0178 17:12	1d
3940	Sat	5	611	Fri, Sep 17, 0179 23:33	Fri, Sep 17, 0179 18:16	2d
3941	Wed	14	407	Wed, Sep 6, 0180 8:22	Wed, Sep 6, 0180 10:07	2d
3942	Tue	11	996	Tue, Sep 25, 0181 5:55	Tue, Sep 25, 0181 10:14	2d
3943	Sat	20	792	Sat, Sep 14, 0182 14:44	Sat, Sep 14, 0182 18:13	3d
3944	Thu	5	588	Wed, Sep 3, 0183 23:32	Wed, Sep 3, 0183 19:36	2d
3945	Wed	3	97	Tue, Sep 21, 0184 21:05	Tue, Sep 21, 0184 13:08	1d
3946	Sun	11	973	Sun, Sep 11, 0185 5:54	Sat, Sep 10, 0185 15:46	1d
3947	Thu	20	769	Thu, Aug 31, 0186 14:42	Thu, Aug 31, 0186 1:42	2d
3948	Wed	18	278	Wed, Sep 19, 0187 12:15	Wed, Sep 19, 0187 1:50	2d
3949	Mon	3	74	Sun, Sep 7, 0188 21:04	Sun, Sep 7, 0188 18:01	2d

Year	Day	Hrs	Pts	Molad of Tishrei	Conjunction	Skw
3950	Fri	11	950	Fri, Aug 28, 0189 5:52	Fri, Aug 28, 0189 9:07	2d
3951	Thu	9	459	Thu, Sep 16, 0190 3:25	Thu, Sep 16, 0190 8:00	2d
3952	Mon	18	255	Mon, Sep 5, 0191 12:14	Mon, Sep 5, 0191 13:57	2d
3953	Sun	15	844	Sun, Sep 23, 0192 9:46	Sun, Sep 23, 0192 8:16	2d
3954	Fri	0	640	Thu, Sep 12, 0193 18:35	Thu, Sep 12, 0193 8:06	1d
3955	Tue	9	436	Tue, Sep 2, 0194 3:24	Mon, Sep 1, 0194 12:47	1d
3956	Mon	6	1025	Mon, Sep 21, 0195 0:56	Sun, Sep 20, 0195 11:08	1d
3957	Fri	15	821	Fri, Sep 9, 0196 9:45	Fri, Sep 9, 0196 1:23	2d
3958	Wed	0	617	Tue, Aug 29, 0197 18:34	Tue, Aug 29, 0197 17:48	1d
3959	Mon	22	126	Mon, Sep 17, 0198 16:07	Mon, Sep 17, 0198 18:16	3d
3960	Sat	6	1002	Sat, Sep 7, 0199 0:55	Sat, Sep 7, 0199 5:20	2d
3961	Fri	4	511	Thu, Sep 25, 0200 22:28	Fri, Sep 26, 0200 1:53	2d
3962	Tue	13	307	Tue, Sep 15, 0201 7:17	Tue, Sep 15, 0201 2:53	2d
3963	Sat	22	103	Sat, Sep 4, 0202 16:05	Sat, Sep 4, 0202 3:33	2d
3964	Fri	19	692	Fri, Sep 23, 0203 13:38	Thu, Sep 22, 0203 23:33	2d
3965	Wed	4	488	Tue, Sep 11, 0204 22:27	Tue, Sep 11, 0204 9:44	1d
3966	Sun	13	284	Sun, Sep 1, 0205 7:15	Sun, Sep 1, 0205 1:11	2d
3967	Sat	10	873	Sat, Sep 20, 0206 4:48	Sat, Sep 20, 0206 2:19	2d
3968	Wed	19	669	Wed, Sep 9, 0207 13:37	Wed, Sep 9, 0207 17:03	2d
3969	Mon	4	465	Sun, Aug 28, 0208 22:25	Mon, Aug 29, 0208 2:13	2d
3970	Sun	1	1054	Sat, Sep 16, 0209 19:58	Sat, Sep 16, 0209 21:23	2d
3971	Thu	10	850	Thu, Sep 6, 0210 4:47	Wed, Sep 5, 0210 21:33	2d
3972	Wed	8	359	Wed, Sep 25, 0211 2:19	Tue, Sep 24, 0211 15:37	1d
3973	Sun	17	155	Sun, Sep 13, 0212 11:08	Sat, Sep 12, 0212 20:34	2d
3974	Fri	1	1031	Thu, Sep 2, 0213 19:57	Thu, Sep 2, 0213 8:47	1d
3975	Wed	23	540	Wed, Sep 21, 0214 17:30	Wed, Sep 21, 0214 9:41	2d
3976	Mon	8	336	Mon, Sep 11, 0215 2:18	Mon, Sep 11, 0215 1:56	2d

Year	Day	Hrs	Pts	Molad of Tishrei	Conjunction	Skw
3977	Fri	17	132	Fri, Aug 30, 0216 11:07	Fri, Aug 30, 0216 15:30	2d
3978	Thu	14	721	Thu, Sep 18, 0217 8:40	Thu, Sep 18, 0217 13:05	2d
3979	Mon	23	517	Mon, Sep 7, 0218 17:28	Mon, Sep 7, 0218 16:33	2d
3980	Sun	21	26	Sun, Sep 26, 0219 15:01	Sun, Sep 26, 0219 10:18	2d
3981	Fri	5	902	Thu, Sep 14, 0220 23:50	Thu, Sep 14, 0220 11:02	1d
3982	Tue	14	698	Tue, Sep 4, 0221 8:38	Mon, Sep 3, 0221 18:16	2d
3983	Mon	12	207	Mon, Sep 23, 0222 6:11	Sun, Sep 22, 0222 17:55	1d
3984	Fri	21	3	Fri, Sep 12, 0223 15:00	Fri, Sep 12, 0223 9:24	2d
3985	Wed	5	879	Tue, Aug 31, 0224 23:48	Wed, Sep 1, 0224 1:27	2d
3986	Tue	3	388	Mon, Sep 19, 0225 21:21	Tue, Sep 20, 0225 1:07	2d
3987	Sat	12	184	Sat, Sep 9, 0226 6:10	Sat, Sep 9, 0226 9:42	2d
3988	Wed	20	1060	Wed, Aug 29, 0227 14:58	Wed, Aug 29, 0227 11:34	2d
3989	Tue	18	569	Tue, Sep 16, 0228 12:31	Tue, Sep 16, 0228 4:51	2d
3990	Sun	3	365	Sat, Sep 5, 0229 21:20	Sat, Sep 5, 0229 7:05	1d
3991	Sat	0	954	Fri, Sep 24, 0230 18:53	Fri, Sep 24, 0230 4:31	1d
3992	Wed	9	750	Wed, Sep 14, 0231 3:41	Tue, Sep 13, 0231 16:55	1d
3993	Sun	18	546	Sun, Sep 2, 0232 12:30	Sun, Sep 2, 0232 9:11	2d
3994	Sat	16	55	Sat, Sep 21, 0233 10:03	Sat, Sep 21, 0233 10:12	2d
3995	Thu	0	931	Wed, Sep 10, 0234 18:51	Wed, Sep 10, 0234 23:20	2d
3996	Mon	9	727	Mon, Aug 31, 0235 3:40	Mon, Aug 31, 0235 5:54	2d
3997	Sun	7	236	Sun, Sep 18, 0236 1:13	Sat, Sep 17, 0236 23:55	2d
3998	Thu	16	32	Thu, Sep 7, 0237 10:01	Wed, Sep 6, 0237 23:45	2d
3999	Wed	13	621	Wed, Sep 26, 0238 7:34	Tue, Sep 25, 0238 18:41	2d
4000	Sun	22	417	Sun, Sep 15, 0239 16:23	Sun, Sep 15, 0239 2:12	2d
4001	Fri	7	213	Fri, Sep 4, 0240 1:11	Thu, Sep 3, 0240 16:18	1d
4002	Thu	4	802	Wed, Sep 22, 0241 22:44	Wed, Sep 22, 0241 17:44	1d
4003	Mon	13	598	Mon, Sep 12, 0242 7:33	Mon, Sep 12, 0242 9:32	2d

Year	Day	Hrs	Pts	Molad of Tishrei	Conjunction	Skw
4004	Fri	22	394	Fri, Sep 1, 0243 16:21	Fri, Sep 1, 0243 21:07	3d
4005	Thu	19	983	Thu, Sep 19, 0244 13:54	Thu, Sep 19, 0244 17:20	2d
4006	Tue	4	779	Mon, Sep 8, 0245 22:43	Mon, Sep 8, 0245 18:45	2d
4007	Sat	13	575	Sat, Aug 29, 0246 7:31	Fri, Aug 28, 0246 19:12	2d
4008	Fri	11	84	Fri, Sep 17, 0247 5:04	Thu, Sep 16, 0247 14:44	1d
4009	Tue	19	960	Tue, Sep 5, 0248 13:53	Tue, Sep 5, 0248 0:30	2d
4010	Mon	17	469	Mon, Sep 24, 0249 11:26	Mon, Sep 24, 0249 1:13	2d
4011	Sat	2	265	Fri, Sep 13, 0250 20:14	Fri, Sep 13, 0250 17:24	1d
4012	Wed	11	61	Wed, Sep 3, 0251 5:03	Wed, Sep 3, 0251 8:33	2d
4013	Tue	8	650	Tue, Sep 21, 0252 2:36	Tue, Sep 21, 0252 7:17	2d
4014	Sat	17	446	Sat, Sep 10, 0253 11:24	Sat, Sep 10, 0253 13:16	2d
4015	Thu	2	242	Wed, Aug 30, 0254 20:13	Wed, Aug 30, 0254 13:42	1d
4016	Tue	23	831	Tue, Sep 18, 0255 17:46	Tue, Sep 18, 0255 7:08	2d
4017	Sun	8	627	Sun, Sep 7, 0256 2:34	Sat, Sep 6, 0256 11:34	1d
4018	Sat	6	136	Sat, Sep 26, 0257 0:07	Fri, Sep 25, 0257 10:18	1d
4019	Wed	14	1012	Wed, Sep 15, 0258 8:56	Wed, Sep 15, 0258 0:31	2d
4020	Sun	23	808	Sun, Sep 4, 0259 17:44	Sun, Sep 4, 0259 17:02	2d
4021	Sat	21	317	Sat, Sep 22, 0260 15:17	Sat, Sep 22, 0260 17:44	2d
4022	Thu	6	113	Thu, Sep 12, 0261 0:06	Thu, Sep 12, 0261 4:49	2d
4023	Mon	14	989	Mon, Sep 1, 0262 8:54	Mon, Sep 1, 0262 8:52	2d
4024	Sun	12	498	Sun, Sep 20, 0263 6:27	Sun, Sep 20, 0263 2:05	2d
4025	Thu	21	294	Thu, Sep 8, 0264 15:16	Thu, Sep 8, 0264 2:33	2d
4026	Tue	6	90	Tue, Aug 29, 0265 0:05	Mon, Aug 28, 0265 9:11	1d
4027	Mon	3	679	Sun, Sep 16, 0266 21:37	Sun, Sep 16, 0266 8:34	1d
4028	Fri	12	475	Fri, Sep 6, 0267 6:26	Fri, Sep 6, 0267 0:02	2d
4029	Thu	9	1064	Thu, Sep 24, 0268 3:59	Thu, Sep 24, 0268 1:45	2d
4030	Mon	18	860	Mon, Sep 13, 0269 12:47	Mon, Sep 13, 0269 16:34	2d

Year	Day	Hrs	Pts	Molad of Tishrei	Conjunction	Skw
4031	Sat	3	656	Fri, Sep 2, 0270 21:36	Sat, Sep 3, 0270 1:49	2d
4032	Fri	1	165	Thu, Sep 21, 0271 19:09	Thu, Sep 21, 0271 20:47	2d
4033	Tue	9	1041	Tue, Sep 10, 0272 3:57	Mon, Sep 9, 0272 20:54	2d
4034	Sat	18	837	Sat, Aug 30, 0273 12:46	Fri, Aug 29, 0273 22:43	2d
4035	Fri	16	346	Fri, Sep 18, 0274 10:19	Thu, Sep 17, 0274 19:22	2d
4036	Wed	1	142	Tue, Sep 7, 0275 19:07	Tue, Sep 7, 0275 7:24	1d
4037	Mon	22	731	Mon, Sep 25, 0276 16:40	Mon, Sep 25, 0276 8:52	2d
4038	Sat	7	527	Sat, Sep 15, 0277 1:29	Sat, Sep 15, 0277 1:13	2d
4039	Wed	16	323	Wed, Sep 4, 0278 10:17	Wed, Sep 4, 0278 14:58	2d
4040	Tue	13	912	Tue, Sep 23, 0279 7:50	Tue, Sep 23, 0279 12:38	2d
4041	Sat	22	708	Sat, Sep 11, 0280 16:39	Sat, Sep 11, 0280 16:09	2d
4042	Thu	7	504	Thu, Sep 1, 0281 1:28	Wed, Aug 31, 0281 16:02	1d
4043	Wed	5	13	Tue, Sep 19, 0282 23:00	Tue, Sep 19, 0282 10:05	1d
4044	Sun	13	889	Sun, Sep 9, 0283 7:49	Sat, Sep 8, 0283 16:59	1d
4045	Thu	22	685	Thu, Aug 28, 0284 16:38	Thu, Aug 28, 0284 6:44	2d
4046	Wed	20	194	Wed, Sep 16, 0285 14:10	Wed, Sep 16, 0285 8:17	2d
4047	Mon	4	1070	Sun, Sep 5, 0286 22:59	Mon, Sep 6, 0286 0:30	2d
4048	Sun	2	579	Sat, Sep 24, 0287 20:32	Sun, Sep 25, 0287 0:40	2d
4049	Thu	11	375	Thu, Sep 13, 0288 5:20	Thu, Sep 13, 0288 9:23	2d
4050	Mon	20	171	Mon, Sep 2, 0289 14:09	Mon, Sep 2, 0289 11:19	2d
4051	Sun	17	760	Sun, Sep 21, 0290 11:42	Sun, Sep 21, 0290 4:15	2d
4052	Fri	2	556	Thu, Sep 10, 0291 20:30	Thu, Sep 10, 0291 6:13	1d
4053	Tue	11	352	Tue, Aug 30, 0292 5:19	Mon, Aug 29, 0292 15:21	1d
4054	Mon	8	941	Mon, Sep 18, 0293 2:52	Sun, Sep 17, 0293 15:35	1d
4055	Fri	17	737	Fri, Sep 7, 0294 11:40	Fri, Sep 7, 0294 7:51	2d
4056	Thu	15	246	Thu, Sep 26, 0295 9:13	Thu, Sep 26, 0295 9:32	2d
4057	Tue	0	42	Mon, Sep 14, 0296 18:02	Mon, Sep 14, 0296 22:51	2d

Year	Day	Hrs	Pts	Molad of Tishrei	Conjunction	Skw
4058	Sat	8	918	Sat, Sep 4, 0297 2:51	Sat, Sep 4, 0297 5:35	2d
4059	Fri	6	427	Fri, Sep 23, 0298 0:23	Thu, Sep 22, 0298 23:35	2d
4060	Tue	15	223	Tue, Sep 12, 0299 9:12	Mon, Sep 11, 0299 23:18	2d
4061	Sun	0	19	Sat, Sep 1, 0300 18:01	Sat, Sep 1, 0300 3:11	1d
4062	Fri	21	608	Fri, Sep 20, 0301 15:33	Fri, Sep 20, 0301 0:58	2d
4063	Wed	6	404	Wed, Sep 10, 0302 0:22	Tue, Sep 9, 0302 14:50	1d
4064	Sun	15	200	Sun, Aug 30, 0303 9:11	Sun, Aug 30, 0303 7:28	2d
4065	Sat	12	789	Sat, Sep 17, 0304 6:43	Sat, Sep 17, 0304 8:38	2d
4066	Wed	21	585	Wed, Sep 6, 0305 15:32	Wed, Sep 6, 0305 20:29	3d
4067	Tue	19	94	Tue, Sep 25, 0306 13:05	Tue, Sep 25, 0306 17:04	2d
4068	Sun	3	970	Sat, Sep 14, 0307 21:53	Sat, Sep 14, 0307 18:33	2d
4069	Thu	12	766	Thu, Sep 3, 0308 6:42	Wed, Sep 2, 0308 18:51	2d
4070	Wed	10	275	Wed, Sep 22, 0309 4:15	Tue, Sep 21, 0309 13:55	1d
4071	Sun	19	71	Sun, Sep 11, 0310 13:03	Sat, Sep 10, 0310 23:18	2d
4072	Fri	3	947	Thu, Aug 31, 0311 21:52	Thu, Aug 31, 0311 14:28	1d
4073	Thu	1	456	Wed, Sep 18, 0312 19:25	Wed, Sep 18, 0312 16:06	1d
4074	Mon	10	252	Mon, Sep 8, 0313 4:14	Mon, Sep 8, 0313 7:28	2d
4075	Sun	7	841	Sun, Sep 27, 0314 1:46	Sun, Sep 27, 0314 6:51	2d
4076	Thu	16	637	Thu, Sep 16, 0315 10:35	Thu, Sep 16, 0315 13:01	2d
4077	Tue	1	433	Mon, Sep 4, 0316 19:24	Mon, Sep 4, 0316 13:29	1d
4078	Sun	22	1022	Sun, Sep 23, 0317 16:56	Sun, Sep 23, 0317 6:46	2d
4079	Fri	7	818	Fri, Sep 13, 0318 1:45	Thu, Sep 12, 0318 10:52	1d
4080	Tue	16	614	Tue, Sep 2, 0319 10:34	Mon, Sep 1, 0319 22:19	2d
4081	Mon	14	123	Mon, Sep 20, 0320 8:06	Sun, Sep 19, 0320 23:06	2d
4082	Fri	22	999	Fri, Sep 9, 0321 16:55	Fri, Sep 9, 0321 15:35	2d
4083	Wed	7	795	Wed, Aug 30, 0322 1:44	Wed, Aug 30, 0322 5:55	2d
4084	Tue	5	304	Mon, Sep 17, 0323 23:16	Tue, Sep 18, 0323 4:14	2d

Year	Day	Hrs	Pts	Molad of Tishrei	Conjunction	Skw
4085	Sat	14	100	Sat, Sep 6, 0324 8:05	Sat, Sep 6, 0324 8:29	2d
4086	Fri	11	689	Fri, Sep 25, 0325 5:38	Fri, Sep 25, 0325 1:56	2d
4087	Tue	20	485	Tue, Sep 14, 0326 14:26	Tue, Sep 14, 0326 2:15	2d
4088	Sun	5	281	Sat, Sep 3, 0327 23:15	Sat, Sep 3, 0327 8:34	1d
4089	Sat	2	870	Fri, Sep 21, 0328 20:48	Fri, Sep 21, 0328 7:25	1d
4090	Wed	11	666	Wed, Sep 11, 0329 5:37	Tue, Sep 10, 0329 22:38	2d
4091	Sun	20	462	Sun, Aug 31, 0330 14:25	Sun, Aug 31, 0330 15:01	2d
4092	Sat	17	1051	Sat, Sep 19, 0331 11:58	Sat, Sep 19, 0331 15:30	2d
4093	Thu	2	847	Wed, Sep 7, 0332 20:47	Thu, Sep 8, 0332 1:03	2d
4094	Wed	0	356	Tue, Sep 26, 0333 18:19	Tue, Sep 26, 0333 20:36	2d
4095	Sun	9	152	Sun, Sep 16, 0334 3:08	Sat, Sep 15, 0334 20:44	2d
4096	Thu	17	1028	Thu, Sep 5, 0335 11:57	Wed, Sep 4, 0335 22:22	2d
4097	Wed	15	537	Wed, Sep 23, 0336 9:29	Tue, Sep 22, 0336 18:44	2d
4098	Mon	0	333	Sun, Sep 12, 0337 18:18	Sun, Sep 12, 0337 6:24	1d
4099	Fri	9	129	Fri, Sep 2, 0338 3:07	Thu, Sep 1, 0338 22:26	2d
4100	Thu	6	718	Thu, Sep 21, 0339 0:39	Wed, Sep 20, 0339 23:49	2d
4101	Mon	15	514	Mon, Sep 9, 0340 9:28	Mon, Sep 9, 0340 13:45	2d
4102	Sat	0	310	Fri, Aug 29, 0341 18:17	Fri, Aug 29, 0341 21:18	2d
4103	Thu	21	899	Thu, Sep 17, 0342 15:49	Thu, Sep 17, 0342 15:49	2d
4104	Tue	6	695	Tue, Sep 7, 0343 0:38	Mon, Sep 6, 0343 15:41	1d
4105	Mon	4	204	Sun, Sep 24, 0344 22:11	Sun, Sep 24, 0344 9:50	1d
4106	Fri	13	0	Fri, Sep 14, 0345 7:00	Thu, Sep 13, 0345 16:26	1d
4107	Tue	21	876	Tue, Sep 3, 0346 15:48	Tue, Sep 3, 0346 5:51	2d
4108	Mon	19	385	Mon, Sep 22, 0347 13:21	Mon, Sep 22, 0347 6:56	2d
4109	Sat	4	181	Fri, Sep 10, 0348 22:10	Fri, Sep 10, 0348 23:05	2d
4110	Wed	12	1057	Wed, Aug 31, 0349 6:58	Wed, Aug 31, 0349 11:33	2d
4111	Tue	10	566	Tue, Sep 19, 0350 4:31	Tue, Sep 19, 0350 8:40	2d

Year	Day	Hrs	Pts	Molad of Tishrei	Conjunction	Skw
4112	Sat	19	362	Sat, Sep 8, 0351 13:20	Sat, Sep 8, 0351 10:45	2d
4113	Fri	16	951	Fri, Sep 26, 0352 10:52	Fri, Sep 26, 0352 4:09	2d
4114	Wed	1	747	Tue, Sep 15, 0353 19:41	Tue, Sep 15, 0353 5:57	1d
4115	Sun	10	543	Sun, Sep 5, 0354 4:30	Sat, Sep 4, 0354 14:49	1d
4116	Sat	8	52	Sat, Sep 24, 0355 2:02	Fri, Sep 23, 0355 14:37	1d
4117	Wed	16	928	Wed, Sep 12, 0356 10:51	Wed, Sep 12, 0356 6:38	2d
4118	Mon	1	724	Sun, Sep 1, 0357 19:40	Sun, Sep 1, 0357 22:12	2d
4119	Sat	23	233	Sat, Sep 20, 0358 17:12	Sat, Sep 20, 0358 21:41	3d
4120	Thu	8	29	Thu, Sep 10, 0359 2:01	Thu, Sep 10, 0359 4:40	2d
4121	Mon	16	905	Mon, Aug 29, 0360 10:50	Mon, Aug 29, 0360 5:33	2d
4122	Sun	14	414	Sun, Sep 17, 0361 8:23	Sat, Sep 16, 0361 23:01	2d
4123	Thu	23	210	Thu, Sep 6, 0362 17:11	Thu, Sep 6, 0362 2:42	2d
4124	Wed	20	799	Wed, Sep 25, 0363 14:44	Wed, Sep 25, 0363 0:27	2d
4125	Mon	5	595	Sun, Sep 13, 0364 23:33	Sun, Sep 13, 0364 14:01	1d
4126	Fri	14	391	Fri, Sep 3, 0365 8:21	Fri, Sep 3, 0365 6:26	2d
4127	Thu	11	980	Thu, Sep 22, 0366 5:54	Thu, Sep 22, 0366 7:17	2d
4128	Mon	20	776	Mon, Sep 11, 0367 14:43	Mon, Sep 11, 0367 19:15	3d
4129	Sat	5	572	Fri, Aug 30, 0368 23:31	Sat, Aug 31, 0368 0:14	2d
4130	Fri	3	81	Thu, Sep 18, 0369 21:04	Thu, Sep 18, 0369 18:03	2d
4131	Tue	11	957	Tue, Sep 8, 0370 5:53	Mon, Sep 7, 0370 18:16	2d
4132	Mon	9	466	Mon, Sep 27, 0371 3:25	Sun, Sep 26, 0371 13:40	1d
4133	Fri	18	262	Fri, Sep 15, 0372 12:14	Thu, Sep 14, 0372 22:50	2d
4134	Wed	3	58	Tue, Sep 4, 0373 21:03	Tue, Sep 4, 0373 13:46	1d
4135	Tue	0	647	Mon, Sep 23, 0374 18:35	Mon, Sep 23, 0374 14:56	1d
4136	Sat	9	443	Sat, Sep 13, 0375 3:24	Sat, Sep 13, 0375 6:12	2d
4137	Wed	18	239	Wed, Sep 1, 0376 12:13	Wed, Sep 1, 0376 16:22	2d
4138	Tue	15	828	Tue, Sep 20, 0377 9:46	Tue, Sep 20, 0377 12:10	2d

Year	Day	Hrs	Pts	Molad of Tishrei	Conjunction	Skw
4139	Sun	0	624	Sat, Sep 9, 0378 18:34	Sat, Sep 9, 0378 12:42	1d
4140	Thu	9	420	Thu, Aug 30, 0379 3:23	Wed, Aug 29, 0379 14:05	1d
4141	Wed	6	1009	Wed, Sep 17, 0380 0:56	Tue, Sep 16, 0380 10:27	1d
4142	Sun	15	805	Sun, Sep 6, 0381 9:44	Sat, Sep 5, 0381 21:44	2d
4143	Sat	13	314	Sat, Sep 25, 0382 7:17	Fri, Sep 24, 0382 22:19	2d
4144	Wed	22	110	Wed, Sep 14, 0383 16:06	Wed, Sep 14, 0383 14:36	2d
4145	Mon	6	986	Mon, Sep 3, 0384 0:54	Mon, Sep 3, 0384 4:51	2d
4146	Sun	4	495	Sat, Sep 21, 0385 22:27	Sun, Sep 22, 0385 3:05	2d
4147	Thu	13	291	Thu, Sep 11, 0386 7:16	Thu, Sep 11, 0386 7:30	2d
4148	Mon	22	87	Mon, Aug 31, 0387 16:04	Mon, Aug 31, 0387 7:32	2d
4149	Sun	19	676	Sun, Sep 18, 0388 13:37	Sun, Sep 18, 0388 1:44	2d
4150	Fri	4	472	Thu, Sep 7, 0389 22:26	Thu, Sep 7, 0389 7:53	1d
4151	Thu	1	1061	Wed, Sep 26, 0390 19:58	Wed, Sep 26, 0390 6:59	1d
4152	Mon	10	857	Mon, Sep 16, 0391 4:47	Sun, Sep 15, 0391 21:59	2d
4153	Fri	19	653	Fri, Sep 4, 0392 13:36	Fri, Sep 4, 0392 14:13	2d
4154	Thu	17	162	Thu, Sep 23, 0393 11:09	Thu, Sep 23, 0393 14:19	2d
4155	Tue	1	1038	Mon, Sep 12, 0394 19:57	Mon, Sep 12, 0394 23:56	2d
4156	Sat	10	834	Sat, Sep 2, 0395 4:46	Sat, Sep 2, 0395 2:36	2d
4157	Fri	8	343	Fri, Sep 20, 0396 2:19	Thu, Sep 19, 0396 20:01	2d
4158	Tue	17	139	Tue, Sep 9, 0397 11:07	Mon, Sep 8, 0397 21:31	2d
4159	Sun	1	1015	Sat, Aug 29, 0398 19:56	Sat, Aug 29, 0398 5:58	1d
4160	Fri	23	524	Fri, Sep 17, 0399 17:29	Fri, Sep 17, 0399 5:52	2d
4161	Wed	8	320	Wed, Sep 6, 0400 2:17	Tue, Sep 5, 0400 21:49	2d
4162	Tue	5	909	Mon, Sep 24, 0401 23:50	Mon, Sep 24, 0401 22:54	2d
4163	Sat	14	705	Sat, Sep 14, 0402 8:39	Sat, Sep 14, 0402 12:45	2d
4164	Wed	23	501	Wed, Sep 3, 0403 17:27	Wed, Sep 3, 0403 20:21	3d
4165	Tue	21	10	Tue, Sep 21, 0404 15:00	Tue, Sep 21, 0404 14:55	2d

Year	Day	Hrs	Pts	Molad of Tishrei	Conjunction	Skw
4166	Sun	5	886	Sat, Sep 10, 0405 23:49	Sat, Sep 10, 0405 14:45	1d
4167	Thu	14	682	Thu, Aug 31, 0406 8:37	Wed, Aug 30, 0406 18:00	1d
4168	Wed	12	191	Wed, Sep 19, 0407 6:10	Tue, Sep 18, 0407 15:47	1d
4169	Sun	20	1067	Sun, Sep 7, 0408 14:59	Sun, Sep 7, 0408 5:09	2d
4170	Sat	18	576	Sat, Sep 26, 0409 12:32	Sat, Sep 26, 0409 6:21	2d
4171	Thu	3	372	Wed, Sep 15, 0410 21:20	Wed, Sep 15, 0410 22:22	2d
4172	Mon	12	168	Mon, Sep 5, 0411 6:09	Mon, Sep 5, 0411 10:48	2d
4173	Sun	9	757	Sun, Sep 23, 0412 3:42	Sun, Sep 23, 0412 7:39	2d
4174	Thu	18	553	Thu, Sep 12, 0413 12:30	Thu, Sep 12, 0413 9:50	2d
4175	Tue	3	349	Mon, Sep 1, 0414 21:19	Mon, Sep 1, 0414 9:57	1d
4176	Mon	0	938	Sun, Sep 20, 0415 18:52	Sun, Sep 20, 0415 5:07	1d
4177	Fri	9	734	Fri, Sep 9, 0416 3:40	Thu, Sep 8, 0416 13:51	1d
4178	Tue	18	530	Tue, Aug 29, 0417 12:29	Tue, Aug 29, 0417 4:43	2d
4179	Mon	16	39	Mon, Sep 17, 0418 10:02	Mon, Sep 17, 0418 6:03	2d
4180	Sat	0	915	Fri, Sep 6, 0419 18:50	Fri, Sep 6, 0419 21:36	2d
4181	Thu	22	424	Thu, Sep 24, 0420 16:23	Thu, Sep 24, 0420 20:46	3d
4182	Tue	7	220	Tue, Sep 14, 0421 1:12	Tue, Sep 14, 0421 3:49	2d
4183	Sat	16	16	Sat, Sep 3, 0422 10:00	Sat, Sep 3, 0422 4:42	2d
4184	Fri	13	605	Fri, Sep 22, 0423 7:33	Thu, Sep 21, 0423 22:08	2d
4185	Tue	22	401	Tue, Sep 10, 0424 16:22	Tue, Sep 10, 0424 1:37	2d
4186	Sun	7	197	Sun, Aug 31, 0425 1:10	Sat, Aug 30, 0425 12:31	1d
4187	Sat	4	786	Fri, Sep 18, 0426 22:43	Fri, Sep 18, 0426 13:21	1d
4188	Wed	13	582	Wed, Sep 8, 0427 7:32	Wed, Sep 8, 0427 5:48	2d
4189	Tue	11	91	Tue, Sep 26, 0428 5:05	Tue, Sep 26, 0428 6:37	2d
4190	Sat	19	967	Sat, Sep 15, 0429 13:53	Sat, Sep 15, 0429 18:35	3d
4191	Thu	4	763	Wed, Sep 4, 0430 22:42	Wed, Sep 4, 0430 23:36	2d
4192	Wed	2	272	Tue, Sep 23, 0431 20:15	Tue, Sep 23, 0431 17:11	1d

Year	Day	Hrs	Pts	Molad of Tishrei	Conjunction	Skw
4193	Sun	11	68	Sun, Sep 12, 0432 5:03	Sat, Sep 11, 0432 17:16	1d
4194	Thu	19	944	Thu, Sep 1, 0433 13:52	Wed, Aug 31, 0433 22:52	2d
4195	Wed	17	453	Wed, Sep 20, 0434 11:25	Tue, Sep 19, 0434 21:54	2d
4196	Mon	2	249	Sun, Sep 9, 0435 20:13	Sun, Sep 9, 0435 12:50	1d
4197	Fri	11	45	Fri, Aug 29, 0436 5:02	Fri, Aug 29, 0436 5:25	2d
4198	Thu	8	634	Thu, Sep 17, 0437 2:35	Thu, Sep 17, 0437 5:40	2d
4199	Mon	17	430	Mon, Sep 6, 0438 11:23	Mon, Sep 6, 0438 15:53	2d
4200	Sun	14	1019	Sun, Sep 25, 0439 8:56	Sun, Sep 25, 0439 11:23	2d
4201	Thu	23	815	Thu, Sep 13, 0440 17:45	Thu, Sep 13, 0440 11:56	2d
4202	Tue	8	611	Tue, Sep 3, 0441 2:33	Mon, Sep 2, 0441 13:04	1d
4203	Mon	6	120	Mon, Sep 22, 0442 0:06	Sun, Sep 21, 0442 9:23	1d
4204	Fri	14	996	Fri, Sep 11, 0443 8:55	Thu, Sep 10, 0443 20:31	2d
4205	Tue	23	792	Tue, Aug 30, 0444 17:44	Tue, Aug 30, 0444 12:32	2d
4206	Mon	21	301	Mon, Sep 18, 0445 15:16	Mon, Sep 18, 0445 14:02	2d
4207	Sat	6	97	Sat, Sep 8, 0446 0:05	Sat, Sep 8, 0446 4:22	2d
4208	Fri	3	686	Thu, Sep 26, 0447 21:38	Fri, Sep 27, 0447 2:29	2d
4209	Tue	12	482	Tue, Sep 15, 0448 6:26	Tue, Sep 15, 0448 6:58	2d
4210	Sat	21	278	Sat, Sep 4, 0449 15:15	Sat, Sep 4, 0449 6:55	2d
4211	Fri	18	867	Fri, Sep 23, 0450 12:48	Fri, Sep 23, 0450 0:46	2d
4212	Wed	3	663	Tue, Sep 12, 0451 21:36	Tue, Sep 12, 0451 6:38	1d
4213	Sun	12	459	Sun, Sep 1, 0452 6:25	Sat, Aug 31, 0452 19:39	2d
4214	Sat	9	1048	Sat, Sep 20, 0453 3:58	Fri, Sep 19, 0453 21:06	2d
4215	Wed	18	844	Wed, Sep 9, 0454 12:46	Wed, Sep 9, 0454 13:28	2d
4216	Mon	3	640	Sun, Aug 29, 0455 21:35	Mon, Aug 30, 0455 2:35	2d
4217	Sun	1	149	Sat, Sep 16, 0456 19:08	Sat, Sep 16, 0456 23:32	2d
4218	Thu	9	1025	Thu, Sep 6, 0457 3:56	Thu, Sep 6, 0457 2:15	2d
4219	Wed	7	534	Wed, Sep 25, 0458 1:29	Tue, Sep 24, 0458 19:18	2d

Year	Day	Hrs	Pts	Molad of Tishrei	Conjunction	Skw
4220	Sun	16	330	Sun, Sep 14, 0459 10:18	Sat, Sep 13, 0459 20:33	2d
4221	Fri	1	126	Thu, Sep 2, 0460 19:07	Thu, Sep 2, 0460 4:41	1d
4222	Wed	22	715	Wed, Sep 21, 0461 16:39	Wed, Sep 21, 0461 4:42	2d
4223	Mon	7	511	Mon, Sep 11, 0462 1:28	Sun, Sep 10, 0462 20:41	2d
4224	Fri	16	307	Fri, Aug 31, 0463 10:17	Fri, Aug 31, 0463 12:43	2d
4225	Thu	13	896	Thu, Sep 18, 0464 7:49	Thu, Sep 18, 0464 12:20	2d
4226	Mon	22	692	Mon, Sep 7, 0465 16:38	Mon, Sep 7, 0465 20:04	3d
4227	Sun	20	201	Sun, Sep 26, 0466 14:11	Sun, Sep 26, 0466 14:26	2d
4228	Fri	4	1077	Thu, Sep 15, 0467 22:59	Thu, Sep 15, 0467 14:11	1d
4229	Tue	13	873	Tue, Sep 4, 0468 7:48	Mon, Sep 3, 0468 17:08	1d
4230	Mon	11	382	Mon, Sep 23, 0469 5:21	Sun, Sep 22, 0469 14:35	1d
4231	Fri	20	178	Fri, Sep 12, 0470 14:09	Fri, Sep 12, 0470 3:45	2d
4232	Wed	4	1054	Tue, Sep 1, 0471 22:58	Tue, Sep 1, 0471 20:19	2d
4233	Tue	2	563	Mon, Sep 19, 0472 20:31	Mon, Sep 19, 0472 21:40	2d
4234	Sat	11	359	Sat, Sep 9, 0473 5:19	Sat, Sep 9, 0473 10:18	2d
4235	Wed	20	155	Wed, Aug 29, 0474 14:08	Wed, Aug 29, 0474 16:05	2d
4236	Tue	17	744	Tue, Sep 17, 0475 11:41	Tue, Sep 17, 0475 9:31	2d
4237	Sun	2	540	Sat, Sep 5, 0476 20:30	Sat, Sep 5, 0476 9:31	1d
4238	Sat	0	49	Fri, Sep 24, 0477 18:02	Fri, Sep 24, 0477 4:12	1d
4239	Wed	8	925	Wed, Sep 14, 0478 2:51	Tue, Sep 13, 0478 12:36	1d
4240	Sun	17	721	Sun, Sep 3, 0479 11:40	Sun, Sep 3, 0479 3:15	2d
4241	Sat	15	230	Sat, Sep 21, 0480 9:12	Sat, Sep 21, 0480 4:58	2d
4242	Thu	0	26	Wed, Sep 10, 0481 18:01	Wed, Sep 10, 0481 20:42	2d
4243	Mon	8	902	Mon, Aug 31, 0482 2:50	Mon, Aug 31, 0482 7:43	2d
4244	Sun	6	411	Sun, Sep 19, 0483 0:22	Sun, Sep 19, 0483 3:35	2d
4245	Thu	15	207	Thu, Sep 7, 0484 9:11	Thu, Sep 7, 0484 4:32	2d
4246	Wed	12	796	Wed, Sep 26, 0485 6:44	Tue, Sep 25, 0485 21:38	2d

Year	Day	Hrs	Pts	Molad of Tishrei	Conjunction	Skw
4247	Sun	21	592	Sun, Sep 15, 0486 15:32	Sun, Sep 15, 0486 0:47	2d
4248	Fri	6	388	Fri, Sep 5, 0487 0:21	Thu, Sep 4, 0487 11:19	1d
4249	Thu	3	977	Wed, Sep 22, 0488 21:54	Wed, Sep 22, 0488 12:01	1d
4250	Mon	12	773	Mon, Sep 12, 0489 6:42	Mon, Sep 12, 0489 4:28	2d
4251	Fri	21	569	Fri, Sep 1, 0490 15:31	Fri, Sep 1, 0490 19:24	3d
4252	Thu	19	78	Thu, Sep 20, 0491 13:04	Thu, Sep 20, 0491 18:08	3d
4253	Tue	3	954	Mon, Sep 8, 0492 21:53	Mon, Sep 8, 0492 23:21	2d
4254	Sat	12	750	Sat, Aug 29, 0493 6:41	Fri, Aug 28, 0493 23:34	2d
4255	Fri	10	259	Fri, Sep 17, 0494 4:14	Thu, Sep 16, 0494 16:53	1d
4256	Tue	19	55	Tue, Sep 6, 0495 13:03	Mon, Sep 5, 0495 22:10	2d
4257	Mon	16	644	Mon, Sep 24, 0496 10:35	Sun, Sep 23, 0496 20:41	2d
4258	Sat	1	440	Fri, Sep 13, 0497 19:24	Fri, Sep 13, 0497 11:25	1d
4259	Wed	10	236	Wed, Sep 3, 0498 4:13	Wed, Sep 3, 0498 3:58	2d
4260	Tue	7	825	Tue, Sep 22, 0499 1:45	Tue, Sep 22, 0499 4:49	2d
4261	Sat	16	621	Sat, Sep 11, 0500 10:34	Sat, Sep 11, 0500 15:18	2d
4262	Thu	1	417	Wed, Aug 31, 0501 19:23	Wed, Aug 31, 0501 18:42	2d
4263	Tue	22	1006	Tue, Sep 19, 0502 16:55	Tue, Sep 19, 0502 11:47	2d
4264	Sun	7	802	Sun, Sep 9, 0503 1:44	Sat, Sep 8, 0503 12:46	1d
4265	Sat	5	311	Fri, Sep 26, 0504 23:17	Fri, Sep 26, 0504 8:36	1d
4266	Wed	14	107	Wed, Sep 16, 0505 8:05	Tue, Sep 15, 0505 19:22	2d
4267	Sun	22	983	Sun, Sep 5, 0506 16:54	Sun, Sep 5, 0506 11:07	2d
4268	Sat	20	492	Sat, Sep 24, 0507 14:27	Sat, Sep 24, 0507 12:45	2d
4269	Thu	5	288	Wed, Sep 12, 0508 23:16	Thu, Sep 13, 0508 3:18	2d
4270	Mon	14	84	Mon, Sep 2, 0509 8:04	Mon, Sep 2, 0509 11:53	2d
4271	Sun	11	673	Sun, Sep 21, 0510 5:37	Sun, Sep 21, 0510 6:45	2d
4272	Thu	20	469	Thu, Sep 10, 0511 14:26	Thu, Sep 10, 0511 6:43	2d
4273	Tue	5	265	Mon, Aug 29, 0512 23:14	Mon, Aug 29, 0512 9:16	1d

Year	Day	Hrs	Pts	Molad of Tishrei	Conjunction	Skw
4274	Mon	2	854	Sun, Sep 17, 0513 20:47	Sun, Sep 17, 0513 5:58	1d
4275	Fri	11	650	Fri, Sep 7, 0514 5:36	Thu, Sep 6, 0514 18:37	2d
4276	Thu	9	159	Thu, Sep 26, 0515 3:08	Wed, Sep 25, 0515 19:43	2d
4277	Mon	17	1035	Mon, Sep 14, 0516 11:57	Mon, Sep 14, 0516 12:05	2d
4278	Sat	2	831	Fri, Sep 3, 0517 20:46	Sat, Sep 4, 0517 1:21	2d
4279	Fri	0	340	Thu, Sep 22, 0518 18:18	Thu, Sep 22, 0518 23:00	2d
4280	Tue	9	136	Tue, Sep 12, 0519 3:07	Tue, Sep 12, 0519 1:54	2d
4281	Sat	17	1012	Sat, Aug 31, 0520 11:56	Sat, Aug 31, 0520 1:55	2d
4282	Fri	15	521	Fri, Sep 19, 0521 9:28	Thu, Sep 18, 0521 20:17	2d
4283	Wed	0	317	Tue, Sep 8, 0522 18:17	Tue, Sep 8, 0522 4:05	1d
4284	Mon	21	906	Mon, Sep 27, 0523 15:50	Mon, Sep 27, 0523 3:34	2d
4285	Sat	6	702	Sat, Sep 16, 0524 0:39	Fri, Sep 15, 0524 19:19	2d
4286	Wed	15	498	Wed, Sep 5, 0525 9:27	Wed, Sep 5, 0525 11:18	2d
4287	Tue	13	7	Tue, Sep 24, 0526 7:00	Tue, Sep 24, 0526 11:18	2d
4288	Sat	21	883	Sat, Sep 13, 0527 15:49	Sat, Sep 13, 0527 19:20	3d
4289	Thu	6	679	Thu, Sep 2, 0528 0:37	Wed, Sep 1, 0528 20:47	2d
4290	Wed	4	188	Tue, Sep 20, 0529 22:10	Tue, Sep 20, 0529 14:02	1d
4291	Sun	12	1064	Sun, Sep 10, 0530 6:59	Sat, Sep 9, 0530 16:47	1d
4292	Thu	21	860	Thu, Aug 30, 0531 15:47	Thu, Aug 30, 0531 2:49	2d
4293	Wed	19	369	Wed, Sep 17, 0532 13:20	Wed, Sep 17, 0532 2:47	2d
4294	Mon	4	165	Sun, Sep 6, 0533 22:09	Sun, Sep 6, 0533 19:05	2d
4295	Sun	1	754	Sat, Sep 25, 0534 19:41	Sat, Sep 25, 0534 20:18	2d
4296	Thu	10	550	Thu, Sep 15, 0535 4:30	Thu, Sep 15, 0535 9:08	2d
4297	Mon	19	346	Mon, Sep 3, 0536 13:19	Mon, Sep 3, 0536 15:08	2d
4298	Sun	16	935	Sun, Sep 22, 0537 10:51	Sun, Sep 22, 0537 9:13	2d
4299	Fri	1	731	Thu, Sep 11, 0538 19:40	Thu, Sep 11, 0538 9:09	1d
4300	Tue	10	527	Tue, Sep 1, 0539 4:29	Mon, Aug 31, 0539 13:58	1d

Year	Day	Hrs	Pts	Molad of Tishrei	Conjunction	Skw
4301	Mon	8	36	Mon, Sep 19, 0540 2:02	Sun, Sep 18, 0540 12:04	1d
4302	Fri	16	912	Fri, Sep 8, 0541 10:50	Fri, Sep 8, 0541 2:25	2d
4303	Thu	14	421	Thu, Sep 27, 0542 8:23	Thu, Sep 27, 0542 3:39	2d
4304	Mon	23	217	Mon, Sep 16, 0543 17:12	Mon, Sep 16, 0543 19:21	3d
4305	Sat	8	13	Sat, Sep 5, 0544 2:00	Sat, Sep 5, 0544 6:30	2d
4306	Fri	5	602	Thu, Sep 23, 0545 23:33	Fri, Sep 24, 0545 2:53	2d
4307	Tue	14	398	Tue, Sep 13, 0546 8:22	Tue, Sep 13, 0546 3:56	2d
4308	Sat	23	194	Sat, Sep 2, 0547 17:10	Sat, Sep 2, 0547 4:43	2d
4309	Fri	20	783	Fri, Sep 20, 0548 14:43	Fri, Sep 20, 0548 0:28	2d
4310	Wed	5	579	Tue, Sep 9, 0549 23:32	Tue, Sep 9, 0549 10:46	1d
4311	Sun	14	375	Sun, Aug 30, 0550 8:20	Sun, Aug 30, 0550 2:18	2d
4312	Sat	11	964	Sat, Sep 18, 0551 5:53	Sat, Sep 18, 0551 3:18	2d
4313	Wed	20	760	Wed, Sep 6, 0552 14:42	Wed, Sep 6, 0552 18:09	3d
4314	Tue	18	269	Tue, Sep 25, 0553 12:14	Tue, Sep 25, 0553 17:01	2d
4315	Sun	3	65	Sat, Sep 14, 0554 21:03	Sat, Sep 14, 0554 22:28	2d
4316	Thu	11	941	Thu, Sep 4, 0555 5:52	Wed, Sep 3, 0555 22:43	2d
4317	Wed	9	450	Wed, Sep 22, 0556 3:25	Tue, Sep 21, 0556 16:35	1d
4318	Sun	18	246	Sun, Sep 11, 0557 12:13	Sat, Sep 10, 0557 21:39	2d
4319	Fri	3	42	Thu, Aug 31, 0558 21:02	Thu, Aug 31, 0558 9:58	1d
4320	Thu	0	631	Wed, Sep 19, 0559 18:35	Wed, Sep 19, 0559 10:38	1d
4321	Mon	9	427	Mon, Sep 8, 0560 3:23	Mon, Sep 8, 0560 2:59	2d
4322	Sun	6	1016	Sun, Sep 27, 0561 0:56	Sun, Sep 27, 0561 3:30	2d
4323	Thu	15	812	Thu, Sep 16, 0562 9:45	Thu, Sep 16, 0562 14:08	2d
4324	Tue	0	608	Mon, Sep 5, 0563 18:33	Mon, Sep 5, 0563 17:41	1d
4325	Sun	22	117	Sun, Sep 23, 0564 16:06	Sun, Sep 23, 0564 11:16	2d
4326	Fri	6	993	Fri, Sep 13, 0565 0:55	Thu, Sep 12, 0565 12:07	1d
4327	Tue	15	789	Tue, Sep 2, 0566 9:43	Mon, Sep 1, 0566 19:29	2d

Year	Day	Hrs	Pts	Molad of Tishrei	Conjunction	Skw
4328	Mon	13	298	Mon, Sep 21, 0567 7:16	Sun, Sep 20, 0567 18:52	2d
4329	Fri	22	94	Fri, Sep 9, 0568 16:05	Fri, Sep 9, 0568 10:26	2d
4330	Wed	6	970	Wed, Aug 30, 0569 0:53	Wed, Aug 30, 0569 2:33	2d
4331	Tue	4	479	Mon, Sep 17, 0570 22:26	Tue, Sep 18, 0570 2:06	2d
4332	Sat	13	275	Sat, Sep 7, 0571 7:15	Sat, Sep 7, 0571 10:47	2d
4333	Fri	10	864	Fri, Sep 25, 0572 4:48	Fri, Sep 25, 0572 5:55	2d
4334	Tue	19	660	Tue, Sep 14, 0573 13:36	Tue, Sep 14, 0573 5:55	2d
4335	Sun	4	456	Sat, Sep 3, 0574 22:25	Sat, Sep 3, 0574 8:18	1d
4336	Sat	1	1045	Fri, Sep 22, 0575 19:58	Fri, Sep 22, 0575 5:31	1d
4337	Wed	10	841	Wed, Sep 11, 0576 4:46	Tue, Sep 10, 0576 18:02	2d
4338	Sun	19	637	Sun, Aug 31, 0577 13:35	Sun, Aug 31, 0577 10:21	2d
4339	Sat	17	146	Sat, Sep 19, 0578 11:08	Sat, Sep 19, 0578 11:09	2d
4340	Thu	1	1022	Wed, Sep 8, 0579 19:56	Thu, Sep 9, 0579 0:22	2d
4341	Tue	23	531	Tue, Sep 26, 0580 17:29	Tue, Sep 26, 0580 21:54	3d
4342	Sun	8	327	Sun, Sep 16, 0581 2:18	Sun, Sep 16, 0581 0:56	2d
4343	Thu	17	123	Thu, Sep 5, 0582 11:06	Thu, Sep 5, 0582 0:53	2d
4344	Wed	14	712	Wed, Sep 24, 0583 8:39	Tue, Sep 23, 0583 19:40	2d
4345	Sun	23	508	Sun, Sep 12, 0584 17:28	Sun, Sep 12, 0584 3:20	2d
4346	Fri	8	304	Fri, Sep 2, 0585 2:16	Thu, Sep 1, 0585 17:31	1d
4347	Thu	5	893	Wed, Sep 20, 0586 23:49	Wed, Sep 20, 0586 18:40	2d
4348	Mon	14	689	Mon, Sep 10, 0587 8:38	Mon, Sep 10, 0587 10:33	2d
4349	Fri	23	485	Fri, Aug 29, 0588 17:26	Fri, Aug 29, 0588 22:13	3d
4350	Thu	20	1074	Thu, Sep 17, 0589 14:59	Thu, Sep 17, 0589 18:18	3d
4351	Tue	5	870	Mon, Sep 6, 0590 23:48	Mon, Sep 6, 0590 19:49	2d
4352	Mon	3	379	Sun, Sep 25, 0591 21:21	Sun, Sep 25, 0591 13:17	1d
4353	Fri	12	175	Fri, Sep 14, 0592 6:09	Thu, Sep 13, 0592 15:51	1d
4354	Tue	20	1051	Tue, Sep 3, 0593 14:58	Tue, Sep 3, 0593 1:45	2d

Year	Day	Hrs	Pts	Molad of Tishrei	Conjunction	Skw
4355	Mon	18	560	Mon, Sep 22, 0594 12:31	Mon, Sep 22, 0594 2:13	2d
4356	Sat	3	356	Fri, Sep 11, 0595 21:19	Fri, Sep 11, 0595 18:28	2d
4357	Wed	12	152	Wed, Aug 31, 0596 6:08	Wed, Aug 31, 0596 9:42	2d
4358	Tue	9	741	Tue, Sep 19, 0597 3:41	Tue, Sep 19, 0597 8:13	2d
4359	Sat	18	537	Sat, Sep 8, 0598 12:29	Sat, Sep 8, 0598 14:17	2d
4360	Fri	16	46	Fri, Sep 27, 0599 10:02	Fri, Sep 27, 0599 8:20	2d
4361	Wed	0	922	Tue, Sep 16, 0600 18:51	Tue, Sep 16, 0600 8:11	1d
4362	Sun	9	718	Sun, Sep 6, 0601 3:39	Sat, Sep 5, 0601 12:46	1d
4363	Sat	7	227	Sat, Sep 25, 0602 1:12	Fri, Sep 24, 0602 11:20	1d
4364	Wed	16	23	Wed, Sep 14, 0603 10:01	Wed, Sep 14, 0603 1:39	2d
4365	Mon	0	899	Sun, Sep 2, 0604 18:49	Sun, Sep 2, 0604 18:14	2d
4366	Sat	22	408	Sat, Sep 21, 0605 16:22	Sat, Sep 21, 0605 18:39	3d
4367	Thu	7	204	Thu, Sep 11, 0606 1:11	Thu, Sep 11, 0606 5:48	2d
4368	Mon	16	0	Mon, Aug 31, 0607 10:00	Mon, Aug 31, 0607 9:56	2d
4369	Sun	13	589	Sun, Sep 18, 0608 7:32	Sun, Sep 18, 0608 3:03	2d
4370	Thu	22	385	Thu, Sep 7, 0609 16:21	Thu, Sep 7, 0609 3:39	2d
4371	Wed	19	974	Wed, Sep 26, 0610 13:54	Tue, Sep 25, 0610 23:34	2d
4372	Mon	4	770	Sun, Sep 15, 0611 22:42	Sun, Sep 15, 0611 9:44	1d
4373	Fri	13	566	Fri, Sep 4, 0612 7:31	Fri, Sep 4, 0612 1:19	2d
4374	Thu	11	75	Thu, Sep 23, 0613 5:04	Thu, Sep 23, 0613 2:44	2d
4375	Mon	19	951	Mon, Sep 12, 0614 13:52	Mon, Sep 12, 0614 17:36	2d
4376	Sat	4	747	Fri, Sep 1, 0615 22:41	Sat, Sep 2, 0615 2:55	2d
4377	Fri	2	256	Thu, Sep 19, 0616 20:14	Thu, Sep 19, 0616 21:42	2d
4378	Tue	11	52	Tue, Sep 9, 0617 5:02	Mon, Sep 8, 0617 21:55	2d
4379	Mon	8	641	Mon, Sep 28, 0618 2:35	Sun, Sep 27, 0618 15:38	1d
4380	Fri	17	437	Fri, Sep 17, 0619 11:24	Thu, Sep 16, 0619 20:29	2d
4381	Wed	2	233	Tue, Sep 5, 0620 20:12	Tue, Sep 5, 0620 8:40	1d

Year	Day	Hrs	Pts	Molad of Tishrei	Conjunction	Skw
4382	Mon	23	822	Mon, Sep 24, 0621 17:45	Mon, Sep 24, 0621 9:54	2d
4383	Sat	8	618	Sat, Sep 14, 0622 2:34	Sat, Sep 14, 0622 2:20	2d
4384	Wed	17	414	Wed, Sep 3, 0623 11:23	Wed, Sep 3, 0623 16:08	2d
4385	Tue	14	1003	Tue, Sep 21, 0624 8:55	Tue, Sep 21, 0624 13:31	2d
4386	Sat	23	799	Sat, Sep 10, 0625 17:44	Sat, Sep 10, 0625 17:07	2d
4387	Thu	8	595	Thu, Aug 31, 0626 2:33	Wed, Aug 30, 0626 17:06	1d
4388	Wed	6	104	Wed, Sep 19, 0627 0:05	Tue, Sep 18, 0627 11:05	1d
4389	Sun	14	980	Sun, Sep 7, 0628 8:54	Sat, Sep 6, 0628 18:09	2d
4390	Sat	12	489	Sat, Sep 26, 0629 6:27	Fri, Sep 25, 0629 17:52	1d
4391	Wed	21	285	Wed, Sep 15, 0630 15:15	Wed, Sep 15, 0630 9:28	2d
4392	Mon	6	81	Mon, Sep 5, 0631 0:04	Mon, Sep 5, 0631 1:46	2d
4393	Sun	3	670	Sat, Sep 22, 0632 21:37	Sun, Sep 23, 0632 1:37	2d
4394	Thu	12	466	Thu, Sep 12, 0633 6:25	Thu, Sep 12, 0633 10:23	2d
4395	Mon	21	262	Mon, Sep 1, 0634 15:14	Mon, Sep 1, 0634 12:23	2d
4396	Sun	18	851	Sun, Sep 20, 0635 12:47	Sun, Sep 20, 0635 5:10	2d
4397	Fri	3	647	Thu, Sep 8, 0636 21:35	Thu, Sep 8, 0636 7:17	1d
4398	Thu	1	156	Wed, Sep 27, 0637 19:08	Wed, Sep 27, 0637 4:22	1d
4399	Mon	9	1032	Mon, Sep 17, 0638 3:57	Sun, Sep 16, 0638 16:45	1d
4400	Fri	18	828	Fri, Sep 6, 0639 12:46	Fri, Sep 6, 0639 9:08	2d
4401	Thu	16	337	Thu, Sep 24, 0640 10:18	Thu, Sep 24, 0640 10:33	2d
4402	Tue	1	133	Mon, Sep 13, 0641 19:07	Mon, Sep 13, 0641 23:54	2d
4403	Sat	9	1009	Sat, Sep 3, 0642 3:56	Sat, Sep 3, 0642 6:41	2d
4404	Fri	7	518	Fri, Sep 22, 0643 1:28	Fri, Sep 22, 0643 0:26	2d
4405	Tue	16	314	Tue, Sep 10, 0644 10:17	Tue, Sep 10, 0644 0:17	2d
4406	Sun	1	110	Sat, Aug 30, 0645 19:06	Sat, Aug 30, 0645 4:17	1d
4407	Fri	22	699	Fri, Sep 18, 0646 16:38	Fri, Sep 18, 0646 2:02	2d
4408	Wed	7	495	Wed, Sep 8, 0647 1:27	Tue, Sep 7, 0647 16:05	1d

Year	Day	Hrs	Pts	Molad of Tishrei	Conjunction	Skw
4409	Tue	5	4	Mon, Sep 25, 0648 23:00	Mon, Sep 25, 0648 17:46	1d
4410	Sat	13	880	Sat, Sep 15, 0649 7:48	Sat, Sep 15, 0649 9:48	2d
4411	Wed	22	676	Wed, Sep 4, 0650 16:37	Wed, Sep 4, 0650 21:42	3d
4412	Tue	20	185	Tue, Sep 23, 0651 14:10	Tue, Sep 23, 0651 17:58	2d
4413	Sun	4	1061	Sat, Sep 11, 0652 22:58	Sat, Sep 11, 0652 19:32	2d
4414	Thu	13	857	Thu, Sep 1, 0653 7:47	Wed, Aug 31, 0653 19:56	2d
4415	Wed	11	366	Wed, Sep 20, 0654 5:20	Tue, Sep 19, 0654 14:53	1d
4416	Sun	20	162	Sun, Sep 9, 0655 14:09	Sun, Sep 9, 0655 0:26	2d
4417	Sat	17	751	Sat, Sep 27, 0656 11:41	Sat, Sep 27, 0656 0:59	2d
4418	Thu	2	547	Wed, Sep 16, 0657 20:30	Wed, Sep 16, 0657 17:18	1d
4419	Mon	11	343	Mon, Sep 6, 0658 5:19	Mon, Sep 6, 0658 8:44	2d
4420	Sun	8	932	Sun, Sep 25, 0659 2:51	Sun, Sep 25, 0659 7:49	2d
4421	Thu	17	728	Thu, Sep 13, 0660 11:40	Thu, Sep 13, 0660 14:02	2d
4422	Tue	2	524	Mon, Sep 2, 0661 20:29	Mon, Sep 2, 0661 14:34	1d
4423	Mon	0	33	Sun, Sep 21, 0662 18:01	Sun, Sep 21, 0662 7:38	1d
4424	Fri	8	909	Fri, Sep 11, 0663 2:50	Thu, Sep 10, 0663 11:54	1d
4425	Tue	17	705	Tue, Aug 30, 0664 11:39	Mon, Aug 29, 0664 23:29	2d
4426	Mon	15	214	Mon, Sep 18, 0665 9:11	Mon, Sep 18, 0665 0:14	2d
4427	Sat	0	10	Fri, Sep 7, 0666 18:00	Fri, Sep 7, 0666 16:52	1d
4428	Thu	21	599	Thu, Sep 26, 0667 15:33	Thu, Sep 26, 0667 17:58	2d
4429	Tue	6	395	Tue, Sep 15, 0668 0:21	Tue, Sep 15, 0668 5:21	2d
4430	Sat	15	191	Sat, Sep 4, 0669 9:10	Sat, Sep 4, 0669 9:39	2d
4431	Fri	12	780	Fri, Sep 23, 0670 6:43	Fri, Sep 23, 0670 2:49	2d
4432	Tue	21	576	Tue, Sep 12, 0671 15:32	Tue, Sep 12, 0671 3:15	2d
4433	Sun	6	372	Sun, Sep 1, 0672 0:20	Sat, Aug 31, 0672 9:41	1d
4434	Sat	3	961	Fri, Sep 19, 0673 21:53	Fri, Sep 19, 0673 8:28	1d
4435	Wed	12	757	Wed, Sep 9, 0674 6:42	Tue, Sep 8, 0674 23:50	2d

Year	Day	Hrs	Pts	Molad of Tishrei	Conjunction	Skw
4436	Tue	10	266	Tue, Sep 28, 0675 4:14	Tue, Sep 28, 0675 1:37	2d
4437	Sat	19	62	Sat, Sep 16, 0676 13:03	Sat, Sep 16, 0676 16:41	2d
4438	Thu	3	938	Wed, Sep 5, 0677 21:52	Thu, Sep 6, 0677 2:16	2d
4439	Wed	1	447	Tue, Sep 24, 0678 19:24	Tue, Sep 24, 0678 21:30	2d
4440	Sun	10	243	Sun, Sep 14, 0679 4:13	Sat, Sep 13, 0679 21:44	2d
4441	Thu	19	39	Thu, Sep 2, 0680 13:02	Wed, Sep 1, 0680 23:29	2d
4442	Wed	16	628	Wed, Sep 21, 0681 10:34	Tue, Sep 20, 0681 19:39	2d
4443	Mon	1	424	Sun, Sep 10, 0682 19:23	Sun, Sep 10, 0682 7:28	1d
4444	Fri	10	220	Fri, Aug 31, 0683 4:12	Thu, Aug 30, 0683 23:40	2d
4445	Thu	7	809	Thu, Sep 18, 0684 1:44	Thu, Sep 18, 0684 1:01	2d
4446	Mon	16	605	Mon, Sep 7, 0685 10:33	Mon, Sep 7, 0685 15:01	2d
4447	Sun	14	114	Sun, Sep 26, 0686 8:06	Sun, Sep 26, 0686 13:08	2d
4448	Thu	22	990	Thu, Sep 15, 0687 16:55	Thu, Sep 15, 0687 16:54	2d
4449	Tue	7	786	Tue, Sep 4, 0688 1:43	Mon, Sep 3, 0688 16:51	1d
4450	Mon	5	295	Sun, Sep 22, 0689 23:16	Sun, Sep 22, 0689 10:43	1d
4451	Fri	14	91	Fri, Sep 12, 0690 8:05	Thu, Sep 11, 0690 17:27	1d
4452	Tue	22	967	Tue, Sep 1, 0691 16:53	Tue, Sep 1, 0691 7:00	2d
4453	Mon	20	476	Mon, Sep 19, 0692 14:26	Mon, Sep 19, 0692 8:02	2d
4454	Sat	5	272	Fri, Sep 8, 0693 23:15	Sat, Sep 9, 0693 0:19	2d
4455	Fri	2	861	Thu, Sep 27, 0694 20:47	Fri, Sep 28, 0694 0:46	2d
4456	Tue	11	657	Tue, Sep 17, 0695 5:36	Tue, Sep 17, 0695 9:48	2d
4457	Sat	20	453	Sat, Sep 5, 0696 14:25	Sat, Sep 5, 0696 11:57	2d
4458	Fri	17	1042	Fri, Sep 24, 0697 11:57	Fri, Sep 24, 0697 5:03	2d
4459	Wed	2	838	Tue, Sep 13, 0698 20:46	Tue, Sep 13, 0698 6:58	1d
4460	Sun	11	634	Sun, Sep 3, 0699 5:35	Sat, Sep 2, 0699 15:57	1d
4461	Sat	9	143	Sat, Sep 22, 0700 3:07	Fri, Sep 21, 0700 15:36	1d
4462	Wed	17	1019	Wed, Sep 11, 0701 11:56	Wed, Sep 11, 0701 7:45	2d

Year	Day	Hrs	Pts	Molad of Tishrei	Conjunction	Skw
4463	Mon	2	815	Sun, Aug 31, 0702 20:45	Sun, Aug 31, 0702 23:28	2d
4464	Sun	0	324	Sat, Sep 19, 0703 18:18	Sat, Sep 19, 0703 22:52	2d
4465	Thu	9	120	Thu, Sep 8, 0704 3:06	Thu, Sep 8, 0704 5:55	2d
4466	Wed	6	709	Wed, Sep 27, 0705 0:39	Wed, Sep 27, 0705 0:16	2d
4467	Sun	15	505	Sun, Sep 16, 0706 9:28	Sun, Sep 16, 0706 0:05	2d
4468	Fri	0	301	Thu, Sep 5, 0707 18:16	Thu, Sep 5, 0707 3:53	1d
4469	Wed	21	890	Wed, Sep 23, 0708 15:49	Wed, Sep 23, 0708 1:23	2d
4470	Mon	6	686	Mon, Sep 13, 0709 0:38	Sun, Sep 12, 0709 15:04	1d
4471	Fri	15	482	Fri, Sep 2, 0710 9:26	Fri, Sep 2, 0710 7:36	2d
4472	Thu	12	1071	Thu, Sep 21, 0711 6:59	Thu, Sep 21, 0711 8:26	2d
4473	Mon	21	867	Mon, Sep 9, 0712 15:48	Mon, Sep 9, 0712 20:30	3d
4474	Sun	19	376	Sun, Sep 28, 0713 13:20	Sun, Sep 28, 0713 17:26	2d
4475	Fri	4	172	Thu, Sep 17, 0714 22:09	Thu, Sep 17, 0714 19:09	2d
4476	Tue	12	1048	Tue, Sep 7, 0715 6:58	Mon, Sep 6, 0715 19:29	2d
4477	Mon	10	557	Mon, Sep 25, 0716 4:30	Sun, Sep 24, 0716 14:36	1d
4478	Fri	19	353	Fri, Sep 14, 0717 13:19	Thu, Sep 13, 0717 23:51	2d
4479	Wed	4	149	Tue, Sep 3, 0718 22:08	Tue, Sep 3, 0718 14:53	1d
4480	Tue	1	738	Mon, Sep 22, 0719 19:41	Mon, Sep 22, 0719 15:59	1d
4481	Sat	10	534	Sat, Sep 11, 0720 4:29	Sat, Sep 11, 0720 7:22	2d
4482	Wed	19	330	Wed, Aug 31, 0721 13:18	Wed, Aug 31, 0721 17:39	2d
4483	Tue	16	919	Tue, Sep 19, 0722 10:51	Tue, Sep 19, 0722 13:19	2d
4484	Sun	1	715	Sat, Sep 8, 0723 19:39	Sat, Sep 8, 0723 13:56	1d
4485	Fri	23	224	Fri, Sep 26, 0724 17:12	Fri, Sep 26, 0724 7:28	2d
4486	Wed	8	20	Wed, Sep 16, 0725 2:01	Tue, Sep 15, 0725 11:31	1d
4487	Sun	16	896	Sun, Sep 5, 0726 10:49	Sat, Sep 4, 0726 22:54	2d
4488	Sat	14	405	Sat, Sep 24, 0727 8:22	Fri, Sep 23, 0727 23:17	2d
4489	Wed	23	201	Wed, Sep 12, 0728 17:11	Wed, Sep 12, 0728 15:41	2d

Year	Day	Hrs	Pts	Molad of Tishrei	Conjunction	Skw
4490	Mon	7	1077	Mon, Sep 2, 0729 1:59	Mon, Sep 2, 0729 6:03	2d
4491	Sun	5	586	Sat, Sep 20, 0730 23:32	Sun, Sep 21, 0730 4:13	2d
4492	Thu	14	382	Thu, Sep 10, 0731 8:21	Thu, Sep 10, 0731 8:44	2d
4493	Wed	11	971	Wed, Sep 28, 0732 5:53	Wed, Sep 28, 0732 2:29	2d
4494	Sun	20	767	Sun, Sep 17, 0733 14:42	Sun, Sep 17, 0733 2:50	2d
4495	Fri	5	563	Thu, Sep 6, 0734 23:31	Thu, Sep 6, 0734 9:06	1d
4496	Thu	3	72	Wed, Sep 25, 0735 21:04	Wed, Sep 25, 0735 7:56	1d
4497	Mon	11	948	Mon, Sep 14, 0736 5:52	Sun, Sep 13, 0736 23:01	2d
4498	Fri	20	744	Fri, Sep 3, 0737 14:41	Fri, Sep 3, 0737 15:21	2d
4499	Thu	18	253	Thu, Sep 22, 0738 12:14	Thu, Sep 22, 0738 15:23	2d
4500	Tue	3	49	Mon, Sep 11, 0739 21:02	Tue, Sep 12, 0739 1:07	2d
4501	Sat	11	925	Sat, Aug 31, 0740 5:51	Sat, Aug 31, 0740 3:53	2d
4502	Fri	9	434	Fri, Sep 19, 0741 3:24	Thu, Sep 18, 0741 21:08	2d
4503	Tue	18	230	Tue, Sep 8, 0742 12:12	Mon, Sep 7, 0742 22:45	2d
4504	Mon	15	819	Mon, Sep 27, 0743 9:45	Sun, Sep 26, 0743 19:20	2d
4505	Sat	0	615	Fri, Sep 15, 0744 18:34	Fri, Sep 15, 0744 6:56	1d
4506	Wed	9	411	Wed, Sep 5, 0745 3:22	Tue, Sep 4, 0745 22:58	2d
4507	Tue	6	1000	Tue, Sep 24, 0746 0:55	Mon, Sep 23, 0746 23:54	2d
4508	Sat	15	796	Sat, Sep 13, 0747 9:44	Sat, Sep 13, 0747 13:51	2d
4509	Thu	0	592	Wed, Sep 1, 0748 18:32	Wed, Sep 1, 0748 21:34	2d
4510	Tue	22	101	Tue, Sep 20, 0749 16:05	Tue, Sep 20, 0749 16:01	2d
4511	Sun	6	977	Sun, Sep 10, 0750 0:54	Sat, Sep 9, 0750 15:58	1d
4512	Sat	4	486	Fri, Sep 28, 0751 22:27	Fri, Sep 28, 0751 10:21	1d
4513	Wed	13	282	Wed, Sep 17, 0752 7:15	Tue, Sep 16, 0752 16:54	1d
4514	Sun	22	78	Sun, Sep 6, 0753 16:04	Sun, Sep 6, 0753 6:20	2d
4515	Sat	19	667	Sat, Sep 25, 0754 13:37	Sat, Sep 25, 0754 7:17	2d
4516	Thu	4	463	Wed, Sep 14, 0755 22:25	Wed, Sep 14, 0755 23:24	2d

Year	Day	Hrs	Pts	Molad of Tishrei	Conjunction	Skw
4517	Mon	13	259	Mon, Sep 3, 0756 7:14	Mon, Sep 3, 0756 11:56	2d
4518	Sun	10	848	Sun, Sep 22, 0757 4:47	Sun, Sep 22, 0757 8:42	2d
4519	Thu	19	644	Thu, Sep 11, 0758 13:35	Thu, Sep 11, 0758 10:59	2d
4520	Tue	4	440	Mon, Aug 31, 0759 22:24	Mon, Aug 31, 0759 11:14	1d
4521	Mon	1	1029	Sun, Sep 18, 0760 19:57	Sun, Sep 18, 0760 6:15	1d
4522	Fri	10	825	Fri, Sep 8, 0761 4:45	Thu, Sep 7, 0761 15:06	1d
4523	Thu	8	334	Thu, Sep 27, 0762 2:18	Wed, Sep 26, 0762 15:06	1d
4524	Mon	17	130	Mon, Sep 16, 0763 11:07	Mon, Sep 16, 0763 7:06	2d
4525	Sat	1	1006	Fri, Sep 4, 0764 19:55	Fri, Sep 4, 0764 22:44	2d
4526	Thu	23	515	Thu, Sep 23, 0765 17:28	Thu, Sep 23, 0765 21:45	3d
4527	Tue	8	311	Tue, Sep 13, 0766 2:17	Tue, Sep 13, 0766 4:54	2d
4528	Sat	17	107	Sat, Sep 2, 0767 11:05	Sat, Sep 2, 0767 5:55	2d
4529	Fri	14	696	Fri, Sep 20, 0768 8:38	Thu, Sep 19, 0768 23:14	2d
4530	Tue	23	492	Tue, Sep 9, 0769 17:27	Tue, Sep 9, 0769 2:50	2d
4531	Mon	21	1	Mon, Sep 28, 0770 15:00	Mon, Sep 28, 0770 0:52	2d
4532	Sat	5	877	Fri, Sep 17, 0771 23:48	Fri, Sep 17, 0771 14:27	1d
4533	Wed	14	673	Wed, Sep 6, 0772 8:37	Wed, Sep 6, 0772 6:57	2d
4534	Tue	12	182	Tue, Sep 25, 0773 6:10	Tue, Sep 25, 0773 7:32	2d
4535	Sat	20	1058	Sat, Sep 14, 0774 14:58	Sat, Sep 14, 0774 19:36	3d
4536	Thu	5	854	Wed, Sep 3, 0775 23:47	Thu, Sep 4, 0775 0:44	2d
4537	Wed	3	363	Tue, Sep 21, 0776 21:20	Tue, Sep 21, 0776 18:14	2d
4538	Sun	12	159	Sun, Sep 11, 0777 6:08	Sat, Sep 10, 0777 18:26	2d
4539	Thu	20	1035	Thu, Aug 31, 0778 14:57	Thu, Aug 31, 0778 0:11	2d
4540	Wed	18	544	Wed, Sep 19, 0779 12:30	Tue, Sep 18, 0779 23:03	2d
4541	Mon	3	340	Sun, Sep 7, 0780 21:18	Sun, Sep 7, 0780 14:05	1d
4542	Sun	0	929	Sat, Sep 26, 0781 18:51	Sat, Sep 26, 0781 15:22	1d
4543	Thu	9	725	Thu, Sep 16, 0782 3:40	Thu, Sep 16, 0782 6:41	2d

Year	Day	Hrs	Pts	Molad of Tishrei	Conjunction	Skw
4544	Mon	18	521	Mon, Sep 5, 0783 12:28	Mon, Sep 5, 0783 17:00	2d
4545	Sun	16	30	Sun, Sep 23, 0784 10:01	Sun, Sep 23, 0784 12:22	2d
4546	Fri	0	906	Thu, Sep 12, 0785 18:50	Thu, Sep 12, 0785 13:00	1d
4547	Tue	9	702	Tue, Sep 2, 0786 3:39	Mon, Sep 1, 0786 14:17	1d
4548	Mon	7	211	Mon, Sep 21, 0787 1:11	Sun, Sep 20, 0787 10:31	1d
4549	Fri	16	7	Fri, Sep 9, 0788 10:00	Thu, Sep 8, 0788 21:46	2d
4550	Thu	13	596	Thu, Sep 28, 0789 7:33	Wed, Sep 27, 0789 22:42	2d
4551	Mon	22	392	Mon, Sep 17, 0790 16:21	Mon, Sep 17, 0790 15:05	2d
4552	Sat	7	188	Sat, Sep 7, 0791 1:10	Sat, Sep 7, 0791 5:29	2d
4553	Fri	4	777	Thu, Sep 24, 0792 22:43	Fri, Sep 25, 0792 3:23	2d
4554	Tue	13	573	Tue, Sep 14, 0793 7:31	Tue, Sep 14, 0793 7:58	2d
4555	Sat	22	369	Sat, Sep 3, 0794 16:20	Sat, Sep 3, 0794 8:03	2d
4556	Fri	19	958	Fri, Sep 22, 0795 13:53	Fri, Sep 22, 0795 1:49	2d
4557	Wed	4	754	Tue, Sep 10, 0796 22:41	Tue, Sep 10, 0796 7:50	1d
4558	Sun	13	550	Sun, Aug 31, 0797 7:30	Sat, Aug 30, 0797 20:58	2d
4559	Sat	11	59	Sat, Sep 19, 0798 5:03	Fri, Sep 18, 0798 22:14	2d
4560	Wed	19	935	Wed, Sep 8, 0799 13:51	Wed, Sep 8, 0799 14:41	2d
4561	Tue	17	444	Tue, Sep 26, 0800 11:24	Tue, Sep 26, 0800 14:46	2d
4562	Sun	2	240	Sat, Sep 15, 0801 20:13	Sun, Sep 16, 0801 0:31	2d
4563	Thu	11	36	Thu, Sep 5, 0802 5:02	Thu, Sep 5, 0802 3:20	2d
4564	Wed	8	625	Wed, Sep 24, 0803 2:34	Tue, Sep 23, 0803 20:16	2d
4565	Sun	17	421	Sun, Sep 12, 0804 11:23	Sat, Sep 11, 0804 21:39	2d
4566	Fri	2	217	Thu, Sep 1, 0805 20:12	Thu, Sep 1, 0805 5:55	1d
4567	Wed	23	806	Wed, Sep 20, 0806 17:44	Wed, Sep 20, 0806 5:50	2d
4568	Mon	8	602	Mon, Sep 10, 0807 2:33	Sun, Sep 9, 0807 21:55	2d
4569	Sun	6	111	Sun, Sep 28, 0808 0:06	Sat, Sep 27, 0808 23:19	2d
4570	Thu	14	987	Thu, Sep 17, 0809 8:54	Thu, Sep 17, 0809 13:20	2d

Year	Day	Hrs	Pts	Molad of Tishrei	Conjunction	Skw
4571	Mon	23	783	Mon, Sep 6, 0810 17:43	Mon, Sep 6, 0810 21:09	3d
4572	Sun	21	292	Sun, Sep 25, 0811 15:16	Sun, Sep 25, 0811 15:20	2d
4573	Fri	6	88	Fri, Sep 14, 0812 0:04	Thu, Sep 13, 0812 15:11	1d
4574	Tue	14	964	Tue, Sep 3, 0813 8:53	Mon, Sep 2, 0813 18:16	2d
4575	Mon	12	473	Mon, Sep 22, 0814 6:26	Sun, Sep 21, 0814 15:40	1d
4576	Fri	21	269	Fri, Sep 11, 0815 15:14	Fri, Sep 11, 0815 4:59	2d
4577	Wed	6	65	Wed, Aug 31, 0816 0:03	Tue, Aug 30, 0816 21:40	2d
4578	Tue	3	654	Mon, Sep 18, 0817 21:36	Mon, Sep 18, 0817 22:45	2d
4579	Sat	12	450	Sat, Sep 8, 0818 6:25	Sat, Sep 8, 0818 11:27	2d
4580	Fri	9	1039	Fri, Sep 27, 0819 3:57	Fri, Sep 27, 0819 8:11	2d
4581	Tue	18	835	Tue, Sep 15, 0820 12:46	Tue, Sep 15, 0820 10:29	2d
4582	Sun	3	631	Sat, Sep 4, 0821 21:35	Sat, Sep 4, 0821 10:35	1d
4583	Sat	1	140	Fri, Sep 23, 0822 19:07	Fri, Sep 23, 0822 5:11	1d
4584	Wed	9	1016	Wed, Sep 13, 0823 3:56	Tue, Sep 12, 0823 13:44	1d
4585	Sun	18	812	Sun, Sep 1, 0824 12:45	Sun, Sep 1, 0824 4:31	2d
4586	Sat	16	321	Sat, Sep 20, 0825 10:17	Sat, Sep 20, 0825 6:06	2d
4587	Thu	1	117	Wed, Sep 9, 0826 19:06	Wed, Sep 9, 0826 21:55	2d
4588	Tue	22	706	Tue, Sep 28, 0827 16:39	Tue, Sep 28, 0827 21:18	3d
4589	Sun	7	502	Sun, Sep 17, 0828 1:27	Sun, Sep 17, 0828 4:33	2d
4590	Thu	16	298	Thu, Sep 6, 0829 10:16	Thu, Sep 6, 0829 5:34	2d
4591	Wed	13	887	Wed, Sep 25, 0830 7:49	Tue, Sep 24, 0830 22:31	2d
4592	Sun	22	683	Sun, Sep 14, 0831 16:37	Sun, Sep 14, 0831 1:48	2d
4593	Fri	7	479	Fri, Sep 3, 0832 1:26	Thu, Sep 2, 0832 12:28	1d
4594	Thu	4	1068	Wed, Sep 21, 0833 22:59	Wed, Sep 21, 0833 13:07	1d
4595	Mon	13	864	Mon, Sep 11, 0834 7:48	Mon, Sep 11, 0834 5:42	2d
4596	Fri	22	660	Fri, Aug 31, 0835 16:36	Fri, Aug 31, 0835 20:43	3d
4597	Thu	20	169	Thu, Sep 18, 0836 14:09	Thu, Sep 18, 0836 19:10	3d

Year	Day	Hrs	Pts	Molad of Tishrei	Conjunction	Skw
4598	Tue	4	1045	Mon, Sep 7, 0837 22:58	Tue, Sep 8, 0837 0:27	2d
4599	Mon	2	554	Sun, Sep 26, 0838 20:30	Sun, Sep 26, 0838 17:48	1d
4600	Fri	11	350	Fri, Sep 16, 0839 5:19	Thu, Sep 15, 0839 17:52	1d
4601	Tue	20	146	Tue, Sep 4, 0840 14:08	Mon, Sep 3, 0840 23:14	2d
4602	Mon	17	735	Mon, Sep 23, 0841 11:40	Sun, Sep 22, 0841 21:42	2d
4603	Sat	2	531	Fri, Sep 12, 0842 20:29	Fri, Sep 12, 0842 12:35	1d
4604	Wed	11	327	Wed, Sep 2, 0843 5:18	Wed, Sep 2, 0843 5:16	2d
4605	Tue	8	916	Tue, Sep 20, 0844 2:50	Tue, Sep 20, 0844 5:54	2d
4606	Sat	17	712	Sat, Sep 9, 0845 11:39	Sat, Sep 9, 0845 16:27	2d
4607	Fri	15	221	Fri, Sep 28, 0846 9:12	Fri, Sep 28, 0846 12:04	2d
4608	Wed	0	17	Tue, Sep 17, 0847 18:00	Tue, Sep 17, 0847 12:44	1d
4609	Sun	8	893	Sun, Sep 6, 0848 2:49	Sat, Sep 5, 0848 13:48	1d
4610	Sat	6	402	Sat, Sep 25, 0849 0:22	Fri, Sep 24, 0849 9:30	1d
4611	Wed	15	198	Wed, Sep 14, 0850 9:11	Tue, Sep 13, 0850 20:25	2d
4612	Sun	23	1074	Sun, Sep 3, 0851 17:59	Sun, Sep 3, 0851 12:19	2d
4613	Sat	21	583	Sat, Sep 21, 0852 15:32	Sat, Sep 21, 0852 13:52	2d
4614	Thu	6	379	Thu, Sep 11, 0853 0:21	Thu, Sep 11, 0853 4:31	2d
4615	Mon	15	175	Mon, Aug 31, 0854 9:09	Mon, Aug 31, 0854 13:10	2d
4616	Sun	12	764	Sun, Sep 19, 0855 6:42	Sun, Sep 19, 0855 7:45	2d
4617	Thu	21	560	Thu, Sep 7, 0856 15:31	Thu, Sep 7, 0856 7:47	2d
4618	Wed	19	69	Wed, Sep 26, 0857 13:03	Wed, Sep 26, 0857 1:17	2d
4619	Mon	3	945	Sun, Sep 15, 0858 21:52	Sun, Sep 15, 0858 6:57	1d
4620	Fri	12	741	Fri, Sep 5, 0859 6:41	Thu, Sep 4, 0859 19:43	2d
4621	Thu	10	250	Thu, Sep 23, 0860 4:13	Wed, Sep 22, 0860 20:47	2d
4622	Mon	19	46	Mon, Sep 12, 0861 13:02	Mon, Sep 12, 0861 13:16	2d
4623	Sat	3	922	Fri, Sep 1, 0862 21:51	Sat, Sep 2, 0862 2:39	2d
4624	Fri	1	431	Thu, Sep 20, 0863 19:23	Fri, Sep 21, 0863 0:03	2d

Year	Day	Hrs	Pts	Molad of Tishrei	Conjunction	Skw
4625	Tue	10	227	Tue, Sep 9, 0864 4:12	Tue, Sep 9, 0864 3:00	2d
4626	Mon	7	816	Mon, Sep 28, 0865 1:45	Sun, Sep 27, 0865 20:03	2d
4627	Fri	16	612	Fri, Sep 17, 0866 10:34	Thu, Sep 16, 0866 21:13	2d
4628	Wed	1	408	Tue, Sep 6, 0867 19:22	Tue, Sep 6, 0867 5:07	1d
4629	Mon	22	997	Mon, Sep 24, 0868 16:55	Mon, Sep 24, 0868 4:31	2d
4630	Sat	7	793	Sat, Sep 14, 0869 1:44	Fri, Sep 13, 0869 20:24	2d
4631	Wed	16	589	Wed, Sep 3, 0870 10:32	Wed, Sep 3, 0870 12:32	2d
4632	Tue	14	98	Tue, Sep 22, 0871 8:05	Tue, Sep 22, 0871 12:25	2d
4633	Sat	22	974	Sat, Sep 10, 0872 16:54	Sat, Sep 10, 0872 20:30	3d
4634	Thu	7	770	Thu, Aug 31, 0873 1:42	Wed, Aug 30, 0873 22:03	2d
4635	Wed	5	279	Tue, Sep 18, 0874 23:15	Tue, Sep 18, 0874 15:00	1d
4636	Sun	14	75	Sun, Sep 8, 0875 8:04	Sat, Sep 7, 0875 17:51	1d
4637	Sat	11	664	Sat, Sep 26, 0876 5:36	Fri, Sep 25, 0876 14:49	1d
4638	Wed	20	460	Wed, Sep 15, 0877 14:25	Wed, Sep 15, 0877 3:46	2d
4639	Mon	5	256	Sun, Sep 4, 0878 23:14	Sun, Sep 4, 0878 20:13	2d
4640	Sun	2	845	Sat, Sep 23, 0879 20:46	Sat, Sep 23, 0879 21:24	2d
4641	Thu	11	641	Thu, Sep 12, 0880 5:35	Thu, Sep 12, 0880 10:19	2d
4642	Mon	20	437	Mon, Sep 1, 0881 14:24	Mon, Sep 1, 0881 16:24	2d
4643	Sun	17	1026	Sun, Sep 20, 0882 11:57	Sun, Sep 20, 0882 10:14	2d
4644	Fri	2	822	Thu, Sep 9, 0883 20:45	Thu, Sep 9, 0883 10:16	1d
4645	Thu	0	331	Wed, Sep 27, 0884 18:18	Wed, Sep 27, 0884 4:48	1d
4646	Mon	9	127	Mon, Sep 17, 0885 3:07	Sun, Sep 16, 0885 12:59	1d
4647	Fri	17	1003	Fri, Sep 6, 0886 11:55	Fri, Sep 6, 0886 3:27	2d
4648	Thu	15	512	Thu, Sep 25, 0887 9:28	Thu, Sep 25, 0887 4:38	2d
4649	Tue	0	308	Mon, Sep 13, 0888 18:17	Mon, Sep 13, 0888 20:28	2d
4650	Sat	9	104	Sat, Sep 3, 0889 3:05	Sat, Sep 3, 0889 7:44	2d
4651	Fri	6	693	Fri, Sep 22, 0890 0:38	Fri, Sep 22, 0890 3:58	2d

Year	Day	Hrs	Pts	Molad of Tishrei	Conjunction	Skw
4652	Tue	15	489	Tue, Sep 11, 0891 9:27	Tue, Sep 11, 0891 5:06	2d
4653	Sun	0	285	Sat, Aug 30, 0892 18:15	Sat, Aug 30, 0892 5:59	1d
4654	Fri	21	874	Fri, Sep 18, 0893 15:48	Fri, Sep 18, 0893 1:26	2d
4655	Wed	6	670	Wed, Sep 8, 0894 0:37	Tue, Sep 7, 0894 11:48	1d
4656	Tue	4	179	Mon, Sep 26, 0895 22:09	Mon, Sep 26, 0895 11:57	1d
4657	Sat	12	1055	Sat, Sep 15, 0896 6:58	Sat, Sep 15, 0896 4:19	2d
4658	Wed	21	851	Wed, Sep 4, 0897 15:47	Wed, Sep 4, 0897 19:18	3d
4659	Tue	19	360	Tue, Sep 23, 0898 13:20	Tue, Sep 23, 0898 18:06	3d
4660	Sun	4	156	Sat, Sep 12, 0899 22:08	Sat, Sep 12, 0899 23:38	2d
4661	Thu	12	1032	Thu, Sep 2, 0900 6:57	Wed, Sep 1, 0900 23:59	2d
4662	Wed	10	541	Wed, Sep 21, 0901 4:30	Tue, Sep 20, 0901 17:34	1d
4663	Sun	19	337	Sun, Sep 10, 0902 13:18	Sat, Sep 9, 0902 22:44	2d
4664	Sat	16	926	Sat, Sep 29, 0903 10:51	Fri, Sep 28, 0903 21:00	2d
4665	Thu	1	722	Wed, Sep 17, 0904 19:40	Wed, Sep 17, 0904 11:33	1d
4666	Mon	10	518	Mon, Sep 7, 0905 4:28	Mon, Sep 7, 0905 4:02	2d
4667	Sun	8	27	Sun, Sep 26, 0906 2:01	Sun, Sep 26, 0906 4:32	2d
4668	Thu	16	903	Thu, Sep 15, 0907 10:50	Thu, Sep 15, 0907 15:16	2d
4669	Tue	1	699	Mon, Sep 3, 0908 19:38	Mon, Sep 3, 0908 18:55	2d
4670	Sun	23	208	Sun, Sep 22, 0909 17:11	Sun, Sep 22, 0909 12:18	2d
4671	Fri	8	4	Fri, Sep 12, 0910 2:00	Thu, Sep 11, 0910 13:16	1d
4672	Tue	16	880	Tue, Sep 1, 0911 10:48	Mon, Aug 31, 0911 20:43	2d
4673	Mon	14	389	Mon, Sep 19, 0912 8:21	Sun, Sep 18, 0912 19:48	2d
4674	Fri	23	185	Fri, Sep 8, 0913 17:10	Fri, Sep 8, 0913 11:27	2d
4675	Thu	20	774	Thu, Sep 27, 0914 14:43	Thu, Sep 27, 0914 12:33	2d
4676	Tue	5	570	Mon, Sep 16, 0915 23:31	Tue, Sep 17, 0915 3:10	2d
4677	Sat	14	366	Sat, Sep 5, 0916 8:20	Sat, Sep 5, 0916 11:58	2d
4678	Fri	11	955	Fri, Sep 24, 0917 5:53	Fri, Sep 24, 0917 6:59	2d

Year	Day	Hrs	Pts	Molad of Tishrei	Conjunction	Skw
4679	Tue	20	751	Tue, Sep 13, 0918 14:41	Tue, Sep 13, 0918 7:04	2d
4680	Sun	5	547	Sat, Sep 2, 0919 23:30	Sat, Sep 2, 0919 9:34	1d
4681	Sat	3	56	Fri, Sep 20, 0920 21:03	Fri, Sep 20, 0920 6:29	1d
4682	Wed	11	932	Wed, Sep 10, 0921 5:51	Tue, Sep 9, 0921 19:04	2d
4683	Tue	9	441	Tue, Sep 29, 0922 3:24	Mon, Sep 28, 0922 19:49	2d
4684	Sat	18	237	Sat, Sep 18, 0923 12:13	Sat, Sep 18, 0923 12:06	2d
4685	Thu	3	33	Wed, Sep 6, 0924 21:01	Thu, Sep 7, 0924 1:27	2d
4686	Wed	0	622	Tue, Sep 25, 0925 18:34	Tue, Sep 25, 0925 22:56	2d
4687	Sun	9	418	Sun, Sep 15, 0926 3:23	Sun, Sep 15, 0926 2:04	2d
4688	Thu	18	214	Thu, Sep 4, 0927 12:11	Thu, Sep 4, 0927 2:08	2d
4689	Wed	15	803	Wed, Sep 22, 0928 9:44	Tue, Sep 21, 0928 20:42	2d
4690	Mon	0	599	Sun, Sep 11, 0929 18:33	Sun, Sep 11, 0929 4:27	1d
4691	Fri	9	395	Fri, Sep 1, 0930 3:21	Thu, Aug 31, 0930 18:44	2d
4692	Thu	6	984	Thu, Sep 20, 0931 0:54	Wed, Sep 19, 0931 19:37	2d
4693	Mon	15	780	Mon, Sep 8, 0932 9:43	Mon, Sep 8, 0932 11:34	2d
4694	Sun	13	289	Sun, Sep 27, 0933 7:16	Sun, Sep 27, 0933 11:08	2d
4695	Thu	22	85	Thu, Sep 16, 0934 16:04	Thu, Sep 16, 0934 19:22	3d
4696	Tue	6	961	Tue, Sep 6, 0935 0:53	Mon, Sep 5, 0935 21:01	2d
4697	Mon	4	470	Sun, Sep 23, 0936 22:26	Sun, Sep 23, 0936 14:19	1d
4698	Fri	13	266	Fri, Sep 13, 0937 7:14	Thu, Sep 12, 0937 17:00	1d
4699	Tue	22	62	Tue, Sep 2, 0938 16:03	Tue, Sep 2, 0938 3:00	2d
4700	Mon	19	651	Mon, Sep 21, 0939 13:36	Mon, Sep 21, 0939 3:10	2d
4701	Sat	4	447	Fri, Sep 9, 0940 22:24	Fri, Sep 9, 0940 19:30	2d
4702	Fri	1	1036	Thu, Sep 28, 0941 19:57	Thu, Sep 28, 0941 20:17	2d
4703	Tue	10	832	Tue, Sep 18, 0942 4:46	Tue, Sep 18, 0942 9:11	2d
4704	Sat	19	628	Sat, Sep 7, 0943 13:34	Sat, Sep 7, 0943 15:23	2d
4705	Fri	17	137	Fri, Sep 25, 0944 11:07	Fri, Sep 25, 0944 9:20	2d

Year	Day	Hrs	Pts	Molad of Tishrei	Conjunction	Skw
4706	Wed	1	1013	Tue, Sep 14, 0945 19:56	Tue, Sep 14, 0945 9:18	1d
4707	Sun	10	809	Sun, Sep 4, 0946 4:44	Sat, Sep 3, 0946 14:01	1d
4708	Sat	8	318	Sat, Sep 23, 0947 2:17	Fri, Sep 22, 0947 12:22	1d
4709	Wed	17	114	Wed, Sep 11, 0948 11:06	Wed, Sep 11, 0948 2:45	2d
4710	Mon	1	990	Sun, Aug 31, 0949 19:55	Sun, Aug 31, 0949 19:24	2d
4711	Sat	23	499	Sat, Sep 19, 0950 17:27	Sat, Sep 19, 0950 19:35	3d
4712	Thu	8	295	Thu, Sep 9, 0951 2:16	Thu, Sep 9, 0951 6:51	2d
4713	Wed	5	884	Tue, Sep 26, 0952 23:49	Wed, Sep 27, 0952 2:53	2d
4714	Sun	14	680	Sun, Sep 16, 0953 8:37	Sun, Sep 16, 0953 4:07	2d
4715	Thu	23	476	Thu, Sep 5, 0954 17:26	Thu, Sep 5, 0954 4:51	2d
4716	Wed	20	1065	Wed, Sep 24, 0955 14:59	Wed, Sep 24, 0955 0:37	2d
4717	Mon	5	861	Sun, Sep 12, 0956 23:47	Sun, Sep 12, 0956 10:52	1d
4718	Fri	14	657	Fri, Sep 2, 0957 8:36	Fri, Sep 2, 0957 2:31	2d
4719	Thu	12	166	Thu, Sep 21, 0958 6:09	Thu, Sep 21, 0958 3:39	2d
4720	Mon	20	1042	Mon, Sep 10, 0959 14:57	Mon, Sep 10, 0959 18:36	3d
4721	Sun	18	551	Sun, Sep 28, 0960 12:30	Sun, Sep 28, 0960 17:03	2d
4722	Fri	3	347	Thu, Sep 17, 0961 21:19	Thu, Sep 17, 0961 22:40	2d
4723	Tue	12	143	Tue, Sep 7, 0962 6:07	Mon, Sep 6, 0962 23:01	2d
4724	Mon	9	732	Mon, Sep 26, 0963 3:40	Sun, Sep 25, 0963 16:39	1d
4725	Fri	18	528	Fri, Sep 14, 0964 12:29	Thu, Sep 13, 0964 21:37	2d
4726	Wed	3	324	Tue, Sep 3, 0965 21:18	Tue, Sep 3, 0965 9:55	1d
4727	Tue	0	913	Mon, Sep 22, 0966 18:50	Mon, Sep 22, 0966 10:54	1d
4728	Sat	9	709	Sat, Sep 12, 0967 3:39	Sat, Sep 12, 0967 3:23	2d
4729	Wed	18	505	Wed, Aug 31, 0968 12:28	Wed, Aug 31, 0968 17:15	2d
4730	Tue	16	14	Tue, Sep 19, 0969 10:00	Tue, Sep 19, 0969 14:27	2d
4731	Sun	0	890	Sat, Sep 8, 0970 18:49	Sat, Sep 8, 0970 18:11	2d

The Last 30 years:

Year	Day	Hrs	Pts	Molad of Tishrei	Conjunction	Skw
5751	Thu	0	258	Wed, Sep 19, 1990 18:14	Wed, Sep 19, 1990 2:46	1d
5752	Mon	9	54	Mon, Sep 9, 1991 3:03	Sun, Sep 8, 1991 13:01	1d
5753	Sun	6	643	Sun, Sep 27, 1992 0:35	Sat, Sep 26, 1992 12:40	1d
5754	Thu	15	439	Thu, Sep 16, 1993 9:24	Thu, Sep 16, 1993 5:10	2d
5755	Tue	0	235	Mon, Sep 5, 1994 18:13	Mon, Sep 5, 1994 20:33	2d
5756	Sun	21	824	Sun, Sep 24, 1995 15:45	Sun, Sep 24, 1995 18:55	3d
5757	Fri	6	620	Fri, Sep 13, 1996 0:34	Fri, Sep 13, 1996 1:07	2d
5758	Thu	4	129	Wed, Oct 1, 1997 22:07	Wed, Oct 1, 1997 18:52	2d
5759	Mon	12	1005	Mon, Sep 21, 1998 6:55	Sun, Sep 20, 1998 19:01	2d
5760	Fri	21	801	Fri, Sep 10, 1999 15:44	Fri, Sep 10, 1999 0:02	2d
5761	Thu	19	310	Thu, Sep 28, 2000 13:17	Wed, Sep 27, 2000 21:53	2d
5762	Tue	4	106	Mon, Sep 17, 2001 22:05	Mon, Sep 17, 2001 12:27	1d
5763	Sat	12	982	Sat, Sep 7, 2002 6:54	Sat, Sep 7, 2002 5:10	2d
5764	Fri	10	491	Fri, Sep 26, 2003 4:27	Fri, Sep 26, 2003 5:09	2d
5765	Tue	19	287	Tue, Sep 14, 2004 13:15	Tue, Sep 14, 2004 16:29	2d
5766	Mon	16	876	Mon, Oct 3, 2005 10:48	Mon, Oct 3, 2005 12:28	2d
5767	Sat	1	672	Fri, Sep 22, 2006 19:37	Fri, Sep 22, 2006 13:45	1d
5768	Wed	10	468	Wed, Sep 12, 2007 4:26	Tue, Sep 11, 2007 14:44	1d
5769	Tue	7	1057	Tue, Sep 30, 2008 1:58	Mon, Sep 29, 2008 10:12	1d
5770	Sat	16	853	Sat, Sep 19, 2009 10:47	Fri, Sep 18, 2009 20:44	2d
5771	Thu	1	649	Wed, Sep 8, 2010 19:36	Wed, Sep 8, 2010 12:30	1d
5772	Tue	23	158	Tue, Sep 27, 2011 17:08	Tue, Sep 27, 2011 13:09	2d
5773	Sun	7	1034	Sun, Sep 16, 2012 1:57	Sun, Sep 16, 2012 4:11	2d
5774	Thu	16	830	Thu, Sep 5, 2013 10:46	Thu, Sep 5, 2013 13:36	2d
5775	Wed	14	339	Wed, Sep 24, 2014 8:18	Wed, Sep 24, 2014 8:14	2d
5776	Sun	23	135	Sun, Sep 13, 2015 17:07	Sun, Sep 13, 2015 8:41	2d

Year	Day	Hrs	Pts	Molad of Tishrei	Conjunction	Skw
5777	Sat	20	724	Sat, Oct 1, 2016 14:40	Sat, Oct 1, 2016 2:12	2d
5778	Thu	5	520	Wed, Sep 20, 2017 23:28	Wed, Sep 20, 2017 7:30	1d
5779	Mon	14	316	Mon, Sep 10, 2018 8:17	Sun, Sep 9, 2018 20:01	2d
5780	Sun	11	905	Sun, Sep 29, 2019 5:50	Sat, Sep 28, 2019 20:26	2d
5781	Thu	20	701	Thu, Sep 17, 2020 14:38	Thu, Sep 17, 2020 13:00	2d

Appendix B: Global Visibility Maps

At this link I have made available Global Visibility Maps for the years 1999 - 2018. The maps were produced by Dutch Astronomer, Robert H. van Gent.

http://www.sodhaibur.com/van-gent-maps.pdf

From van Gent's website[87]:

> Progress in astronomy and in computing techniques has now made it possible to calculate the geocentric positions of the sun and the moon at any time with stunning precision. However, predicting when the thin sliver of the lunar crescent can first be seen in the sky from a given location after its conjunction with the sun still remains a difficult problem.
>
> The main cause for this problem is the fact that the faint and narrow lunar crescent has to be detected shortly after sunset, when the moon is still close to the western horizon in the twilight sky. It is obvious that weather and the local transparency of the atmosphere are important factors for successfully detecting the lunar crescent, as well as the experience [expertise] of the observer.
>
> Numerous computational methods and algorithms for predicting the visibility of the lunar crescent have been proposed in the past (a comprehensive bibliography is given at the bottom of this webpage) but the method now most favored by astronomers is based on the Yallop algorithm, proposed in 1997 by Bernard D. Yallop of the computing section of HM Nautical Almanac Office.

What was observed by Rabban Gamliel is manifest in these charts, that "sometimes [the moon] travels a long route and sometimes [the moon] travels a short route."

---

[87] http://www.staff.science.uu.nl/~gent0113/babylon/babycal.htm

Appendix C: Three-Day Discrepancies

Whenever the calendar court established Rosh HaShanah there was a presumption by the people that witnesses had actually seen the New Moon. The calendar court, however, was determining Rosh HaShanah based on starting at sunset of the Hebrew day within which the Molad fell. The court simply accepted witnesses on that day, knowing full well that they had not actually seen the moon.

For three-day discrepancies this was complicated by folk wisdom that the New Moon would never be seen after sunset if the Old Moon had been seen before sunrise.

Three-day discrepancies were synonymous with a visible Old Moon Erev Rosh HaShanah.

This was the cause of the conflict between Rabban Gamliel and R' Yehoshua. It was what precipitated the note found by R' Hai Gaon from Hillel ben R' Yehuda, in 358 CE. It also caused the concern of of the Exilarch in 835 CE. And it is almost explicitly stated in the Yerushalmi with regard to the Old Moon seen by R' Hiyya:

רבי חייה רבה הילך לאורו של ישן ארבעת מיל רבי אבון משדי עלוי צררין ואמר לה לא תבהית בני מריך ברמשא אנן בעיין תיתחמי מיכא ואת מיתחמי מיכא מיד איתבלע מן קומוי.

R' Hiyya the Great walked by the light of the Old Moon for four miles. Rabbi Abun threw pebbles at [the Old Moon] and said to it: "Do not upset the children of your Master, tonight we have to see you from this side [i.e. the New Moon], but you are seen from here [the Old Moon is still visible]." Immediately it disappeared.

I like to think that when the redactors of the Talmud included the story of R' Hiyya and the story the conflict between Rabban Gamliel and R' Yehoshua, they did so as a signpost, precisely so that someone like me could gain the insight to write this book. I feel very privileged to have done so.

Year	Day	Hrs	Pts	Molad of Tishrei	Conjunction	Skw
3774	Sat	22	142	Sep 21, 0013 16:07	Sep 21, 0013 20:54	3d
3783	Mon	19	685	Sep 12, 0022 13:38	Sep 12, 0022 18:27	3d
3803	Mon	20	1076	Sep 1, 0042 14:59	Sep 1, 0042 18:40	3d
3819	Wed	22	410	Sep 4, 0058 16:22	Sep 4, 0058 19:36	3d
3835	Fri	23	824	Sep 7, 0074 17:45	Sep 7, 0074 20:35	3d
3844	Sun	21	287	Aug 29, 0083 15:15	Aug 29, 0083 19:23	3d
3881	Mon	21	601	Sep 9, 0120 15:33	Sep 9, 0120 19:04	3d
3897	Wed	22	1015	Sep 12, 0136 16:56	Sep 12, 0136 19:31	3d
3906	Fri	20	478	Sep 3, 0145 14:26	Sep 3, 0145 18:08	3d
3934	Thu	23	249	Sep 23, 0173 17:13	Sep 23, 0173 22:00	3d
3943	Sat	20	792	Sep 14, 0182 14:44	Sep 14, 0182 18:13	3d
3959	Mon	22	126	Sep 17, 0198 16:07	Sep 17, 0198 18:16	3d
4004	Fri	22	394	Sep 1, 0243 16:21	Sep 1, 0243 21:07	3d
4066	Wed	21	585	Sep 6, 0305 15:32	Sep 6, 0305 20:29	3d
4119	Sat	23	233	Sep 20, 0358 17:12	Sep 20, 0358 21:41	3d
4128	Mon	20	776	Sep 11, 0367 14:43	Sep 11, 0367 19:15	3d
4164	Wed	23	501	Sep 3, 0403 17:27	Sep 3, 0403 20:21	3d
4181	Thu	22	424	Sep 24, 0420 16:23	Sep 24, 0420 20:46	3d
4190	Sat	19	967	Sep 15, 0429 13:53	Sep 15, 0429 18:35	3d
4226	Mon	22	692	Sep 7, 0465 16:38	Sep 7, 0465 20:04	3d
4251	Fri	21	569	Sep 1, 0490 15:31	Sep 1, 0490 19:24	3d
4252	Thu	19	78	Sep 20, 0491 13:04	Sep 20, 0491 18:08	3d
4288	Sat	21	883	Sep 13, 0527 15:49	Sep 13, 0527 19:20	3d
4304	Mon	23	217	Sep 16, 0543 17:12	Sep 16, 0543 19:21	3d
4313	Wed	20	760	Sep 6, 0552 14:42	Sep 6, 0552 18:09	3d
4341	Tue	23	531	Sep 26, 0580 17:29	Sep 26, 0580 21:54	3d
4349	Fri	23	485	Aug 29, 0588 17:26	Aug 29, 0588 22:13	3d

Year	Day	Hrs	Pts	Molad of Tishrei	Conjunction	Skw
4350	Thu	20	1074	Sep 17, 0589 14:59	Sep 17, 0589 18:18	3d
4366	Sat	22	408	Sep 21, 0605 16:22	Sep 21, 0605 18:39	3d
4411	Wed	22	676	Sep 4, 0650 16:37	Sep 4, 0650 21:42	3d
4473	Mon	21	867	Sep 9, 0712 15:48	Sep 9, 0712 20:30	3d
4526	Thu	23	515	Sep 23, 0765 17:28	Sep 23, 0765 21:45	3d
4535	Sat	20	1058	Sep 14, 0774 14:58	Sep 14, 0774 19:36	3d
4571	Mon	23	783	Sep 6, 0810 17:43	Sep 6, 0810 21:09	3d
4588	Tue	22	706	Sep 28, 0827 16:39	Sep 28, 0827 21:18	3d
4596	Fri	22	660	Aug 31, 0835 16:36	Aug 31, 0835 20:43	3d
4597	Thu	20	169	Sep 18, 0836 14:09	Sep 18, 0836 19:10	3d
4633	Sat	22	974	Sep 10, 0872 16:54	Sep 10, 0872 20:30	3d
4658	Wed	21	851	Sep 4, 0897 15:47	Sep 4, 0897 19:18	3d
4659	Tue	19	360	Sep 23, 0898 13:20	Sep 23, 0898 18:06	3d
4695	Thu	22	85	Sep 16, 0934 16:04	Sep 16, 0934 19:22	3d
4711	Sat	23	499	Sep 19, 0950 17:27	Sep 19, 0950 19:35	3d
4720	Mon	20	1042	Sep 10, 0959 14:57	Sep 10, 0959 18:36	3d
4756	Wed	23	767	Sep 2, 0995 17:42	Sep 2, 0995 22:50	3d
4757	Tue	21	276	Sep 20, 0996 15:15	Sep 20, 0996 18:51	3d
4773	Thu	22	690	Sep 24, 1012 16:38	Sep 24, 1012 18:55	3d
4818	Mon	22	958	Sep 7, 1057 16:53	Sep 7, 1057 21:39	3d
4819	Sun	20	467	Sep 26, 1058 14:25	Sep 26, 1058 18:22	3d
4880	Sat	22	69	Sep 13, 1119 16:03	Sep 13, 1119 20:30	3d
4933	Tue	23	797	Sep 26, 1172 17:44	Sep 26, 1172 22:00	3d
4942	Thu	21	260	Sep 17, 1181 15:14	Sep 17, 1181 19:58	3d
4978	Sat	23	1065	Sep 9, 1217 17:59	Sep 9, 1217 21:28	3d
5003	Wed	22	942	Sep 3, 1242 16:52	Sep 3, 1242 20:16	3d
5004	Tue	20	451	Sep 22, 1243 14:25	Sep 22, 1243 18:58	3d

Year	Day	Hrs	Pts	Molad of Tishrei	Conjunction	Skw
5040	Thu	23	176	Sep 14, 1279 17:09	Sep 14, 1279 20:15	3d
5065	Mon	22	53	Sep 8, 1304 16:02	Sep 8, 1304 19:20	3d
5102	Tue	22	367	Sep 19, 1341 16:20	Sep 19, 1341 19:29	3d
5118	Thu	23	781	Sep 22, 1357 17:43	Sep 22, 1357 19:33	3d
5127	Sat	21	244	Sep 13, 1366 15:13	Sep 13, 1366 18:31	3d
5163	Mon	23	1049	Sep 6, 1402 17:58	Sep 6, 1402 22:32	3d
5164	Sun	21	558	Sep 25, 1403 15:31	Sep 25, 1403 19:01	3d
5180	Tue	22	972	Sep 28, 1419 16:54	Sep 28, 1419 18:12	3d
5225	Sat	23	160	Sep 10, 1464 17:08	Sep 10, 1464 21:12	3d
5287	Thu	22	351	Sep 16, 1526 16:19	Sep 16, 1526 20:34	3d
5296	Sat	19	894	Sep 7, 1535 13:49	Sep 7, 1535 18:08	3d
5340	Sun	23	1079	Sep 30, 1579 17:59	Sep 30, 1579 21:45	3d
5349	Tue	21	542	Sep 20, 1588 15:30	Sep 20, 1588 19:40	3d
5410	Mon	23	144	Sep 6, 1649 17:08	Sep 6, 1649 19:55	3d
5411	Sun	20	733	Sep 25, 1650 14:40	Sep 25, 1650 18:16	3d
5447	Tue	23	458	Sep 17, 1686 17:25	Sep 17, 1686 20:05	3d
5472	Sat	22	335	Sep 12, 1711 16:18	Sep 12, 1711 19:11	3d
5509	Sun	22	649	Sep 22, 1748 16:36	Sep 22, 1748 19:38	3d
5525	Tue	23	1063	Sep 25, 1764 17:59	Sep 25, 1764 18:48	3d
5571	Fri	21	840	Sep 28, 1810 15:46	Sep 28, 1810 18:37	3d
5632	Thu	23	442	Sep 14, 1871 17:24	Sep 14, 1871 21:10	3d
5641	Sat	20	985	Sep 4, 1880 14:54	Sep 4, 1880 18:52	3d
5694	Tue	22	633	Sep 19, 1933 16:35	Sep 19, 1933 20:21	3d
5756	Sun	21	824	Sep 24, 1995 15:45	Sep 24, 1995 18:55	3d

www.ingramcontent.com/pod-product-compliance
Lightning Source LLC
Chambersburg PA
CBHW031143160426
43193CB00008B/235